# The ideology of the extreme right

## Cas Mudde

Manchester University Press

Manchester and New York

distributed exclusively in the USA by Palgrave

*Published by* Manchester University Press
Oxford Road, Manchester M13 9NR, UK
*and* Room 400, 175 Fifth Avenue, New York, NY 10010, USA
http://www.manchesteruniversitypress.co.uk

*Distributed exclusively in the USA by*
Palgrave, 175 Fifth Avenue, New York,
NY 10010, USA

*Distributed exclusively in Canada by*
UBC Press, University of British Columbia, 2029 West Mall,
Vancouver, BC, Canada V6T 1Z2

*British Library Cataloguing-in-Publication Data*
A catalogue record for this book is available from the British Library

*Library of Congress Cataloging-in-Publication Data applied for*

ISBN 0 7190 5793 0 *hardback*
ISBN 0 7190 6446 5 *paperback*

First published 2000
First published in paperback 2002

07 06 05 04 03 02          10 9 8 7 6 5 4 3 2 1

Typeset in Sabon with Stone Sans
by Northern Phototypesetting Co Ltd, Bolton
Printed in Great Britain
by Bookcraft (Bath) Ltd, Midsomer Norton

# Contents

# Preface

With extreme right parties in government in Austria and Italy, and Jean-Marie Le Pen contesting the run-off in the 2002 presidential elections in France, few people will dispute their continuing relevance in the politics of Western Europe. Indeed, ever since the first small electoral successes of parties like the Centrumpartij in the Netherlands or the Front National in France in the early 1980s, the extreme right has been the most discussed group of parties both in and outside of the scholarly community. Thousands of newspaper articles and hundreds of pieces of scholarly work have been devoted to extreme right parties, predominantly describing their history, leaders or electoral successes, as well as proclaiming their danger. Remarkably little serious attention has been devoted to their ideology, however. This aspect of the extreme right has been considered to be known to everyone. The few scholars that did devote attention to the ideology of the contemporary extreme right parties have primarily been concerned with pointing out similarities with the fascist and National Socialist ideologies of the pre-war period. If the similarities were not found, this was often taken as 'proof' that the extreme right hides its (true) ideologies, rather than as a motivation to look in a different direction.

Although concerned with the ideology of the extreme right, this book is also about so-called 'party families'. In particular, it is about how we can use ideology as a focus for identifying and analysing a specific party family, in this case the extreme right. The study is limited in two ways. First, it is limited in that not every (alleged) extreme right party is included in this study, which only draws from parties in Belgium, Germany and the Netherlands. This limitation derives from the method chosen: an intensive and in-depth analysis of party literature. The second limitation, as a consequence of the method chosen, is that the parties are taken at their word. Since there is no *proof* to the contrary, it is assumed that extreme right parties are as (dis)honest in their propaganda and literature as other political parties. As various other authors have pointed out, (all) political parties hide certain aspects of their ideology from their programmes, mostly for opportunistic reasons. This notwithstanding, when selecting a relatively broad sample of party literature, and when being aware and critical in analysing this material, one can study party ideology in a scholarly way. This is what will be done in this study for this particular group of extreme right parties; it can, of course, also be done in exactly the same way for other families of parties, such as liberal or social democratic parties.

There is another limitation in this study: as the focus is on families of parties, the (whole) political party is the unit of analysis. This means that each (extreme right) political party is considered as a unitary actor, and I look for the ideology of 'the' party. That there are different factions within each party is accepted as a possibility, as is their possible relevance for certain aspects of the party; but they are not the subject of research here. Only when the different factions are so strong and divided on a certain topic or ideological feature that they inhibit the creation of a (majority) view of the party, will this be explicitly discussed.

Finally, the picture of the party ideology developed here is a picture which falls within a certain historical, societal and political context. Various factors have helped to create the party ideology, but these will be only scantily touched upon in this study. Extreme right parties, like all new parties, have to find their place in an already formed political and ideological space (Linz 1967; Ignazi 1996), which influences their behaviour and ideology. To some extent, certain ideological arguments and features only appear in their propaganda as reactions to arguments and features of other parties. Other topics are addressed by (extreme right) parties, only because other parties challenge them on these topics. For example, virtually all extreme right parties are at one time or another linked to anti-Semitism, even if they have never addressed topics such as Jews, Judaism or Israel themselves before that time. It is only in such instances that this study will discuss the interaction of extreme right parties with their political and social environment, and then only briefly. For the rest, the book will deal with the extreme right parties themselves, and most specifically their history, literature and, above all, ideology.

But not before I have said my words of thanks to all who have made it possible for me to write this book. Throughout the years I have profited from financial, material, personal, and intellectual assistance from a great variety of people and organisations. For the collection and analysis of the party literature I have visited various archives, where I have been very kindly assisted by René Blekman (Anne Frank Stichting, Amsterdam), Monika Deniffel (Institut für Zeitgeschichte, Munich), Alois Fischer (Bundesarchiv, Koblenz), Gabrielle Nandlinger (Blick nach Rechts, Bad Godesberg), Roeland Raes and Dirk De Smedt (Vlaams Blok, Brussels). Part of these visits has been made possible by a travel grant from the Dutch Organisation for Scientific Research (NWO); in other instances, such as the visits to party meetings of the Deutsche Volksunion and the Vlaams Blok, I have benefited often from financial aid from the 'Vakgroepsfonds' in Leiden.

I feel privileged to have studied and worked at the Department of Politics in Leiden, which combines a pleasant social climate with a highly stimulating intellectual climate. I want to thank all my former colleagues for contributing to this general climate. I especially want to thank Hans Oversloot, Huib Pellikaan and Margo Trappenburg, for their many hours of small and big discussions on various scholarly topics, and for their help with and reading of earlier parts of this book. *In extremis* this applies to Joop Van Holsteyn, who has been (and still is) the best scholarly colleague and teacher possible. Deepest gratitude is also due (finally) to Peter Mair, whose optimistic support and sharp mind have helped me to develop beyond my originally narrow boundaries; a *Doktorvater* in the truest sense of the word.

I further want to thank all (former) Dutch Ph.D. students in political science, with whom I had the privilege to participate in the so-called 'Promoclub' and 'Polybios' sessions between 1993 and 1997. Since defending my Ph.D. at the University of Leiden in January 1998, I have benefited greatly from the stimulating environment of the Central European University in Budapest. The change of scenery and the unique blend of cultures has helped me to sharpen some of my main thoughts in the book. I thank all my former CEU colleagues and students, wherever they might be now.

In addition, a number of people outside my departments have discussed different queries with me or commented on chapters of the book. I would like to thank all of them, and in particular Uwe Backes, Hans-Georg Betz, Kris Deschouwer, Marc Spruyt, Andreas Umland and Jaap Van Donselaar. I owe special thanks to Roger Eatwell, who through the wonderful world of Internet has become one of my closest colleagues. My friend and colleague Petr Kopecky has helped me in a great many ways, among others by brainstorming on any possible academic and other (i.e. football) matter. Marjo van Ammers and Anna Siskova, the two women in my life, have kept me sane by being less bothered with the book, while at the same time supporting me in my endeavour. A final thanks goes out to Tim Mudde, who has made my scholarly work both difficult and possible. I am grateful for all the help he has extended to me, and even more for the fact that we still respect each other despite our differences of opinion.

Edinburgh

# Acronyms

| Acronym | Original Name | English Name |
|---------|--------------|--------------|
| AN | Alleanza Nazionale | National Alliance |
| ANR | Aktion Neue Rechte | Action New Right |
| BNP | | British National Party |
| BP | Boerenpartij | Farmers Party |
| BPN | Burgerpartij Nederland | Citizens Party Netherlands |
| BR | Bayerische Rundfunk | Bavarian Broadcasting |
| BVD | Binnenlandse Veiligheidsdienst | National Security Service |
| CD | Centrumdemocraten | Centre Democrats |
| *CDa* | *CD-Actueel* | *CD-Up-to-Date* |
| *CDi* | *CD-Info* | *CD-Information* |
| CDU | Christlich-Demokratische Union | Christian Democratic Union |
| *CN* | *Centrumnieuws* | *Centre News* |
| CP | Centrumpartij | Centre Party |
| CP'86 | Centrumpartij'86 | Centre Party'86 |
| CSU | Christlich-Soziale Union | Christian Social Union |
| CVP | Christelijke Volkspartij | Christian People's Party |
| *DA* | *Deutsche Anzeiger* | *German Informant* |
| DLVH | Deutsche Liga für Volk und Heimat | German League for Nation and Fatherland |
| *DNZ* | *Deutsche National-Zeitung* | *German National Newspaper* |
| DP | Deutsche Partei | German Party |
| DRP | Deutsche Reichspartei | German Reich Party |
| *DSZ* | *Deutsche Soldatenzeitung* | *German Soldiers Newspaper* |
| DV | Deutsche Volksunion e.V. | German People's Union |
| DVU | Deutsche Volksunion | German People's Union |

| | | |
|---|---|---|
| DWZ | *Deutsche Wochen-Zeitung* | *German Weekly Newspaper* |
| EC | | European Community |
| EP | | European Parliament |
| EU | | European Union |
| FDP | Freie Demokratische Partei | Free Democratic Party |
| FN | Front National | National Front |
| FPD | Fremskridtspartiet | Progress Party (Denmark) |
| FPN | Fremskittspartiet | Progress Party (Norway) |
| FPÖ | Freiheitliche Partei Österreichs | Austrian Freedom Party |
| FR | Freiheitlicher Rat | Freedom Council |
| FRG | | Federal Republic of Germany |
| GDR | | German Democratic Republic |
| JFN | Jongerenfront Nederland | Youth Front Netherlands |
| JN | Junge Nationaldemokraten | Young National Democrats |
| LL | Lega Lombarda | Lombard League |
| LN | Lega Nord | Northern League |
| MEP | | Member European Parliament |
| MP | | Member of Parliament |
| MSI | Movimento Sociale Italiano | Italian Social Movement |
| NB | Nederlands Blok | Dutch Block |
| NCP | Nationale Centrumpartij | National Centre Party |
| ND | Ny Demokrati | New Democracy |
| NDP | Nationaldemokratische Partei | National Democratic Party |
| NF | | National Front |
| NOS | Nationalistische Omroep-stichting | Nationalist Broadcast Foundation |
| NOU | Nationale Oppositie Unie | National Opposition Union |
| NPD | Nationaldemokratische Partei Deutschlands | German National Democratic Party |
| NSB | Nationaal Socialistische Beweging in Nederland | National Socialist Movement in the Netherlands |
| NSDAP | Nationalsozialistische Deutsche Arbeiterpartei | German National Socialist Workers Party |
| NSV | Nationalistische Studenten-vereniging | Nationalist Students' Association |
| NVI | Nationalistisch Vormings-instituut | Nationalist Educational Institute |
| NVP | Nationale Volkspartij/CP'86 | National People's Party/CP'86 |

| | | |
|---|---|---|
| NVU | Nederlandse Volks-Unie | Dutch People's Union |
| PDS | Partei des Demokratischen Sozialismus | Party of Democratic Socialism |
| PS | Parti Socialiste | Socialist Party |
| PvdA | Partij van de Arbeid | Labour Party |
| RA | *Republikanische Anzeiger* | *Republican Informant* |
| Rep | *Der Republikaner* | *The Republican* |
| REP | Die Republikaner | The Republicans |
| SOPD | Stichting Oud Politieke Delinquenten | Foundation of Former Political Delinquents |
| SP | Socialistische Partij | Socialist Party |
| SPD | Sozialdemokratische Partei Deutschlands | German Social Democratic Party |
| SRP | Sozialistische Reichspartei | Socialist Reich Party |
| VB | Vlaams Blok | Flemish Block |
| VBJ | Vlaams Blok Jongeren | Flemish Block Youth |
| VBM | *Vlaams Blok Magazine* | *Flemish Block Magazine* |
| Verdinaso | Verbond van Dietse Nationaal-Solidaristen | Association of Diets National Solidarists |
| VLB | *Vlaams Blok* | *Flemish Block* (party paper) |
| VLN | *De Vlaams Nationalist* | *The Flemish Nationalist* |
| VMO | Vlaamse Militanten Orde | Order of Flemish Militants |
| VNN | Volksnationalisten Nederland | Ethnic Nationalists Netherlands |
| VNP | Vlaams Nationale Partij | Flemish National Party |
| VNV | Vlaams Nationaal Verbond | Flemish National Union |
| VU | Volksunie | People's Union |
| VVP | Vlaamse Volkspartij | Flemish People's Party |
| WELL | Werkgemeenschap Europa in de Lage Landen | Working Community Europe in the Low Countries |
| Were Di | Verbond van Nederlandse Werkgemeenschappen Were Di | Association of Dutch Working Groups Protect Yourself |

# 1

# The extreme right party family

Studies of political parties have been based on a multiplicity of both scholarly and political theories, and have focused on a variety of internal and external aspects. As is common within the scientific community, complaints have been voiced about the lack of knowledge in particular areas of the field, such as party (as) organisations (Mair 1994), party ideology (Von Beyme 1985), and minor or small parties (Fischer 1980; Müller-Rommel 1991). However, even though a lot of work certainly remains to be done, political parties do constitute one of the most studied fields in political science in general, and comparative politics in particular (Katz and Mair 1992; Janda 1993).

Studies of political parties focus primarily either on the whole group of political parties or on different subgroups within the larger group. The former studies are aimed at determining what characteristics all political parties have in common. They mainly focus on constructing a (general) theory and definition of political parties. Even though many theories have been developed during the past decades, 'there has been no dominant theoretical perspective in the study of political parties' (Crotty 1991: 145). This also holds true for the second group, which deals with defining the political party. There is a wide variety of definitions, based on an almost as wide variety of criteria, but none can claim general acceptance in the field. However, a consensus can be found in the fact that the political party is to be defined primarily on the basis of its function(s). It is also on this basis that the political party will be defined in this study, namely as *any political group identified by an official label that places candidates for public office through elections* (see also Sartori 1976: 63). Although such definitions have sometimes been criticised for being (too) narrow (see Janda 1993), and although this criticism might be valid in certain cases, a 'minimal definition' serves the purposes of this study, i.e. identifying the object.

## The concept of the party family

In addition to the group of scholars that study characteristics that are part of all political parties, a large(r) group centres on the distinction of different subgroups within the larger group. This is generally done by constructing typologies or classifications of political parties. The construction of classifications forces researchers to structure their knowledge and information of the subject at hand, which again helps them to gain a greater understanding and control of that subject (Lazarsfeld and Barton 1951). What variable is chosen as the theoretical basis of the classification, or combination of variables in the case of a typology, depends on the interest and research question of the author (e.g. Mair 1990).

One of the most popular classifications is that of the so-called party family, in which political parties are grouped across countries predominantly on the basis of their ideology. Although this idea has been elaborated at the theoretical level only relatively recently, it has been part implicitly of several of the older studies in the field, going back to the classical studies of Michels (1911/78), Duverger (1951:64) and Lipset and Rokkan (1967). The idea of the party family is not one of the most rigorously tested classifications in political science, however; and, for the most part, it has its vagueness and 'common sense' to thank for its wide usage. However, the distinction of political parties on the basis of ideology has both theoretical and practical merits (see Mair and Mudde 1998).

One of the most authoritative sources on party families is Von Beyme's *Politische Parteien in Westeuropa* (1984; English translation in 1985). In this book he constructs several typologies, based on different criteria, of which the most important criterion is to be found at the ideological level: that of the *familles spirituelles*. It is these ideological 'families' that are compared on the basis of the other criteria. Although his main typology is based on ideology, Von Beyme writes that he has constructed the different types on the basis of Rokkan's famous historical–sociological study of the four critical lines of cleavages (Von Beyme 1985: 23). Where Rokkan distinguishes ten 'ideological groups' on the basis of four major conflicts (cleavages) in Western Europe (Rokkan 1970), Von Beyme specifies only nine 'spiritual families': (i) liberal and radical parties; (ii) conservative parties; (iii) socialist and social democratic parties; (iv) christian democratic parties; (v) communist parties; (vi) agrarian parties; (vii) regional and ethnic parties; (viii) right-wing extremist parties; and (ix) the ecology movement.

The classification of individual parties into these nine party families is done on the basis of two 'ideological' criteria: the *name* of the party, and, when this is not (or no longer) satisfactory, the *voters'* perception of party programmes and ideological position (Von Beyme 1985: 3; my italics).[1]

---

[1] Seiler (1980, 1985) has constructed a typology of *familles partisanes*, which is based even more closely on Rokkan's four cleavages model. He comes, however, to a far greater number

Although party ideology is said to be the most important criterion for classification, it is used only in an indirect way, i.e. through the eyes of the party itself (party name) or of the voters. Thus it is not the researcher who assesses the ideology of the different parties. This is also true for the assessment of the content of the party ideologies, as the attention in the book is predominately directed at the ideology of the different *familles spirituelles*, not at that of the different member parties. Moreover, whether the ideology of a certain party family is identical to that of all its member parties, or whether the individual parties are classified correctly on the basis of (one of) these indirect criteria, is not discussed by the author. His main interest is clearly in the party family as a whole, especially its development, rather than in the individual members that constitute the family.

More recently, Gallagher *et al.* have listed three criteria on the basis of which different party families in Western Europe can be distinguished: (i) 'genetic' origin, (ii) transnational federations and (iii) policies (1995: 181). With a shared genetic origin the authors mean that parties mobilised either in similar historical circumstances or with the intention of representing similar interests. As examples of these families they name socialist (or social-democratic) and agrarian parties. This criterion seems most strongly influenced by Rokkan's cleavage approach.

For the classification of political parties in general and the group of parties that is the concern of this study – (alleged) extreme right parties of the 1980s – in particular, the 'genetic' criterion is of limited use. Although these parties by definition mobilised in similar historical circumstances, Western Europe of the 1980s, they are not the only (group of) parties of this historical period; the green parties, for instance, also mobilised during this period. Nor does the criterion of (the intention of) representing similar interests apply to this specific group. It has been argued that Lipset's thesis of middle-class extremism, originally developed for the pre-war *Nationalsozialistische Deutsche Arbeiterpartei* (German National Socialist Workers Party, NSDAP), is also valid for the post-war extreme right parties (Lipset 1960; Kühnl *et al.* 1969). However, this thesis has come under increasing attack in the last decades (Childers 1983; Falter 1991) and electoral studies have shown that the electorates of modern extreme right parties of the second (Herz 1975; Husbands 1981) and third 'wave' of post-war right-wing extremism are too diverse to speak of middle-class extremism (Betz 1994; Kitschelt 1995).

of families than both Von Beyme and Rokkan. The individual parties are classified on the basis of (1) the historical function performed by the party at its creation; (2a) the sociological structure of the party's electorate, membership and inner group; and (2b) the linkage structure between the party and a given network of pressure groups, movements and associations (Seiler 1985: 81). Many of his *familles partisanes* clearly coincide with the party families generally classified on the basis of ideology, which also seems to be the major criterion for the 'linkage structure' in the third criterion.

The second criterion Gallagher *et al.* mention is based on pragmatic rather than theoretical considerations, i.e. the cross-national linkages that parties have developed among themselves. These linkages are chosen by the parties themselves, and are generally based on (the assumption of) a shared ideology. The most important examples of official organisations of parties from different countries are (i) the party groups in the European Parliament (EP) and (ii) the transnational party federations. Both are primarily organised on the basis of (the assumption of) shared ideological principles (Pridham and Pridham 1979a, 1979b; Bardi 1994).

From the very beginning of the establishment of some form of EP, various groupings of parties have been in place. In the first period only three party groups were represented in the then Common Assembly of the European Coal and Steel Community: the socialists, the christian democrats and the liberals. Since the 1980s, there seems to be a trend towards a closer cooperation between national parties within the existing party groups, on the one hand, and towards competition between these groups instead of between the various national parties, on the other hand. In addition to the three original groups the green parties also form a relatively well organised party group in the EP. Looser coalitions are formed by various regionalist parties in the Rainbow Coalition and during the years 1984–9 and 1989–94 by extreme right parties. This notwithstanding, not all political parties represented in the EP are members of a party group (or 'official' party family) and not every party family is represented as a party group in (every term of) the EP. Moreover, not all political parties that can be described as 'relevant' in the Sartorian sense (Sartori 1976) at the national level are represented at the European level.

Except for the party groups in the EP there are a number of transnational party federations that reach beyond the geographical boundaries of the European Union (EU). In his handbook on political parties of the world Day notes a 'growing inclination of political parties throughout the world to construct or join international organisations of like-minded formations' (Day 1988: ix). Some examples of world-wide federations are the Socialist International (primarily socialist and social-democratic parties), the Socialist Fourth International (Trotskyist parties), and the Liberal International. Even though most of these transnational federations are older than the party groups in the EP, the latter seem to be of bigger importance in the possible foundation of transnational, most likely Euro-, parties (Bardi 1994). However, it will still be a long time before transnational parties will become as relevant as national parties.

Though the criterion of transnational federations has the obvious advantage of being based on clear and open relations between parties, it has severe shortcomings when applied to classifying small parties in general and to the group of extreme right parties of the 1980s in particular. Although there exist several cross-national linkages between parties within the latter group, most of these are neither official nor at the party level. Various linkages are *ad hoc* or only at the individual level. And, although there have been extreme right party groups in the EP, they have always involved only a few of the parties generally considered extreme right (as most of them never made it into the EP). On top of this, the party groups differed considerably in member parties and were highlighted by disputes both within and between the various parties (e.g. Osterhoff 1997; Veen 1997; Fennema and Pollmann 1998). The particular situation of a 'contaminated' family name, finally, makes the more successful parties often cautious to use it, and they often even distance themselves from 'family members' abroad (Pfahl-Traughber 1994).

This leaves us with the third criterion, i.e. policies, or to be more precise 'the extent to which the policies pursued by one party in a country are similar to those pursued by another party in another country' (Gallagher *et al.* 1995: 181). The authors warn that this criterion has the disadvantage that it naively assumes that the same policy means the same thing in different countries. Seiler even went so far as to state that the use of the criterion of 'policies really implemented by political parties' in cross-national research would in practice lead to a typology of countries rather than of parties (1985: 81). The question is how to solve this problem of cross-national comparability. While authors like Seiler have decided to ignore the criterion, Gallagher *et al.* state that 'to ignore professed policies altogether when looking for similarities between parties would clearly be to stick our heads in the sand' (1995: 181).

The problem of cross-national comparability can be circumvented by focusing on the ideology of the parties. Ideologies function as the normative bases of the pursued policies of political parties and have the advantage of being more generally formulated than the more nationally centred policies that are pursued (Christian and Campbell 1974; Sainsbury 1980). Even though the aspect of ideology has been ignored somewhat within the study of party politics, most scholars in the field do accept the importance of it (LaPalombara and Weiner 1966; Janda 1993). This is especially the case in comparative studies, as '[i]deology and program are ... a convenient vehicle for bringing some kind of intellectual order out of what would otherwise be the chaos of competing political groups' (Alexander 1973: xix).

## The study of extreme right parties

The rise of right-wing extremist parties comes in waves, as authors have observed for several West European countries (see Knütter 1991; Zimmermann and Saalfeld 1993; Buijs and Van Donselaar 1994). According to some authors these waves are similar in all or at least most of the countries (e.g. Von Beyme 1988; Stouthuysen 1993; Epstein 1996), whereas others believe that they are for the largest part country specific (e.g. Veen 1997). Buijs and Van Donselaar argue that what seems to be a European development might be no more than a 'temporary and accidental coming together of the national development of a number of countries' (1994: 30). As they state, however, at the moment there is insufficient empirical evidence to support this, in their own words, relativising view (though see Husbands 1996).

Not only do extreme right parties rise in waves, but so do the studies on the subject, with a slight delay. This conjunctural development of scholarly studies on right-wing extremism has been written on and warned against (e.g. Backes 1990a). The recent 'high' in literature on extreme right parties is in line with this development. As extreme right parties either win or maintain their position in the various West European party systems, the number of writings on the phenomenon is exploding. Most of the literature is of a primarily descriptive nature, portraying (the history of) either one extreme right party or extreme right parties in one country. Only fairly recently have some truly comparative studies been undertaken in the field of party ideology (Gardberg 1993; Mudde 1995) and on explanations of the current electoral success of extreme right parties (Betz 1994; Kitschelt 1995).

### The study of the third wave, 1980–2000

The 'third wave' of post-war right-wing extremism (Von Beyme 1988) is without a doubt the most successful period in both the electoral and ideological sense for such parties in almost every West European country (see Suleiman 1995; Taggart 1995). Even though they are still regarded as pariahs in most countries, some extreme right parties have established themselves, at the least, as politically important pariahs, as, for instance, the French *Front National* (National Front, FN) and the Belgian *Vlaams Blok* (Flemish Block, VB). In Italy the *Alleanza Nazionale* (National Alliance, AN) was the first West European extreme right party of the post-war period to make it into government. The extreme right has become a relevant factor in West European politics both within the party system and outside of it (as, for example, the extreme right linked violence in Germany, Austria and elsewhere).

The importance of extreme right parties is also visible in the field of research. Not only has the number of studies on the subject exploded, but also the number of scholars active in the field and the theoretical approaches applied to the field has expanded enormously (see Mudde 1996). Probably the most important development since the early 1980s has been the influx of scholars that originally worked outside the field of right-wing extremism (and historical fascism). This has, on the one hand, brought valuable insights from the study of, for instance, political parties in general and left-libertarian parties in particular (see, most notably, Betz 1994; Kitschelt 1995). On the other hand, it has incorporated the study of extreme right parties into the wider study of political parties, thereby providing useful insights for, among others, the study of small and new parties (e.g. Ignazi 1996). However, these developments have not only made the field broader in volume, but also the number of debates have increased. In comparison to the situation some ten years ago, we now know far more about extreme right parties, yet seem to agree on far less. In particular, there is increasing disagreement on which parties might be properly regarded as extreme right.

### Which parties?

Though formal definitions or derivations based on the history of ideas largely failed to provide a convincing concept for 'right-wing extremism', research work on political parties of the right has not had serious problems in selecting appropriate cases. (Von Beyme 1988: 3)

Von Beyme's observation is valid for most party families: we seem to know *who* they are even though we do not exactly know *what* they are. However, there are some special circumstances for this particular family that make the implications of the remark more serious. First, various other parties have (part) of the family name in their own party name, a feature which is especially obvious in the case of some left-wing families (notably communist and green). This is not true for the right-wing extremist parties, however, which not only reject the term extremist, some even object to the term right-wing (Verbeeck 1994), as is evident, for example, in the case of the two Dutch *Centre*parties. Second, most other party families have some sort of transnational federation in which the various national parties cooperate, whereas this is missing for the extreme right parties.

The 'appropriate cases' that are selected without serious problems by the various researchers involved in the field are listed in appendix A. The political parties listed are those generally considered 'extreme right', which contested national elections at least once in the 1980–95 period. Clearly, not every West European country is mentioned as there is no extreme right party in, for example, Iceland and Ireland that meets the election requirement. Nor is every party mentioned studied with equal care and attention. Parties like the FN and the German *Die Republikaner* (The Republicans, REP) belong to the better-known and studied political parties in Western Europe, while parties such as the Dutch *Centrumpartij'86* (Centre Party'86, CP'86) and the Swiss *Schweizer Demokraten* (Swiss Democrats) are virtually unknown beyond (and even within) their own national boundaries.

The fact that German extreme right parties (not only the REP) are studied so intensively shows that electoral significance is not the only or even main reason for scholarly attention. Even though they have had some electoral success at the *Land* (state) level and once at the European level, the German parties are of mediocre size at the national level in comparison to many of their European counterparts. Still, the REP has been studied by both German and non-German scholars more than, for instance, the almost equally successful Dutch *Centrumdemocraten* (Centre Democrats, CD). The prime reason for this is, of course, the legacy of the past. On top of that and also because of this legacy there are more scholars from Germany working in the field of right-wing extremism than from other countries (Roberts 1994).

A practical reason for the difference in scholarly attention is language. As Müller-Rommel has noted this is a restraining factor in the study of all small parties, especially when primary sources are involved:

> Studying small parties obviously encounters some unique problems especially when it comes to gathering information for a cross-national analysis. In most cases there are clearly language problems. Although it is relatively easy to collect information on party programmes, manifestos and party statutes, it is notably more difficult to read these brochures since (in most cases) they have not been translated into English or another international language. (1991: 2)

Language is the main reason why the scholarly (English-language) community can get more information on, for instance, the British extreme right parties, the *National Front* (NF) and the *British National Party* (BNP), whose electoral relevance is particularly small, than on a party like the Belgian VB, one of the more successful yet still relatively little-known extreme right parties. It might also be one of the main reasons why the 'doyen' of right-wing extremism, the Italian MSI, has been largely ignored by the international scholarly community. However, language does not explain everything, since the MSI has only recently been discovered as a scientific topic by the Italians themselves (Ignazi 1989, 1994c; Ferraresi 1996). Moreover, the relatively new regional leagues have been the subject of intensive study both from Italian and non-Italian scholars, making them the subject of more (inter)national scholarly attention than the almost five times older and still more successful MSI (now AN).

There are also some parties whose extreme right status is disputed by some of the (leading) scholars in the field. One of these borderline cases is the *Lega Nord* (Northern League, LN) and its main predecessor the *Lega Lombarda* (Lombard League, LL), which some authors define as part of the regionalist or sub-nationalist rather than the extreme right party family (see Ignazi 1992; Gallagher *et al.* 1995). This may, except for the obvious regionalist platform and support, be partly the result of the fact that the LL itself chose to be part of the regionalist Rainbow Coalition in the European Parliament in 1989 instead of joining the Technical Fraction of the Euroright; in 1994 the LN joined the Euroliberals.

A party whose ideological status has been the subject of scientific, public and political debate, is the German *Die Republikaner*. Whereas most scholars have defined the party as extreme right there are some who have rejected this labelling. They argue that the REP is fundamentally different from the traditional German extreme right parties (such as the NPD), among other reasons because the REP originated as a splinter from a democratic party (see chapter 2) (Backes 1990b; Veen *et al.* 1993). These scholars have long been 'supported' by the German state, which in its influential *Verfassungs- schutzbericht* did not list the REP among the extreme right groups. How- ever, in December 1992 the German state changed its view and the REP is from that time officially labelled extreme right. Even though this decision has been criticised from both inside and outside the REP as being primarily politically and electorally motivated (Jaschke 1994; More 1994), it has cer- tainly weakened the argument advanced by the 'dissidents'; most have since changed to the new state terminology.

The Austrian *Freiheitliche Partei Österreichs* (Austrian Freedom Party, FPÖ) did not originate from a purely right-wing extremist environment either. The party was founded in 1955/6 as the successor of the *Verband der Unabhängigen* (Alliance of Independents), a coming together of *Deutschna- tionalen* (German-nationalists), liberals and former and new Nazis (Neuge- bauer 1981). After a clearly nationalist beginning the FPÖ developed into a (national-)liberal party, thereby losing some right-wing extremists in the 1966 split *Nationaldemokratische Partei* (National Democratic Party, NDP), until it was eventually accepted as coalition partner of the *Sozialdemokratis- che Partei Österreichs* (Austrian Social Democratic Party) in 1983. However, with the 1986 take-over by Jörg Haider as *Bundesparteiobmann* (national party chairman), a young and energetic populist who had made his political career in the right-wing extremist Carinthian branch of the party, more and more authors came to define the FPÖ as right-wing extremist. This inter- pretation has been strengthened by the increasing grip of Haider (and his clique) over the party, by the split of prominent liberal party members in the Spring of 1993 in the *Liberales Forum* (Liberal Forum), and by the 'expul- sion' of the party from the Liberal International later that year.[2] However, there are still various authors who dispute the right-wing extremist charac- ter of the party as a whole (Merkl 1993) or consider it (still) as part of the liberal party family (Gallagher *et al.* 1995).

Finally, the Scandinavian Progress Parties, the Danish *Fremskridtspartiet* (FPD) and the Norwegian *Fremskrittspartiet* (FPN), which are seen by some as the first of the most recent (third) wave of right-wing extremism (Ignazi 1992; Betz 1994; Svåsand 1998) whereas others consider them to be the last of the (second) wave of more Poujadist-like parties (Von Beyme 1988; Stouthuysen 1993). The main question here is certainly not whether the par- ties are right-wing but whether they are extremist. Various authors see them as either classical right-wing libertarian parties, admittedly primarily 'anti' but certainly not extremist or as part of the secular conservative party family (Gooskens 1994; Gallagher *et al.* 1995).

---

[2] The FPÖ was not formally expelled by the Liberal International, as the party anticipating expulsion, made its own withdrawal (Pfahl-Traughber 1994).

*What right-wing extremism?*

The question of which parties are excluded from the extreme right party family is closely related to the question of what one means by the term extreme right. Almost every scholar in the field points to the lack of a generally accepted definition. Even though the term right-wing extremism itself is accepted by a majority of the scholars, there is no consensus on the exact definition of the term. A variety of authors have defined it in a variety of ways. This has been partly caused by the fact that the term is not only used for scientific purposes but also for political purposes (Knütter 1991; Kowalsky and Schroeder 1994). Several authors define right-wing extremism as a sort of anti-thesis against their own beliefs and/or as (closely) linked to their 'democratic' political opponent.[3]

Notwithstanding these political disputes, there is a rather broad consensus in the field that the term right-wing extremism describes primarily an ideology in one form or another (Herz 1975; Mudde 1995).[4] What this ideology holds, again, is a matter of extensive scholarly debate. Some scholars define right-wing extremism on the basis of only one single feature. Hartmann *et al.*, for example, use right-wing extremism as a collective term for all 'progress-hostile forces' (1985: 9). There are some major objections to this restricted though at the same time broad usage. The most important objections are, first, that the term right-wing extremism describes something already described by another and more suitable term (like progress hostility), and, second, that it portrays extreme right parties falsely as (primarily) single-issue movements, thereby obscuring other (sometimes more) important features of their ideologies (see Mitra 1988; Mudde 1999).

Most of the authors involved define right-wing extremism as a political ideology that is constituted of a combination of several different features (see Mudde 1995). The number of features mentioned in the various definitions varies from one or two to more than ten. Examples of short definitions are from Macridis, who defines right-wing extremism as an 'ideology [that] revolves around the same old staples: racism, xenophobia, and nationalism' (1989: 231), and Backes and Jesse, who define it as 'a collective term for anti-democratic dispositions and attempts, that are traditionally positioned at the extreme "right" of the left-right spectre' (1993: 474).

Some definitions are the size of shopping lists, containing eight to ten different features. A good example is the definition of Falter and Schumann,

---

[3] This can also be seen in the fact that many definitions mention mainly negatively formulated features. Moreover, several scholars demonstrate their rejection of the phenomenon by declaring right-wing extremism to be an anti- or non-ideology (see Verbeeck 1994; Fennema 1996).

[4] Some authors add another dimension to the definition, as, for instance, the use of violence (Von Beyme 1988; Benz 1989), and/or a particular party strategy (De Schampheleire 1991; Jäger 1991).

who list no less than ten features as the core (!) of right-extremist thinking: 'extreme nationalism, ethnocentrism, anti-communism, anti-parliamentarianism, anti-pluralism, militarism, law-and-order thinking, a demand for a strong political leader and/or executive, anti-Americanism and cultural pessimism' (1988: 101).

In twenty-six definitions of right-wing extremism that can be derived from the literature no less than fifty-eight different features are mentioned at least once. Only five features are mentioned, in one form or another, by at least half of the authors: nationalism, racism, xenophobia, anti-democracy and the strong state (Mudde 1995: 206). As is clear from the large number of features mentioned in the different definitions, the questions of, how many features together constitute right-wing extremism and what are the minimal combination of features that define right-wing extremism, need some clarification.

Only a few authors explicitly state how many features constitute right-wing extremism. Commonsense would lead us to expect that the more features are mentioned in the definition, the less likely the statement is that all features have to be present. However, there are authors who list a large number of features and still require all features to be present. Pennings and Brants, for example, speak of a 'minimum repertoire' of six features (1985: 44). Even more extreme is the extensive list of Falter and Schumann, mentioned above, who require all ten features to form the core of right extremist thinking.

These authors are an exception, however, not only in their excessive demands, but also in the explicitness of these demands. Most authors either fail to mention or mention only vaguely what combination of features are necessary to constitute right-wing extremism. This notwithstanding, three different approaches can be distinguished: the quantitative, the qualitative, and the mixed approach (Mudde 1995: 218–19). In the first approach all features are considered equally important and only one criterion is used: the number of features. In the second approach one (or more) feature is 'more equal' than others: this is, for instance, the case in the extremism-theoretical tradition, in which at least anti-democracy must be part of the combination to speak of extremism (see Backes 1989; Backes and Jesse 1993). The third approach combines these two approaches: for example, the requirement of at least two features of which one has to be an 'exclusionist' feature, such as xenophobia, and one a 'hierarchic' feature, such as authoritarianism (see Meijerink *et al.* 1998).

### Beyond right-wing extremism?

Even though right-wing extremism is the most commonly used term for the parties under study here (Ueltzhöffer 1991), alternatives are being used. On the one hand, terms that were used to describe right-wing extremist parties of the first and second wave are still used today. Generally speaking, the terms neo-Nazism and to a lesser extent neo-fascism are now used exclusively for parties and groups that explicitly state a desire to restore the Third Reich (in the case of neo-fascism the Italian Social Republic) or quote historical National Socialism (fascism) as their ideological influence. Examples of neo-Nazi parties in the 1980s are rare, most notably the sectarian German *Freiheitliche Deutsche Arbeiterpartei* (German Free Workers Party), though there exists a wide variety of neo-Nazi groupings in Western Europe. The best (and only) example of a neo-fascist party is the Italian MSI, which until its transformation into the AN officially defined itself as a fascist party. Nevertheless, (neo-) Marxist authors in particular keep using the terms, either with or without the prefix 'neo', considering the parties of the 1980s as no more than recent examples of the 1930s phenomenon. Working within the Marxist theory of fascism, most of these authors try to 'prove' the historical continuity and cooperation of the traditional and extreme right (see Schulz 1990; Gossweiler 1995).[5]

Another term that occasionally surfaces in the literature is right-wing radicalism or *Rechtsradikalismus*. This predecessor of the term right-wing extremism is most often used interchangeably with it (e.g. Oswalt 1991; Weinberg 1993), but there are two traditions in which it is used in a different manner. In the German tradition the terms radicalism and extremism are used to describe a certain view *vis-à-vis* democracy, both containing a left-wing and right-wing variant. This tradition is strongly based on the official definition of the German state, which explicitly defines the 'fundamental principles of the free democratic order' and, since 1973, the distinction between radicalism and extremism:

> The term 'radicalism' resp. 'radical' has consequently undergone a change of meaning. What we characterise as 'extremist' today, used to be characterised as 'radical'. Nowadays, attempts that are characterised as 'radical' are those aimed at one-sided solutions that go 'down to the root' of certain problems, without (yet) aiming at the full or partial elimination of the free democratic order. (Frisch 1990: 8–9)

Simply stated, the difference between radicalism and extremism is that the former is *verfassungswidrig* (opposed to the constitution), whereas the latter is *verfassungsfeindlich* (hostile towards the constitution). This difference is of the utmost practical importance for the political parties involved, as extremist parties are extensively watched by the (federal and state) *Verfassungsschutz* and can even be banned, whereas radical parties are free from this control.

In the American tradition the term radical right is still commonly used, yet has a broader and even somewhat different meaning than in the European

---

[5] There are also a few scholars working outside the Marxist tradition who use the term 'fascism' in a generic sense, that is, for all periods – see, for instance, Griffin (1995) and Eatwell (1995).

literature. Authors working within the American tradition use the term 'radical right'

> to denote a wide variety of groups and small political parties that rekindled a special American tradition of right-wing radicalism. This old school of nativism, populism, and hostility to central government was said to have developed into the post-World War II combination of ultranationalism and anti-communism, Christian fundamentalism, militaristic orientation, and anti-alien sentiment. (Sprinzak 1991: 10)

Recently a wide variety of new terms, mainly variants on the term populism, have made their way into the field: right-wing populism, radical right-wing populism, national populism, new populism, neo-populism, etc. The terms not only differ in name but also in their relationship towards the term right-wing extremism. What most definitions have in common, though, is that it is claimed that populism is primarily used to describe a specific political form or style instead of a specific ideology or to distinguish modern from traditional parties of the extreme right. In most cases the difference between political style and ideological feature is not really clear, as authors relate the political style at least indirectly to a specific view of the people. This problem with defining the term populism is not typical for the field of right-wing extremism. Populism has always been a widely applied term in the political and scholarly debate (Canovan 1981; Ionescu and Gellner 1969).

Generally, two different uses of the term populism in relationship to the term extremism can be distinguished. In the first, authors clearly distinguish between the two, where the former is used primarily to describe the more moderate parties of the extreme right (Backes 1991; Betz 1994). In the second, the term populism is used exclusively to describe a certain political style used by right-wing extremist parties (Pfahl-Traughber 1994). All in all, most definitions of (whatever) populism do not differ that much in content from the definitions of right-wing extremism. They are usually more focused on political style and less on anti-democratic features. On top of that, the term populism is often used by authors who stress the newness of the (success of the) parties in question (Taggart 1995).

When the whole range of different terms and definitions used in the field is surveyed, there are striking similarities, with the various terms often being used synonymously and without any clear intention. Only a few authors, most notably those working within the extremist-theoretical tradition, clearly distinguish between the various terms. In addition, every term suffers from excessive variations in definitions and applications. All in all, the differences in definitions vary as much between terms as within terms, though they all point to some sort of ideology that is constituted from several different features. These features again refer back to the ideological features of historical fascism and National Socialism (cf. Scheuch and Klingemann 1976). Hence, the ultimate choice of what term is used is often primarily determined by the theoretical school the author adheres to (see Mudde 1996).

### Subgroups within the extreme right party family

Recently, there has been an increasing number of studies in which various subgroups within the broader extreme right party family have been distinguished on the basis of party ideology. These studies sometimes implicitly acknowledge the similarity of all parties with regard to some features of right-wing extremism, but point to differences between them with respect to other features or with respect to the intensity or importance of the feature(s) for the party ideology.

One of the early classifications is constructed by the German Stöss, who distinguishes four different types of right-wing extremism in Germany on the basis of the party's stand on the German question (1988: 36; also 1991: 26–8). Only two of the four groups have any real significance: the 'Old Nationalism' or the 'Old Right-Wing' and the 'New Nationalism' or the 'New Right-Wing'. The main difference between the two has to do with their ideological basis, whether it is 'Old', i.e. based on the ideas of the *Deutschnationalen* and the Nazis, or 'New', i.e. seeking modern paths adapted to changing national and international (post-war) conditions. The former are further characterised by 'a leaning towards statist and militarist thinking and a foreign policy preference for pro-Western or European-neutralist approaches', as well as a fierce anti-communism (Stöss 1988: 37). The parties of the New Nationalism want to find a 'new political credo' and look for a so-called 'third way'; a concept that has always remained rather vague and is mostly used to indicate an economic system different from both capitalism and communism and a foreign policy of a neutral Europe free of both the East and West, i.e. of the United States.

There are some problems with Stöss' distinction. First, it is developed for the German context, which is a rather specific one. Even if the concept of 'Old Nationalism' is extended to extreme right thinking of the inter-war period in general, the possibility of applying the classification outside of Germany (and possibly Austria) remains difficult. Second, the classification has limited value when applied strictly to political parties with some electoral relevance. Indeed, according to Stöss only two parties fall within the 'New' category, both of which never made it into the federal or even a state parliament.

These problems are for a large part overcome by the fairly similar classification of the Italian Ignazi, who distinguishes 'old' and 'new' extreme right parties. The whole family of extreme right parties is classified according to three ideological[6] criteria (1992: 7): (1) placement at the far right of the

---

[6] Ignazi himself speaks of three 'distinct' criteria and claims that his definition is, in contrast to others listed in his work, not solely based on 'party's ideology and/or issues' (1994b: 5). This

national political spectrum (spatial criterion); (2) fascist features in the party ideology (historic-ideological criterion); and (3) negative attitude toward the political system (attitudinal-systemic criterion). The new extreme right parties are selected on the basis of the first and third criterion, and are essentially right-wing anti-system parties. The old extreme right parties combine all three criteria. As prototypes of the new extreme right parties, Ignazi lists, among others, the CD, FN, REP and VB. The prototype of the old extreme right parties is the Italian MSI, which is according to Ignazi the inspiration for all extreme right-wing parties up until the 1970s. Other old extreme right parties are the BNP, CP'86, *Deutsche Volksunion-Liste D* (German People's Union-List D, DVU), and NPD (Ignazi 1992).

In his more recent work Ignazi has renamed the 'old' into 'traditional', and the 'new' into 'post-industrial' extreme right parties (1994a, 1994b). Even though the basis for classification remains the same, there are some changes in the actual classification of the individual parties. Former borderline cases such as the FPD, FPN and FPÖ are now included in the group of post-industrial extreme right parties. The VB is 'for certain aspects' included in the traditional group, but also in the post-industrial group, albeit with a question mark (1994a: 243–5; also 1994b). However, this problem of classification should by no means be limited to the case of the VB, as it can be argued for all parties involved. The problem stems from the vagueness of the historic-ideological criterion, which Ignazi summarises as: 'references to myths, symbols, slogans of the interwar fascist experience, often veiled as nostalgia, or in terms of a more explicit reference to at least part of the ideological corpus of fascism' (1992: 10). As he lists a rather broad and varied 'fascist corpus' including features like 'limitations on personal and collective freedoms' and 'acceptance of hierarchical criteria for social organisation' (1992: 10), not many of the new or post-industrial extreme right parties will escape this criterion when applied rigorously. Nevertheless, Ignazi has taken the distinction between 'new' and 'old' extreme right parties a step further by making it less German (thereby making it a bit too much Italian with its focus on Italian fascism and the MSI) and making it applicable to a wider range of (electorally relevant) political parties.

An alternative classification is constructed by Betz, who distinguishes two 'faces of radical right-wing populism': 'neo-liberal' or 'libertarian' populism, on the one hand, and 'authoritarian' or 'national' populism, on the other (1993: 680; 1994: 108). The main difference between these two 'ideal types' is defined in relative terms: 'What ultimately determines whether a party should be characterised as a neo-liberal populist party or a national

---

is primarily the result of the fact that Ignazi seems to have opted for a more restrictive use of ideology, requiring it to be 'structured and coherent' (1994b: 8), whereas I define ideology in a more inclusive way (see below).

populist party is the relative weight it attributes to the respective elements in its program' (Betz 1994: 108).[7] The distinction is far from static as parties can develop and have developed from one type into the other, partly as a result of the changing social base of their electorate. However, Betz notes that since the late 1980s there have been clear signs of an increasing importance of national-populist elements in the programmes of all the parties. The one exception to this development is the LN.

Betz' classification has both theoretical and empirical relevance but struggles with the problem of determining the relative weight of the two elements. How do you weigh the neo-liberal substance of a programme? Even though the author claims to provide 'a comprehensive analysis of the basic elements of the radical right-wing populist program and the shifts in emphasis of its two main components' (1994: 109), the actual analysis he provides is a rather general account on the basis of some election programmes and pamphlets of the various parties. While this might suffice to note 'a' shift in emphasis, it is hardly a solid basis for a meaningful classification.

## Putting the extreme right party family to the test

As can be seen from this short overview, different scholars group different parties together and do this under different labels. In addition, even scholars that use the same term often mean different things. Some consensus can nevertheless be uncovered. First, the term extreme right (or right-wing extremist) is still broadly accepted as the most satisfying collective noun. Second, this term is generally used to describe an ideology containing a combination of several distinct features. Third, despite several borderline cases there is a large number of political parties whose extreme right status is not debated. On the basis of this consensus, we can construct the following propositions:

1   The extreme right party family consists of a distinct group of parties that share a common ideological core.
2   This common ideological core includes (at least) that combination of features generally defined as right-wing extremist.
3   Within the broader extreme right party family at least two subgroups can be distinguished on the basis of ideological extremity.

The term proposition is used as none of these points has ever been empirically validated. Moreover, as far as there has been empirical research into a common ideological core of alleged extreme right parties, the results have rejected rather than supported the propositions. In an earlier study I have

---

[7] Betz explicitly mentions the following parties as representatives of neoliberal populism: *Autopartei* (Car Party), FPD, FPN, FPÖ, LN and *Ny Demokrati* (New Democracy, ND); and of national populism: FN, REP and VB.

tested the (first two) propositions on a small number of parties (Mudde 1995). After defining right-wing extremism as a combination of five distinct features (i.e. nationalism, racism, xenophobia, anti-democracy, and the strong state), the literature of three parties was analysed on the basis of the presence of these features. Only three features were found in all three cases and could thus be said to constitute the ideological core of the(se) extreme right parties. So, though an ideological core was found (prop. 1), it did not include all the features generally described as constituting right-wing extremism (prop. 2). As all three parties – CP'86, NDP and NPD – belong to the 'old' subgroup (see Ignazi 1992), it could be expected that the more 'moderate' extreme right parties, which are also electorally more relevant, will hold even fewer features (generally described as constituting right-wing extremism).

In her parallel comparative study Gardberg focused on four 'new' extreme right parties: the FN, REP, VB and ND. The goal of her study was to find the most appropriate label for their ideologies, using a list of six different labels or categories: neo-fascism, extreme right, nationalism, xenophobia or racism, neo-conservative and neo-liberal ideas, and populism or protest (1993: 8–9). On the basis of an analysis of (some) party programmes and interviews she concludes that 'it is indeed difficult to agree on a common label or category for them' (1993: 121). As far as there is an appropriate label for all four parties, it is the label 'new right'. However, this label has the disadvantage of being rather vague, i.e. meaning a combination of neo-liberal and neo-conservative ideas, and is applicable to a far broader range of parties, such as those normally labelled 'conservative' (1993: 122).

These two studies show that although there exists a rather broad consensus on the existence of a distinct extreme right party family that entails (at least two) different subgroups, this consensus is no more than a proposition at this time. The few empirical studies provide only (moderate) support for the first proposition: that these parties share an ideological core. However, that this core is indeed right-wing extremist, as the second proposition holds, remains doubtful. Finally, the third proposition, asserting the existence of subgroups, has as yet not been tested at all. This study therefore intends not only to test all three propositions, but also to do this on the basis of a broader selection of cases and material than was employed in either of the two earlier studies. Indeed, both studies suffer from limitations, most notably in the particular group of parties selected (Mudde 1995) and the limited number of party documents studied (Gardberg 1993).

For the purposes of this analysis the following parties were selected according to both intrinsic and practical criteria: *Die Republikaner* and the *Deutsche Volksunion* in Germany, the *Vlaams Blok* in Belgium, and the *Centrumdemocraten* and the *Centrumpartij'86* in the Netherlands. The principal intrinsic criteria were that (i) the party has to have contested at least one parliamentary election; (ii) it has to be reputed generally as extreme right in the scholarly literature; (iii) it has to be part of the 'third wave' of right-wing extremism, i.e. have been politically active since the 1980s. In addition, the selected parties must differ in ideological extremity to study the third proposition. Ideologically, the CP'86 and the DVU are classified as part of the (more) 'radical' subgroup of the old/traditional extreme right parties, whereas the CD and the REP are classified as part of the (more) 'moderate' subgroup of the new/post-industrial extreme right parties, with the VB being partly in both groups though mainly in the first (Ignazi 1992, 1994b). The parties also differ in terms of electoral success. The VB belongs to the electorally successful extreme right parties in Western Europe (in 1994), gaining around 12 per cent of the Flemish votes;[8] the rest are not successful, gaining under 5 per cent on average in national elections. The CD and the REP are more successful (or better: less unsuccessful) with around 2.5 per cent compared to the under 1 percent parties CP'86 and DVU. The most important practical criteria of the study were (accessibility of) language and the availability of party literature. Having selected the parties to be studied, we now have to determine how we can best study party ideology.

## Studying party ideology

Although party ideology is normally given a chapter or paragraph in studies on political parties, there are only a few studies that adopt an 'ideological approach', i.e. in which 'the substance and prevalence of a party's ideology are of primary interest to the investigator' (Lawson 1976: 15). The number is even less in the case of comparative studies.[9] Especially in studies of party families the ideologies of the individual parties have been of secondary interest. Often it seems to be assumed that (all and only) the member parties share the family ideology as the core of their respective ideologies. The few comparative studies that have adopted the ideological approach compare either one party through time (Sainsbury 1980; Dittrich et al. 1986) or a number of parties from the same country (Hoogerwerf 1971; Borg 1966; see also most of the contributions in Budge et al. 1987) or like-minded parties in different countries (Gardberg 1993; Mudde 1995).

---

[8] Some authors list the score that the VB gets at the federal level (i.e. in the whole of Belgium, which was 6.6 per cent in 1991, see Betz 1994; Kitschelt 1995). However, as is the case for all Flemish parties, the VB contests elections only in the Flemish part of Belgium, and in the area of Brussels, and the federal score thus provides a distorted picture of the party's real strength.

[9] Janda, on the other hand, speaks of 'the outpouring of empirical research on comparative party ideologies' (1993: 169). This difference of opinion is for the largest part due to the fact that he also includes studies on party's positions on issues (even when these 'do not fit common ideological concepts'), i.e. studies that work with a single left–right dimension. Most of these studies are not only very limited in scope, as they primarily or exclusively focus on the socioeconomic views of parties, but their interest in party ideology is also often only secondary.

This lack of comparative research into the ideologies of political parties can possibly be explained by the fact that during the so-called 'Golden Age of comparative politics' (Dalton 1991), i.e. the late 1950s and early 1960s, the importance of ideology in party politics was severely challenged by the 'end-of-ideology' thesis. This held that the major political parties in the West had converged so much ideologically that politics had become more a matter of administration (see in Bell 1960; also Lipset 1960). Not surprisingly, the few studies of that period that adopted the ideological approach were aimed at testing this thesis empirically. Hoogerwerf (1971), for instance, demonstrated on the basis of a both synchronic and diachronic comparative analysis of the 1948 and 1963 election programmes of the four major Dutch parties that a larger correspondence in socio-economic policies had come into being. The ideological differences that existed in 1948 were altered into differences in strategy and means in 1963. Thomas came to similar findings in a comparison of the major parties of six countries, which led him to the conclusion that without an ideological revival West European parties 'could be headed toward the kind of partisan consensus which now characterises American politics' (1980: 364). This revival seemed very unlikely to him, as the major parties had too much to loose and new parties had never proved to be very successful over time. Even though the end-of-ideology thesis was disputed both on empirical and theoretical grounds (see LaPalombara 1966; Seliger 1976), and seemed to have disappeared in the 1970s, it regained its influence within the political science community in the late 1980s.

### Defining party ideology

Ideology has been defined in numerous ways, and often the definitions are based on some normative idea. Seliger, for example, distinguishes two uses of the term ideology: restrictive and inclusive (1976: 14). In the restrictive use the term is confined to belief systems of the extreme left and right in the post-war Western world. Seliger argues against this use, describing it as a manifestation of political conviction and 'a concomitant of the latest theory, that of the end of ideology, whose major proponents did not disguise that what they claimed to be ending was that which they wished to be ending' (1976: 26). In accordance with Seliger I reject the restrictive use, as it limits not only our view of the phenomenon at hand, but also its usage in comparative research; what is extremist and ideological in one context can be moderate and non-ideological in another.

In this study the term ideology is used in an inclusive way, i.e. as 'a body of normative or normative-related ideas about the nature of man and society as well as the organisation and purposes of society' (Sainsbury 1980: 8). It thus includes both ideas on how society or man *ought to be* and ideas on how they *are*. Following this definition, party ideology is defined as *a party's body of normative(-related) ideas about the nature of man and society as well as the organisation and purposes of society*. Once the different ideas (or fea-

tures) of the ideology are conceptualised properly, i.e. in a manner 'suffi-
ciently abstract to travel across national boundaries' (Rose 1991: 447), the
criterion of ideology should lead to no distinctive problems in cross-national
comparative research.

### Which sources of party ideology?

Most studies on party ideology use election programmes as data for analyses. Programmes have the advantage that they are, in general, officially
endorsed by the members of the party and, consequently, can be 'considered
to represent and express the policy collectively adopted by the party' (Borg
1966: 97; also Anckar and Ramstedt-Silén 1981). Nevertheless, some
authors take the view that election programmes are not satisfactory, because
out of tactical considerations they do not show the true face of the parties.
Election programmes of political parties are aimed at, among other things,
the attraction of voters and the enhancement of the profile of the party. They
thus have a predominantly external orientation (Flohr 1968; Raschke
1970), and in the case of extreme right parties it has often been argued that
there exists a radical 'back-stage' behind this (relative) moderate 'front-
stage' (Van Donselaar 1991: 16; also Fleck and Müller 1998).[10] However,
extreme right parties do not have the exclusive rights to a discrepancy
between views expressed in the official election programmes and those proclaimed elsewhere or supported 'truly'.[11] Flechtheim, among many others
(e.g. Sainsbury 1980; Dierickx 1996), has argued that this is customary with
all political parties:

> The programmes alone will hardly fully open the true nature of the party – for
> that purpose political programmes are as a rule too much of an ideological cov-
> ering. With those parties that are explicit ideological creations ... at least much
> of what could be compromising will be left unsaid. (1974: 179)

One of the more popular methods to determine the 'real' ideology of
(extreme right) parties has therefore been to focus attention on the 'political
origins' of the party leaders and officials instead of on the party programmes
(see Müller 1989; Van Donselaar 1991). There are several problems with
this approach. First, the political origin of the individuals can only be interpreted when the ideology of the original party can be established. And then,

---

[10] Eatwell makes a similar distinction between the '*esoteric* and *exoteric* appeal. The former
refers to the ideological nature of discussion among converts, or in closed circles. The latter
refers more to what it is considered wise to say in public' (1992: 174).

[11] An explanation for the particular focus on extreme right parties in this regard can be found
in the fact that most authors define the extreme right as 'the other' of which they are no part
and are often also openly hostile toward. As Naess perceptively states: 'An important ingredi-
ent in descriptions of outgroups is the hypothesis that the outgroup says one thing, but means
another' (1980: 136).

of course, the original question returns: how is this to be done? Second, which leaders and officials are representative of the (whole) party? In the case of the REP, for example, there are (and were) leaders that have been members of 'openly' extreme right parties like the NPD, and maybe even of neo-Nazi groups, but there are (were) also leaders who have never been part of these groups – several have even been (sometimes prominent) members of democratic parties. Which official counts more and on what grounds?

The problem of representativeness is also at the root of two other alternative methods, interviewing leading party members and using 'observers'. How do we know if the opinion of the interviewee(s) is representative of the (majority) view of the party (Dierickx 1996)? The volatility of the leadership of many extreme (right) parties makes this a particularly pressing problem. This can be seen in the study of Gardberg (1993), for example, who interviewed five of the six members of the REP fraction in the EP. Unfortunately, all five members had left the REP either already at the time of the interview or slightly afterwards, and the only remaining representative and then party leader, Franz Schönhuber, had objected to an interview. Gardberg was thus stuck with the views of REP dissidents, not REP leaders. The second approach, using 'observers' (see Janda 1980), cannot be evaluated on its scientific merits as it is not made clear who these observers in question are, nor what they observe and how they observe this.

To overcome the danger of being stuck with only the front stage of the extreme right parties, I have chosen to analyse not only primarily externally oriented party literature, but also party material whose primary orientation is internal: party papers. It seems plausible that this literature will hide 'the true nature of the party' to a far lesser extent than externally directed literature since it is aimed at a different group of recipients, i.e. the party members (the internal arena), as against the whole electorate (the external arena; cf. Sjöblom 1968). A second advantage of party papers is that they are the official organ aimed at the members on behalf of the party leadership, and although they are not officially endorsed by the members it can be assumed that they are officially endorsed by the collective party leadership. These two sources together (party programmes and party papers) should provide us with a fairly broad and detailed insight into the 'institutionalised party ideology' (Sainsbury 1980: 17; also Holzer 1981).

This selection, though broader than most studies on party ideology, still contains restrictions. The fact that only the *manifest* party ideology is studied means that the 'latent party ideology', appearing in unofficial documents (e.g. pamphlets of party dissidents or of individual party members), is left outside of the analysis (Helenius 1969; Sainsbury 1980). Moreover, the fact that only documents from the *national* party are studied means that material, whether official or unofficial, from regional or local party branches is left aside. Finally, the focus throughout rests on what the party says (party literature) and not on what the party does (party policy). However, since most right-wing extremist parties in Western Europe, and all parties selected for this analysis, are seen and treated as pariah parties and kept out of power at all governmental levels, the distinction between what they say and what they do is largely academic.

### What method of analysis?

Studies that deal either primarily or secondarily with party ideology generally adopt a qualitative approach to textual analysis; the selected material is 'read carefully' and the most important ideological features, according to the researcher, are presented (often with illustratory quotations). Although this type of textual analysis is still by far the most popular and has proven its value (especially in explorative studies), it has been criticised for being 'subjective, idiosyncratic, and overinterpretive' (Livingstone 1989: 188). According to some critics genuine textual analysis or content analysis is quantitative by nature and uses computerised methods to come to 'exact' and 'scientific' results. As Gerring has noted for the mostly quantitative studies of party ideology in America: 'the focus is usually on the *general function* of ideology ... rather than on the *specific content* and history of the ideologies in question' (1998: 288, my italics). This is also the case for the ECPR-organised manifesto project, which dominates the comparative study of party ideology in Europe (see Budge *et al.* 1987; Klingemann *et al.* 1994). However, because of both its method and sources, the manifesto project data are better used to analyse policies of parties and party families than their ideologies (e.g. Budge and Keman 1990; Laver and Schofield 1990).

Moreover, differences between qualitative and quantitative analysis in general are not as big as is often claimed (Coffey and Atkinson 1996) and this is also true for the particular case of textual analysis (Thomas 1994). The choice between the two approaches is not a matter of principle, but a difference in attention and emphasis.

> Three major differences in qualitative and quantitative emphasis deserve attention: (1) the distinction between explanation and understanding as the purpose of inquiry; (2) the distinction between a personal and impersonal role for the researcher, and (3) a distinction between knowledge discovered and knowledge constructed. (Stake 1995: 37)

As this study is explorative, aimed at understanding rather than explanation, and at discovering rather than constructing, a qualitative approach is clearly more suitable. Moreover, given the complex nature of (party) ideology, classification or coding is vital. Though a human coder introduces an element of subjectivity, this should not be seen as 'a failing needing to be eliminated but as an essential element of understanding' (Stake 1995: 45; also Gerring 1998: 297–8). Moreover, the choice between a machine (computer) and a human coder (researcher) is often in essence a choice between reliability and validity (also Kepplinger 1989; Livingstone 1989). Whereas computerised methods are superior in regard to reliability, both in terms of completed measurement and future replaceability (Thomas 1994), they are bound to the categories chosen on forehand and cannot interpret the context of these categories, and therefore may be inferior in regard to validity. Also, compared to the human coder the machine is far less flexible and less able to learn during the process. As Coffey and Atkinson write:

> codes are organising principles that are not set in stone. They are our own creations, in that we identify and select them ourselves. They are tools to think with. They can be expanded, changed, or scrapped altogether as our ideas develop through repeated interactions with the data. Starting to create categories is a way of beginning to read and think about the data in a systematic and organised way. (1996: 32)

On the basis of these arguments I have chosen a form of qualitative textual analysis that is partly structured by a preliminary list of possibly relevant ideological features and themes. This list has been constructed on the basis of a variety of sources: (1) ideological features mentioned in the literature on right-wing extremism (Mudde 1995); (2) themes used in other content analyses that were expected to be relevant (Borg 1966; Budge et al. 1987); and (3) an initial study of (a sample of) party programmes of the parties in question (see appendix B). On the basis of this list the *content* of the ideological features of the different parties will be captured.

The *importance* of the various features within the party ideology as a whole, however, will be determined by the use of the *causal chain approach*. This approach is aimed at discovering the hierarchy of the various features that are found to be part of the ideology. This is done by following the direction of the argumentation and assessing what is the prime argument, what is the secondary argument, etc. (see also Naess 1980). This can best be explained by a short (self-invented) story:

> Crime is sweeping our cities! Even within the police force there is nostalgia for the time that policemen and bankrobbers were on a first name base and arrests could still be made without the use of weapons. But these days are long gone, as the criminals of today are violent sociopaths. This is especially true for the immigrant youth, by far the majority of the hardened criminals. They have monopolised the drugs market and made the white criminal an exception in our own prisons. We should, however, not only blame these criminal black youngsters, as they are also victims. They have been torn away from their own culture and, under strong pressure from left-wing welfare people and politicians, forced to integrate. As we all know, this is impossible and the loss of identity and a consequent life of crime were the logical conclusions. Even though these black hoodlums should be punished severely, after having been sent back to their own countries, the problem can't be solved by this end alone. Not unless we punish the traitors in power and return to a pure Dutch society, will we have our peace and safety back on the streets again.

This story initially seems to deal with the problem of rising crime, based on the feature of law and order. However, it is not crime itself that is the main problem, but a specific sort of crime; crime committed by black youngsters. Moreover, it is not even their criminality, but the root of it, the fact that (young) immigrants are 'torn away from their own culture', that is the prime concern of the story. This is a typical example of ethnopluralist reasoning, which lies behind the law-and-order theme (and behind the xenophobic and anti-elite views). It is this sort of analysis that is developed by the causal chain approach.

## Outline of the book

The book is composed in the following manner: the five parties are ordered by country and each of the three countries is addressed in a different section. Each section begins with a short introduction of the history of post-war right-wing extremism in the country up until the founding of the parties under study. Except for the Flemish part, which entails only one party, each part contains two chapters. Each chapter describes the history, literature and ideology of a single party in different sections.

The section on the ideology is subdivided into themes and ideological features. Some features are discussed for all parties, as they constitute main features of right-wing extremism (e.g. nationalism, exclusionism, the strong state). Other features and themes are mentioned in the case of some parties, depending on their salience in the party literature. Though the subdivisions might at times appear artificial or overlapping, they serve first and foremost to structure the presentation of the analysis of the ideology. The conclusions will provide for a concise and integrated description of the whole party ideology. The book concludes with a chapter in which the literature and ideology of the different parties are compared and the question of the validity of the propositions is addressed.

# Part I

# Germany: 'Deutschland den Deutschen!'

## The extreme right in Germany, 1945–80

After the capitulation of Nazi Germany, the country was briefly occupied and divided into zones by the main four allied forces (France, the Soviet Union, the United Kingdom and the United States). Because of the occupation and the allied denazification policy, political organisations were initially severely hindered in their development. They could, for instance, only organise at the community and later the zone level (Backes and Jesse 1993). Moreover, the fact that only parties with a democratic character could contest elections limited the electoral possibilities of right-wing extremist movements. The ending of the Allied controlled licence duty for political parties in 1948 and the increasing polarisation of the East–West relations, with the divided Germany at its heart, created some space for them.

Between 1946 and 1952 several extreme right parties were founded and allowed in the three zones of the western part of Germany, which in 1949 became the Federal Republic of Germany (further Germany or FRG). Most of these parties never grew beyond a regional basis. One of the few parties that did have a wider impact was the *Deutsche Konservative Partei-Deutsche Rechtspartei* (German Conservative Party, German Right-Wing Party). It received 8.1 per cent of the votes in the 1949 state election in Lower Saxony, which gave it the right to five seats in the *Bundestag* (the German parliament).[1] After several ideological disputes within the parliamentary faction, the majority of the delegates founded a new party in 1950, the *Deutsche*

[1] Until 1956 the '5 per cent hurdle' applied only at the state (*Land*) level. If a party gained more than five per cent in one state it gained entry in the federal parliament. With the amendments to the electoral law in 1953 and 1956 the electoral system became as follows: every German has two votes, the *Erststimme* (first vote) is cast for a candidate in a constituency, the *Zweitstimme* (second vote) for a party list at the state level. The second vote determines the final percentage of parliamentary seats, the first vote (in part) the people that occupy these seats. A party needs more than 5 per cent at the federal level, or the majority in three constituencies, to gain entry in the Bundestag (Von Beyme 1983: 26).

*Reichspartei* (German Reich Party, DRP).[2] The main representative of the first right-wing extremist wave,[3] however, was the *Sozialistische Reichspartei* (SRP), which received 11.0 and 7.7 per cent in the 1951 state elections in respectively Lower Saxony and Bremen.[4] After October 1952 the first wave ebbed away after the SRP had been banned on the grounds of its neo-Nazi character. In the following three months more than sixty-one successors to the SRP were also banned (Knütter 1991).

Consequently, the DRP remained as the strongest right-wing extremist party in (West-)Germany. However, the party soon suffered various set-backs. In 1961 it suffered a defeat at the parliamentary election, gaining a mere 0.8 per cent, which led to an internal power struggle and a split of the militant faction of the party. As a reaction to its marginalisation DRP leaders contacted prominent members of other nationalist parties, among them members of the folding *Deutsche Partei* (German Party, DP) and the *Gesamtdeutsche Partei* (All-German Party). Their primary goal was to found a new political party, which would become the reservoir of the fragmented German nationalist right-wing. On 28 November 1964 it was founded under the name *Nationaldemokratische Partei Deutschlands* (NPD). The second wave of German right-wing extremism had begun.

The NPD wanted to create the appearance of being a national-conservative party with a leadership without a Nazi past. The chairman of the party became Fritz Thielen, in 1945 co-founder of the *Christlich-Demokratische Union* (Christian Democratic Union, CDU) in Bremen and later chairman of the national-conservative DP. The choice of Thielen also served another purpose, namely that the NPD was a collection of different (national-conservative) parties rather than a revamping of the (extreme right) DRP. The real power, however, was in the hands of former DRP leader Adolf von Thadden.[5] Moreover, a large group within the leadership did have a Nazi past: two-thirds of the party executive had been member of Hitler's NSDAP, from which another two-thirds had either joined before 1933 (the year it took over power) or had occupied a high position in the Nazi regime (Niethammer 1967).

---

[2] For an overview of the histories of these parties, see the relevant chapters in Tauber (1967); Stöss (1983/84); Dudek and Jaschke (1984).

[3] Three (short) waves of right-wing extremism in (West-)Germany are generally distinguished in the literature (see Knütter 1991; Zimmermann and Saalfeld 1993; Wetzel 1994). The first wave was characterised by the short-lived electoral success of the SRP in the 1948–52 period; the second wave by that of the NPD between 1964 and 1969; the third wave started at the beginning of the 1980s, increasing at the end of that decade with the successes of the REP and to a lesser extent the DVU.

[4] Unless indicated differently, all electoral results cited here are based on Stöss (1991).

[5] Niethammer (1967: 26) describes von Thadden as 'the spder in the web of the party leadership'. For a description of the man who became the personification of Germany's second wave of right-wing extremism, see Jesse (1990).

The NPD developed into a full-fledged political party within a few years. In 1967 its organisation extended over almost the whole territory of the FRG, relying heavily on the still existing party organisation of the DRP, with a presence in 75 per cent of all German cities and all ten states (Niethammer 1967: 28). Within a short period of time its membership increased dramatically. The party had started with only 473 members at the inaugural meeting in November 1964, yet at the end of 1966 this figure had risen to over 25,000. This was probably for a large part the spillover effect of the ongoing electoral successes. The party began with a modest 2.0 per cent of the votes in the 1965 parliamentary election. This was well under the federal 5 per cent hurdle needed to gain entry into the federal Parliament, but more than twice what its 'predecessor', the DRP, had received at the previous parliamentary election. Within a year the NPD won 7.8 and 7.4 per cent in state elections in Hesse and Bavaria respectively. At the state election in Baden-Württemberg in April 1968 the party reached its peak with 9.8 per cent and with this result it had achieved a total of sixty-one seats in seven (out of ten) German state parliaments and some 600 representatives in regional and local councils throughout the country (Stöss 1991: 147). The ongoing electoral successes also led to a growing interest in the party by the German state. In the late 1960s the government indicated on several occasions that it was considering a constitutional ban of the party because of its alleged extremist character (Dudek and Jaschke 1984).

In 1967 the NPD suffered a short 'power struggle' when Von Thadden decided to step out of the shadow and replaced Thielen as chairman. His 'coup' was little more than a surgical correction and changed nothing in the (electoral) appeal of the party. At the beginning of 1969 the NPD seemed to have reached its goal of becoming the reservoir of the German extreme right with no less than 72 per cent of all 'organised' right-wing extremists[6] in Germany being members of the party (Arndt and Schardt 1989: 284). Most other right-wing extremist parties had either lost their members to the party or had called upon the remaining members to vote for the NPD at elections. The only relevant person in right-wing extremist circles that kept resisting its omnipotence was the influential Gerhard Frey, owner, publisher and chief editor of the most important nationalist newspapers in Germany (see chapter 3). Frey remained sceptical about the party and only reluctantly appealed to his readers to vote NPD in the 1969 parliamentary election (Backes and Jesse 1993: 87).

The 1969 election was approached with much confidence by the NPD. Its slogan *Man kann wieder wählen* (One can vote again) did put the finger at

[6] By 'organised' right-wing extremists are generally meant all persons that are member of any organisation that is officially registered as right-wing extremist by the German State. For an overview of these organisations and the 'official' number of organised right-wing extremists, see the annual *Verfassungsschutzberichten* (further VSB).

the sore spot of German politics of that time: the Grand Coalition. This government coalition of the two major parties, the Union block of the CDU and the Bavarian *Christlich-Soziale Union* (Christian Social Union, CSU) and the *Sozialdemokratische Partei Deutschlands* (German Social Democratic Party, SPD), combined with the traditionally weak opposition of the *Freie Demokratische Partei* (Free Democratic Party, FDP), gave the NPD the opportunity to present itself as the only authentic (right-wing) opposition party. Within the media and scholarly community a substantial electoral success of the NPD was anticipated too. The German left-wing liberal weekly *Die Zeit*, for instance, reported already on 9 February 1968:

> In the fall of 1969, after the parliamentary election, the President will have to welcome a new party and a new parliamentary party leader to the Parliament hall: Adolf v. Thadden and his men of the NPD. There is almost no doubt about this. The only thing that is still unclear is precisely how many national-democrats will enter Parliament – whether 25, as opinion pollers say, or even 50, as optimists in the NPD central office suspect. (reprinted in Dudek and Jaschke 1984: 286–7)

In the event, the election resulted in a complete disaster with the party winning 'only' 4.3 per cent and no seats in the Bundestag. This was the beginning of the end for the NPD, as became clear in the following year. At state elections in among others Bavaria, North Rhine-Westphalia and Hesse the party remained well under the 5 per cent hurdle. The rapid collapse led the government to abandon its preparations for a possible ban on the party. The mere threat of a ban appeared to have been effective, not only outside of the party (scaring away possible voters) but even within (Dudek and Jaschke 1984).

The internal struggle, which had been suppressed by the collective euphoria over the seemingly never ending electoral successes in the preceding years, broke out with great vehemence after the electoral defeats. Militant members openly indicted the parliamentary strategy of the party leadership and called for more extraparliamentary activism, partly in reaction to the highly successful actions of the extreme left *Außerparlamentarische Opposition* (Extraparliamentary Opposition) of that time. In November 1971 Von Thadden stepped down as party chairman, arguing that the NPD had got out of control. Before he went, however, he made sure that his successor was a confidant, Martin Mußgnug. In protest against the continuation of the 'moderate' law-abiding course a group of some 400 militants left the NPD and founded the extraparliamentary group *Aktion Neue Rechte* (Action New Right, ANR) shortly thereafter.[7] Between 1972 and 1979 the NPD became

---

[7] The ANR tried to integrate nationalism and socialism into a 'national-revolutionary' doctrine and, though itself unsuccessful, became a starting point of many right-wing extremist activists of the 1970s (see Bartsch 1975; Dudek and Jaschke 1984).

more and more run down. As electoral successes failed to materialise the number of council seats decreased from 426 in 1971 to only thirteen at the end of 1979 (Arndt and Schardt 1989: 287).[8] However, the problems of the NPD were not restricted to electoral support. The membership dropped dramatically and fluctuated around a mere 8,000 at the end of the 1970s. In a final attempt to turn things for the better, the party leadership tried to come to an agreement with Frey, who even became a member of the NPD in 1975 after having been guaranteed a nomination as vice-chairman by Mußgnug and Von Thadden. But the membership was only short-lived. The nomination met with fierce resistance within the party and Frey was defeated at the party conference. In the summer of 1976 he left the NPD, advising his readership to vote CDU/CSU (Schmollinger 1984).

In the 1970s the law-abiding image of the NPD was badly damaged by neo-Nazi terrorist groups that surfaced in its environment, especially that of its youth movement, the *Junge Nationaldemokraten* (Young National Democrats, JN). The many scandals resulted not only in a dramatic fall in the membership figures of the NPD, but also in its electoral results. By 1971 the party had lost all its seats in the various state parliaments, generally receiving around 3 per cent (Stöss 1991). At the end of the 1970s the ongoing decay had reduced the NPD to a 'less-than-one-per-cent-party'. The decrease in both members and votes (and thus seats) also had a dramatic financial effect on the party. Because of its low electoral support the NPD often could not appeal for the so-called *Wahlkampfkostenrückerstattung*, i.e. a state refund of the costs of the election campaign.[9] As a consequence, it was at the edge of bankruptcy on several occasions.

At the beginning of the 1980s the NPD tried to revitalise as well as improve its image by founding regional single-issue parties. In 1980 the *Bürgerinitiative Ausländerstopp* (Citizens Initiative to Stop Foreign Immigration) was founded in North Rhine-Westphalia and in 1982 the *Kieler Liste für Ausländerbegrenzung* (Kiel List to Limit Foreign Immigration) and *Hamburger Liste für Ausländerstopp* (Hamburg List to Stop Foreign Immigration) followed. These parties presented themselves as independent protest movements with a single issue: foreign immigration. This had been made into one of the most important issues of the NPD since 1979, under strong pressure from the powerful JN. Nevertheless, the ideological renewal could not stem the lingering malaise of the party. The membership decreased

---

[8] This was not only caused by internal factors. For instance, the end of the Grand Coalition and the subsequent polarisation of domestic and foreign politics between the social-liberal government and the christian democratic opposition made it possible for (moderate) nationalist right-wing voters to support the CDU/CSU again (Stöss 1988).

[9] Since 1967 German political parties that gain a certain percentage of the votes in an election, initially 2.5 and soon after 0.5 per cent, receive state funding of five DM per vote for the party's election campaign (Haller and Deiters 1989: 264; also Conradt 1989: 123).

further and stabilised after 1982 at some 6,200. In the various state and parliamentary elections it remained well below 1 per cent. The once prospering NPD, reservoir of German nationalism during the second wave of post-war right-wing extremism, had become a sectarian group of militant outcasts. The third wave of right-wing extremism would be caused and dominated by two new political parties.

# 2

# Die Republikaner

## The ups and downs of a discorded party

While the NPD was slipping further and further into oblivion in the 1980s, dissatisfaction was building up on the right of the *Union* parties. Their open support for the process of European integration and hidden support for (or at least acceptance of) the so-called *Ostpolitik*, the normalisation of relations with the communist states initiated by former SPD premier Willy Brandt, led to much criticism in as well as outside the parties. Originally, the protest was voiced primarily within the CDU/CSU or through non-party political movements (Jaschke 1994). In 1983 CSU leader Franz Josef Strauß supported a credit of over ten billion DM to the German Democratic Republic (GDR), in complete breach with the party's long-term and radical opposition to any measures that might stabilise the GDR economy. Several members left the party in protest, among them two prominent Members of Parliament (MPs), Franz Handlos and Ekkehard Voigt. Together with Franz Schönhuber, a well-known Bavarian journalist, they founded a new political party on 17 November 1983: *Die Republikaner* (The Republicans, REP). Handlos became leader of the new party, Voigt and Schönhuber his deputies.

In the beginning the party considered itself and was treated by the media as a *Rechtsabspaltung* (right-wing breakaway) of the CSU (Pfahl-Traughber 1993). Handlos wanted to build the REP into what Strauß had always been threatening the CDU with, a *bundesweite* (federal) CSU, that is a right-wing conservative party that would contest elections in the whole FRG and not just in Bavaria. Schönhuber also wanted a federal party, but he wanted a more modern right-wing populist party, inspired by the electoral successes of the French FN. The two fought a fierce power struggle in which Handlos accused Schönhuber of wanting to put the REP on a right-wing extremist course. After a failed attempt to expel Schönhuber, Handlos stepped down as party chairman and left the party, followed a year later by Voigt. At the *Bundesparteitag* (federal party meeting) in June 1985 Schönhuber was elected chairman and Harald Neubauer, a former NPD member and Frey-journalist, party secretary. This strengthened the allegations in the media that the REP was right-wing extremist instead of simply right-wing conservative.

Franz Schönhuber has become the personification of the third wave of German right-wing extremism.[1] Born 1923 in a small rural village in Upper Bavaria, he joined the NSDAP at the age of 18 and the *Waffen-SS* a year later. During the war he served for the most time as instructor in the French *Charlemagne* division. Even though Schönhuber fought only once in a real battle (very briefly in Crete) his Waffen-SS experience would remain important to him for the rest of his life (see Schönhuber 1989). After the war he became a journalist, initially as sport reporter for a communist (sympathising) newspaper and later becoming chief editor of the Munich tabloid *tz*. In the 1970s he changed to the *Bayerische Rundfunk* (BR), where he became deputy editor of the television department. Moreover, as presenter of the popular program *Jetzt red i* (Now I speak) Schönhuber became a famous personality in Bavaria. With his move to the CSU-dominated BR he became close to several leading party members (see Hirsch and Sarkowicz 1989: 20). In 1981 Schönhuber published an autobiography of his war-time experiences entitled *Ich war dabei* (I was there), which led to a storm of negative publicity.[2] Schönhuber was accused of trivialising the crimes of the (Waffen-)SS and the Nazi regime. As a consequence, he was fired by the BR in April 1982; it was this experience that led him to the CSU rivals REP.

At the beginning the REP could profit from dissatisfaction with the CSU, which was a consequence of this party's (alleged) abuse of power, patronage and limited internal democracy (Pfahl-Traughber 1993). The membership of the REP increased from 150 in November 1983 to 4,000 in February 1986,[3] among them several local CSU-delegates. The party tried from the outset to establish the image of a federal party. Although the REP had established branches in all German states in 1987, except for Saarland, the majority of the members lived in the two southern states of Baden-Württemberg and Bavaria. After German unification in 1990 the REP organisation was expanded by five new (and weak) state branches, though the situation did not change much in the sense that almost half of the 1994 membership (45 per cent) still lived in the two southern states, with 32 per cent in Bavaria.

The REP experienced its first electoral test in the Bavarian state election of October 1986. The election went surprisingly well for the party, even though it stayed under the 5 per cent hurdle. Nevertheless, the 3.1 per cent

[1] On Franz Schönhuber, see Hirsch and Sarkowicz (1989); Leggewie (1989: 108–29); Jaschke (1994: 94–103); Pfahl-Traughber (1993: 38–43); Dammann (1999).

[2] At the same time it became a bestseller; in 1989 it had sold already over 130,000 copies and was in its eleventh edition (Schönhuber 1989), while ten years later it was estimated to have sold some 220,000 copies (Klußmann 1998).

[3] Unless indicated differently membership figures and electoral results of the REP used in the text are based on Backes and Moreau (1994: 77–103).

brought it not only national media coverage but also 1.28 million DM *Wahlkampfkostenrückerstattung* which it used mainly for the development of its organisational structure (Backes and Moreau 1994: 83). Following this successful electoral debut the party membership increased further, doubling from 4,000 to 8,000 between December 1986 and December 1988. The party failed to translate this upward trend in membership into votes, however. In September 1987 it gained 1.2 per cent in Bremen, in March 1988 1.0 per cent in Baden-Württemberg and in May 1988 just 0.6 per cent in Schleswig-Holstein. In all cases the REP remained behind the scores of 'other' extreme right parties that contested the elections, the DVU and the NPD. These electoral defeats intensified the general idea that the REP was, as its mother party the CSU, a Bavarian phenomenon.

The year 1989 marked the electoral breakthrough of the party. In January it won 7.8 per cent in the West Berlin Senate election, which brought it eleven seats. This result came as a total surprise to both party insiders and outsiders, as the REP never had a big membership in the Berlin area. Moreover, in the period before the election the local leadership had been so divided that it was even thought that the party would not contest the election at all. Commentators agreed that the massive media reaction to its electoral campaign had been the main reason for its electoral success (see Haller and Deiters 1989; Hartel 1989). Later that year the REP won 7.1 per cent in the European election. The support for the party was distributed unequal over Germany: in Baden-Württemberg it received 8.7 per cent, yet the absolute stronghold was Bavaria with 14.6 per cent. The REP entered the European Parliament with a six person parliamentary party, led by Schönhuber, and joined the French FN (eleven delegates) and the Belgian VB (one delegate) in the so-called 'Technical Group of the European Right' (see Fennema and Pollmann 1998), a coalition of convenience rather than ideology. Schönhuber had worked together with VB-leader Dillen to ease the FN away from the MSI, with which party (and the Greek *Ethniki Politiki Enosis*; National Political Union) the FN had constituted a full party group in the previous period. Neither the REP nor the VB wanted to form a group with the MSI, because of a territorial dispute over South Tyrol. Ironically, the FN choose the REP for purely opportunistic reasons, believing that it would be more successful than the MSI in the longer run.

The electoral successes were accompanied by an increase in membership, from 8,500 in January to 25,000 in December 1989. Moreover, they brought about a total REP mania in the German public opinion with hundreds of editorials, articles and books being written about the party (Backes 1990a). Some authors predicted that the REP would become the fifth party of the German party system and they saw themselves supported by voices within the right-wing of the CDU/CSU, which declared the REP a possible coalition partner (e.g. Müller 1989). Others were more sceptical, claiming that the REP had only a small chance of survival in the long turn (e.g. Lepszy

1989; Roth 1989). The successes also strengthened the debate on the character of the party: while some experts argued that it was still part of the democratic right-wing (e.g. Backes and Jesse 1989; Lepszy 1989), the majority considered the party to be part of the extreme right (e.g. Stöss 1991; Pfahl-Traughber 1993). Especially within (extreme) left-wing circles, a comparison between the Bonn Republic of the 1990s and the Weimar Republic of the 1930s became a topic of serious debate (e.g. Hirsch and Sarkowicz 1989).

As quickly as the successes of the REP had come, the defeats followed. In the fourteen elections the party contested in 1990 and 1991, it never surpassed the 5 per cent threshold. In the case of the Bavarian state election the party had been extremely close, gaining 4.9 per cent of the votes. The only other reasonable scores were in the state elections in Saarland (3.3 per cent) and the now united Berlin (3.1 per cent). In the first parliamentary election after the 1990 unification the REP gained only 2.1 per cent of the votes; 2.3 per cent in the former West and 1.3 per cent in the former East (Backes and Jesse 1993: 124). Even though the party was one of the first German (extreme right) parties to try and 'convert' the former East Germans, it never gained a real foothold (Pfahl-Traughber 1993). This might have been caused in part by the fact that the REP had been banned by the last *Volkskammer* (GDR parliament) between February and August 1990.

The ongoing defeats went hand in hand with a stream of quarrels, scandals and splits. In the summer of 1989, for instance, the leadership of two state branches, Berlin and North Rhine-Westphalia, were collectively discharged from their office (Pfahl-Traughber 1993). In 1990 the internal division climaxed in an open power struggle between the 'moderate' Schönhuber and the 'extremist' Neubauer.[4] In May Schönhuber stepped down as party chairman as a result of ongoing criticism of his authoritarian style of leadership and populist style of politics by ('extremist' members of) the party executive. However, a majority of delegates at the party meeting reinstated him as party chairman two months later. In a later purge of extremists by the party leadership, Neubauer and various of his supporters were either expelled or discharged from their leading function. The symbol of the new leadership was the new vice-chairman Rolf Schlierer, a young and well-educated man with a national-conservative background. Schlierer had left the REP shortly in 1988 in protest at its radicalisation, but returned in 1989 to lead the council delegation in his hometown Stuttgart (Backes and Moreau 1994). All in all, the party had become more homogeneous but also smaller: its membership had dropped to 20,093 in December 1990 and 16,843 a year later. As a consequence of the ongoing electoral defeats, the

---

[4] Neubauer was at that time MEP, chairman of the Bavarian branch, federal vice-chairman, and was generally considered heir to Schönhuber (see Backes and Jesse 1993: 298–9).

defections to the *Deutsche Liga für Volk und Heimat* (German League for Ethnic Community and Heimat, DLVH),[5] and the storm of negative publicity, the REP was considered doomed to disappear at the beginning of the 1990s (see Roth 1990).

Despite the gloomy predictions, the REP returned with a blast in the state election of Baden-Württemberg in April 1992. Under the leadership of Schlierer, the party gained 10.9 per cent of the votes and, with fifteen seats, became the third largest party in the state parliament. Again it was proven that the REP was primarily a southern phenomenon: on the same day it gained a mere 1.2 per cent in the state election of Schleswig-Holstein. The electoral success in Baden-Württemberg led to the same public reaction as in 1989. However, the expected REP-avalanche did not follow and the party was again doomed to die. The results in the following elections remained under the 5 per cent threshold, though the REP had been extremely close in the Hamburg *Bürgerschaftwahl* (state council election) in September 1993, gaining 4.8 per cent. The lack of electoral successes led to new internal disputes between 'moderates' and 'radicals', which were strengthened by the mounting pressure of the German state. In December 1992 the Federal Home Secretary had decided to put the party under the surveillance of the *Bundesverfassungsschutz* (Federal Bureau for the Protection of the Constitution) at the repeated request of states that already observed the REP (North Rhine-Westphalia and Hamburg in particular). The REP reacted furiously to the decision and tried to contest the decision in several courts (VSB 1994). Though the decision was more widely accused of being politically motivated (e.g. Jaschke 1994; More 1994), the REP was officially listed as right-wing extremist in 1994 (VSB 1995).[6]

During the *Superwahljahr* (super election year) 1994 the REP contested the parliamentary and European elections, eight state elections and local elections (*Kommunalwahlen*) in ten states (see VSB 1995: 144–8). It started rather well, gaining 3.7 per cent in the Lower Saxony state election (an increase of 2.2 per cent), but soon fell back to 3.2 per cent in the European election and between 1.0 and 1.5 per cent in various Eastern states. Even the

---

[5] In January 1991 the Neubauer group had founded a new political party, the *Deutsche Allianz-Vereinigte Rechte* (German Alliance-United Right-Wing), which on 3 October that year changed into the DLVH. The goal of the party was the same as that of the NPD in 1964, to unite the scattered nationalist camp. The DLVH started well: it was supported by several non-party political groups within the extreme right, among them the influential journal *Nation [und] Europa*, and various delegates from the REP (as well as from the NPD and DVU) joined (Wagner 1992). Among these were three of the five former MEPs of the REP, which under the leadership of Neubauer became the German representative of the Technical Group of the European Right. Despite the good start, the party never posed a serious threat to the REP (or DVU).

[6] In 1999 the REP is still officially registered as an extremist organisation, and is consequently observed by the Federal and all State Bureaux for the Protection of the Constitution, except for those in Berlin and Rhineland-Palantine (*Frankfurter Rundschau*, 27 March 1999).

state election in homeland Bavaria brought only 3.9 per cent. In October the REP gained a mere 1.9 per cent in the parliamentary election. In the simultaneous state elections in Mecklenburg-Vorpommern, Thüringen and Saarland it gained between 1.0 and 1.5 per cent. Only the regional elections in Baden-Württemberg and Rhineland-Palatinate brought the party some minimal local successes.

Electoral fiascos and state monitoring were probably the reason for Schönhuber's remarkable rapprochement with his old enemy Frey. On 22 August 1994 the two party leaders issued a joint communique announcing a new cooperation between the REP and the DVU. The party leadership was totally bombshelled by Schönhuber's one-man show: had not both he and the party always distanced themselves openly from the 'extreme right DVU'? In a hastily convened meeting they dismissed Schönhuber as party leader. Even though not everybody supported the immediate dismissal of Schönhuber,[7] the *Bundesparteitag* of December approved the step and elected Schlierer as new party chairman. He had to watch Schönhuber supporter and former CDU MP Rudolf Krause being elected convincingly as one of the five vice-chairmen however. Having been ruled in an authoritarian style for almost ten years by Schönhuber, the alleged *Führerpartei* had dismissed its *Führer*.

The next year revolved predominantly around the ongoing struggle between the camps of Schlierer and Schönhuber (see Backes 1996). Increasingly, it became a struggle between two different visions of party politics, i.e. a 'united right-wing' (Schönhuber) or an independent party with clear distance to the 'extremists' (Schlierer). Schönhuber's sudden retirement from the party in November 1995 meant that Schlierer had won a battle, but certainly not the war. The internal quarrels had cost the REP many seats and had reduced the membership to some 16,000 at the end of the year (VSB 1996). In addition, the series of unsuccessful state elections, in Bremen and North Rhine-Westphalia the REP remained even under 1 per cent, did little to strengthen Schlierer's position.

The Baden-Württemberg state election of 24 March 1996 were the litmus test for Schlierer's power within the party. At various times he had stated that he would resign as party chairman if the REP would not be reelected to the state Parliament. Against most expectations, the party and its leader succeeded in their task, gaining 9.1 per cent of the vote and fourteen seats (VSB 1997: 124). This was also the only election that year in which the party was successful; though it did almost double its support in Rheinland-Phalantine (to 3.5 per cent). The Baden-Württemberg result did enough to keep

---

[7] Schlierer said, in a interview with the author on 24 May 1995, that he had wanted Schönhuber to stay on until the parliamentary election to limit the electoral impact of the affair, as Schönhuber had already promised not to contest the election for party chairman at the party meeting.

Schlierer in power; at the first post-Schönhuber party meeting, in October 1996, he was reelected by 77 per cent of the delegates, and got his preferred team of vice-chairpersons approved (Nandlinger 1996).

The next year the REP was able to consolidate itself, most notably in terms of finances, during 1996 the party had received some 4.5 million DM from the state (Backes 1997: 138), and in terms of membership, which went slightly up from 15,000 in 1996 to 15,500 the next year (VSB 1998). At the same time, Schlierer's leadership remained disputed and electoral results remained disappointing – at the Hamburg state council election the REP dropped from 4.8 per cent in 1993 to just 1.8 per cent (VSB 1998). The next year the party remained again well below the 5 per cent threshold in various state elections. Particularly in the Bavarian 'homeland', where it had been polled above the 5 per cent benchmark before the election day, the actual result of 3.6 per cent meant a rude awakening, even more so because the party had not faced competition from the DVU. Still even more painful was the Saxony-Anhalt election, were the REP was completely overshadowed by the DVU's record 12.9 per cent.

The parliamentary election of 27 September did not end the loosing streak either: the REP gained a mere 1.8 per cent. Schlierer tried to interpret the result in a positive vein, hailing the increase in the actual number of votes (from 875,000 to 905,000) and the fact that the Republicans remained the leading party in the right-wing spectre (as the DVU and NPD got even less votes). This notwithstanding, the electoral results meant that the criticism against Schlierer and his *Abgrenzungsstrategie* returned to the centre of the party discussion (e.g. Braasch 1998; Moreau and Backes 1998). Vice-chairman Christian Käs became Schlierer's most outspoken opponent, openly challenging him for the party leadership. But a few days before the party meeting of November 1998, Käs withdrew his candidature and Schlierer, the only remaining candidate, was reelected with 81 per cent (VSB 1999). Nevertheless, Schlierer had again to accept Käs as one of his five vice-chairpersons, and, probably under the great pressure of his challenge, met DVU leader Frey and agreed that the two parties should not unnecessarily compete with each other (Nandlinger 1998; Pfahl-Traughber 1999). Notwithstanding the DVU's absence, and despite the traditional optimistic predictions of the party leadership, the June 1999 European election turned out dramatically for the REP, as it gained just 1.7 per cent. In anticipation of inevitable new attacks on his leadership, Schlierer explained the disappointing outcome as the result of voter disception by the Union parties and of the (EU-wide) non-voting by Eurosceptics.

Throughout its existence, the REP has tried to build a strong and broad political organisation, including a variety of auxiliary organisations. Only on paper has the party succeeded. The official youth organisation, *Republikanische Jugend*, founded as an *Arbeitskreis* (working group) in 1990, is organised in just five of the sixteen federal states. It includes all party members between the ages of sixteen and thirty, which is estimated at approximately 200 (Moreau and Backes 1998: 159). The student organisation, *Republikanische Hochschulverband*, has an even more limited reach. Except for the two seats it won in the Marburg university parliament in 1997, of which it lost one already the next year, very little has been heard of it (Moreau and Backes 1998: 160). The *Republikanischer Bund der öffentlich Bediensteten* or *Republikanischer Beamtenbund* (Republicans League of Civil Servants), was founded in October 1993 in reaction to the 1992 decision of the German state to officially register the REP as right-wing extremist. The initiative could not prevent the exodus of civil servants, most notably police officers, from the REP, however, and in 1998 its membership was estimated at a mere 150 (Moreau and Backes 1998: 160). The women organisation of the REP, the *Republikanischer Bund der Frauen* (Republicans League of Women), finally, is probably the smallest and least important. According to the webpage[8] it was founded on 26 August 1995, became an official auxiliary organisation of the REP two months later, and has 'over 70 per cent female members'.

The REP has never been very active in establishing contacts with other parties in and outside of Germany. This was in part because it originally did not want to ally itself with 'contaminated' parties, i.e. parties officially registered as extreme right, whereas 'democratic' parties did not want to ally themselves with the contaminated REP. Within Germany the party has virtually always kept its distance from parties like the NPD and DVU. Internationally, it had a short alliance with the FN and VB, which ended after the 1990 'split' when these parties accepted the group-Neubauer instead of Schönhuber as member of the Technical Group of the European Right. Schönhuber has always looked favourably upon the FPÖ, especially when Jörg Haider took over, but the Austrians kept their distance. During the first years after the fall of communism the German Republikaner were the inspiration of several short-lived initiatives in countries such as Hungary, Ukraine and Latvia, with which Schönhuber was also in contact. The contacts with the only successful East European Republikaner, the Czechoslovak (and later Czech) *Sdruzeni pro Republiku – Republikanska strana Ceskoslovenska* (Association for the Republic – Republican Party of Czechoslovakia), were terminated in 1993 due to the increasing anti-German rhetoric of its leader Miroslav Sladek[9] (Dvoraková 2000; Kopecky 1999).

[8] http://www.republikaner.org/repfrauen/1rbf02.htm
[9] Schönhuber once described the leader of the Czech party, Miroslav Sladek, as a 'Deutschenhasser' (German hater). See his interview with Backes and Hertel (1996: 144).

## Profiling the literature

*Externally oriented: programmes*

The so-called 'party without a programme' (Hirsch and Sarkowicz 1989: 23) has actually issued no less than seven national programmes in its first sixteen years of existence. Especially in its first years the programme was not only changed often, but also comprehensively. The programme of 1985 was a break with the original programme on several points, in part as a result of the succession of Handlos by Schönhuber. During these early years the self-image of the REP changed from being an 'independent, conservative-liberal people's party' to that of a 'society of German patriots, a freedom-loving [freiheitliche] and national party with high social and ecological obligations' (since 1987).

The original programme, entitled *Grundsatzprogramm* (Party of Principle, REP 1983) was adopted at the first *Bundeskongreß* (federal congress) on 26 November 1983. It contained sixteen A4 pages in which seventeen themes were discussed. The programme opened with a preamble, stating the party's democratic credentials, self-definition and (ten) main theses. At the Siegburg party meeting of June 1985, Schönhuber was elected party chairman and a new programme was accepted: *Das Siegburger Manifest* (The Siegburg Manifesto, REP 1985). It ran to just four pages, covering a total of nine points. Except for the difference in tone, which had radicalised, the new programme differed more in what was left out than in what was left in.

The 1987 *Programm der Republikaner* (Programme of the Republicans, REP 1987) was of similar size as the 1983 programme (fifteen pages), yet was more similar to the 1985 manifesto in tone. The structure was completely new, entailing seven basic principles and ten main points. Under the pressure of the rapid developments in the (former) communist states and their consequences for East–West relations the REP revised its programme again in January 1990. The theme of the *Parteiprogramm* (REP 1990) follows clearly from the text on the title page: 'Our Adherence: Germany; Our Goal: Restoration of Germany; Our Demand: Berlin – Capital of Germany'. It entails a preamble, following the theme, and twelve chapters in which various topics are generously elaborated and well structured on the basis of various lists of demands. All together the programme runs to a total of fifty-seven pages (A5 format).

In 1993 the REP again adopted a new programme, entitled *Wir machen uns stark... für deutsche Interessen* (We do our best... for German interests, REP 1993). It is quite similar to the 1990 version, though almost twice as thick (100 A5 pages). It now contains eighteen chapters, primarily as a consequence of a restructuring of the themes. Some chapters are accompanied by the note 'This chapter will be revised by the party council, according to the resolution at the federal party meeting of 26/27.06.1993, and will be put before the next party meeting for decision-making.'[10] The new programme was a reaction to two different events: the unification of Germany and, even more important, the Maastricht Treaty. As a consequence of the latter, European politics has its own chapter. The preamble has been extensively rewritten by the late Hellmut Diwald and opens with a sentence that would become his legacy within the REP: 'He who does not take his right, gives it up' (REP 1993: 3).

The 1998 parliamentary election were contested with a 'short version' of the programme, conveniently called *Partei-programm (Kurzform)* (REP 1998).[11] This pamphlet had a similar form as the DVU-programmes, i.e. one A4 page, printed on both sides, and folded twice. Despite the radical change, i.e. from one hundred pages to some six page sections, the short programme did cover the main themes of the party. For the European election the next year the REP used a more professional programme, *Deutschland und Europa* (Germany and Europe, REP 1999). It entailed thirty-one A5 pages, in which the party discussed thirteen different topics with a special European focus.

### Internally oriented: party paper

The official party paper of the REP was originally called *Der Republikanische Anzeiger* (Republican Informant, *RA*). It looked grim, appeared monthly, and originally contained four, later mostly eight pages (A3 format). Schönhuber started as chief editor, being succeeded by Neubauer in October 1985. In January 1986 the paper was renamed *Der Republikaner* (The Republican, *Rep*). Except for the new name, nothing substantial changed in content or style and also the counting of years of publication was maintained. After September 1988 the paper usually consisted of ten pages.

The power struggle between Schönhuber and Neubauer in 1990 had its resonance in the make-up of the editorial board of the paper. In May 1990 Schönhuber was listed as publisher and Ralph Lorenz as chief editor. The next issue named Hans Dorn and Johanna Grund (then MEP) as publishers and Karl Richter as chief editor; one issue later no publisher(s) was listed, though Richter was still chief editor. The address of the paper had changed from Munich to Landshut. The next journal which the various subscribers received had the same (unlisted) publisher and (listed) chief editor, but was named *Deutsche Rundschau* (German Review). It was presented as the successor to the *Rep*, including the same lay-out and counting. At the same time the REP leadership continued to publish the *Rep*, though through a new publishing company and with Schönhuber as both publisher and chief editor.

---

[10] In fact, it would take until the federal party meeting of 6 October 1996 before these chapters were actually revised.

[11] Information provided by Jürgen Wirtz, webmaster of the REP web page, in an email communication to the author on 8 June 1999.

The *Deutsche Rundschau* would soon after become the official party paper of the DLVH, before being absorbed by *Nation [und] Europa* in 1994.

In April 1992 the *Rep* was enlarged in both format and size. The paper got an additional two pages, making a total of twelve, of which two were filled with advertisements for an increasing range of party products (such as banners and lighters with the party logo). In January 1994 the logo again contained the three colours of the German flag (yellow, red and black). Moreover, the whole paper was more colourful, thereby making it less sombre and more professional. After the struggle between Schlierer and Schönhuber in 1994, the party got into serious organisational and financial problems, which also had their impact on the party paper. While the appearance remained largely the same, from January 1995 the *Rep* appeared only as a bimonthly with just four pages. The setback was overcome already the next year, when the paper returned to its original format (i.e. a monthly of eight pages). In the summer of 1997 it was renamed *Der neue Republikaner* (The New Republican); barring some small details (such as the reintroduction of colors), it remained identical to its predecessor.

The *RA* had always been printed in an edition of some 30,000 copies. The *Rep*'s second issue already had a total claimed circulation of 80,000. This figure has been unstable though, fluctuating around 70,000 in the late 1980s and 85,000 in the early 1990s. As a consequence of the 1994 internal party struggle, the circulation of the *Rep* dropped sharply, stablising at some 20,000 in 1997–8 (see the annual VSB). The party deemed the months before elections particularly important and the circulation was increased heavily. Before the Bavarian state election of 1986, for instance, the number of copies of the *Rep* rose from 100,000 in June to 650,000 in October (the election month). In the month of the 1987 Bremen state election the circulation was increased to 300,000. The all-time record was reached in the month of the parliamentary election of 1990: 4,000,000 copies were said to be printed. Except for the occasional increase in the circulation of the normal party paper, the *Rep* also published a few special issues concerning forthcoming elections.

## From national-conservatism to extreme right

### Nationalism

The primary ideological feature of the party literature is and always has been nationalism. It is telling for the political climate in post-war Germany and the cautiousness of the REP, that the party always denied being nationalist, rather calling itself 'national' or 'patriotic'. This notwithstanding, the REP can without any doubt be labelled nationalist. There are even strong indications of an ethnic nationalist outlook. For one, the REP believes that man is a *Gemeinschaftswesen* and can only develop fully within a community. It identifies various complementary communities, ranging from the smallest, the family, to the largest, the *Volksgemeinschaft* (ethnic community). This latter is considered to be the most important and should decide over its own affairs. This is most clearly depicted in Diwald's introduction: 'The sovereign ethnic community finds its political will in the nation, which releases its internal and external form in the state' (REP 1993: 3).

However, the ethnic community is defined in a both ethnic and state nationalist manner. For instance, some contributors to the party paper argue that membership of the ethnic community is to be defined on the basis of the individual's adherence to the ethnic community (*Rep* 9/87), while others define this adherence in an almost *völkisch* (ethnic) way: 'The instinctive bond to the own ethnic community can develop in perfect form only when one is born into it, is raised in it and so from childhood on identifies with it, thus, so to speak, taking solidarity in with one's mother's milk' (*Rep* 11/87).

This stringent definition of nationality expresses the position of the party accurately. The REP often criticises the alleged ease with which German nationality is given to foreigners. To ensure successful assimilation it pleads for restricting German nationality to foreigners that are genuinely prepared to dedicate themselves to the German nation 'as if it was their own' (*Rep* 11/87). Among other elements, this includes renouncing the old nationality (REP 1993: 22). The most positive statement on (large-scale) assimilation was made by Schönhuber, who acknowledged that the ethnic communities in Central Europe have mixed and that good Germans have come from that (*Rep* 7/88).

The demand for German (re)unification has always featured prominently in the party literature. From the beginning the REP has defined German unification as its highest goal. The 1983 programme presented a three-phase plan for the realisation of German unification,[12] which would lead to a *Gesamtdeutschland* (All-Germany), by which the party at that time seemed to refer only to the FRG and GDR. Over the years the topic was voiced more impatiently and aggressively. The 1987 programme stated: 'The illegal, unnatural and violent crumbling of the German ethnic community and its country in the heart of Europe is a danger to world peace and a humiliation of the people' (REP 1987: 3). Though the party welcomed the 1990 unification it considered this only a first step in the process of full unification that would eventually lead to a Germany having the borders of 1937. Within this vision the 1990 merger was considered a 'small reunification' of West Germany and *Mitteldeutschland* (Central Germany).[13] The real East Germany

---

[12] The three steps were: (1) elaboration of the German–German relations; (2) creation of a German *Bund* between the two German states; and (3) a free, secret and direct election for one national parliament (REP 1983: 11–12).

[13] Before the German unification of 1990, the party generally used three terms in this respect: *Deutschland* for the whole German nation, *Bundesrepublik Deutschland* for West Germany (the FRG), and *"DDR"* for East Germany (the GDR); the quotation marks indicated the party's rejection of both the country and its name (especially the reference to its democratic nature).

are the parts of the 'German Reich' that lay behind the Oder-Neiße border, i.e. the so-called *Ostgebiete* in Poland, Russia, Ukraine and the Czech Republic. Hence, the REP continued its demand for unification and for new negotiations and treaties with the eastern neighbouring states 'with the goal of a peaceful completion of German unity including East Germany' (REP 1993: 9).

The claim to reinstate the 'German Reich within its 1937 borders' has always been based on legal rather than nationalist arguments. The REP argues that these are the borders that are (still) recognised by international law. It speaks of the 'legally still existing German Reich' (REP 1990: 10). Hence it considers the acceptance of the Oder-Neiße border by the German government, as part of the two-plus-four treaty that formed the legal basis of the German unification of 1990, a violation of international law. In its *Deutschlandpolitik* (Germany politics) the party 'appeals to the directive of the constitution and to the ruling of the Federal Constitutional Court, which hold that everything should be done and nothing should be refrained from, that leads to the unity of Germany' (REP 1990: 4).

Though the party at times uses nationalist arguments for German unification it is not consistent in its demand for *external exclusiveness*. According to the ethnic nationalist tenet, *all* nationals have to live within the state (Koch 1991). The REP regards various groups outside of the aspired German state as part of the German ethnic community and nation (Austrians, South Tyroleans and so-called *Siebenbuerger Sachsen* that live in Romania), yet does not strive for the inclusion of these people or their territories. In general, the party limits itself to arguing that the FRG should protect the German character of these groups, for example through the introduction of an autonomous area and by pressuring the state in which they live.

The party does strive consistently for *internal homogenisation*, aptly expressed in its slogan *Deutschland den Deutschen* (Germany for the Germans). Consequently, 'Germany is not allowed to become an immigration country' (REP 1985: 1), meaning that the multi-cultural society is rejected and foreign immigration is to be limited in both the number of people and the period of stay. The party supports the Swiss model of foreign labour, which is said to mean that '(f)oreign workers are allowed to take jobs that are impossible to employ by Germans and only according to a temporary contract and without family members' (*Rep* 10/86). Originally, the party wanted the right to asylum to be reserved, under certain conditions, for real political asylum seekers (among whom it counted, for example, Afghans). In 1992, during the big asylum debate in Germany, the party reversed its position, stating that the fall of communism had made European asylum seekers impossible and, as refugees should be received in their own cultural environment, de facto excluded the possibility of legal asylum seekers in Germany (e.g. *Rep* 1/92). Even the civil war in Bosnia and the Kosovo 'crisis' did not lead to a change in the party's situation, as in both cases the REP vehemently opposed the (generous) adoption of refugees from the former Yugoslavia.

In exceptional cases foreigners are allowed to stay in Germany: first, foreigners who fully integrate (or better: assimilate) into the German society, though they thereby technically cease to be foreigners; second, temporary guest workers who have to leave after their contract expires; and, third, the occasional genuine refugees who have to leave as soon as the situation in their country of origin is safe again. During their stay in Germany all foreigners will be treated as guests, which means hospitably but without certain rights. Most notably, the party opposes the right to vote for foreigners, including those from other EU-countries.

The position of so-called *Aussiedler* – immigrants of German descent that lived in the 'lost territories' and who are by German law considered German citizens – causes the party an interesting nationalist dilemma. On the one hand, it considers them to be Germans, thus having the right to live within the German state. On the other hand, they have become fused with their *Heimat* (outside of the FRG) and, moreover, if all *Aussiedler* would leave, the territories might be really forever lost to Germany. Nevertheless, despite pressure from its electorate, which considered them as 'normal' asylum seekers (e.g. Betz 1990, 1994), the REP has generally championed the rights of the *Aussiedler* to settle in Germany and has often criticised the poor conditions under which they were received (blaming them on the fact that sham refugees take most of the budget).

In conclusion it is difficult to decide whether the REP is an ethnic or state nationalist party. As far as the party literature holds elaborations of the nationalist ideology they fit the ethnic nationalist tenet, emphasising the importance of the ethnic community and putting it over the state. Its nationalism is also mainly voiced in ethnic terms such as *Volksgemeinschaft* and *Heimat*. But at the same time the party accepts the possibility of successful large scale assimilation (at least in the past) and the fact that large parts of the German ethnic community live outside of the German state. So even though the REP adheres foremost to an ethnic nationalist ideology, it is neither elaborated nor applied rigidly.

### Exclusionism

As the REP is almost exclusively centred on Germany and the German ethnic community, a feature like ethnopluralism is seldom openly present in the party literature. One of the few instances is a pseudo-scientific discussion on the naturalness of xenophobia and ethnopluralism, which referred to work of prominent representatives of the (inter)national new right, such as Irenäus Eibl-Eibesfeld (a former student of Konrad Lorenz) and Alain de Benoist, intellectual head of the French *nouvelle droîte* (*Rep* 10/88). In general, however, vague hints of an ethnopluralist view can be derived only from the desired model of Europe.

The first programme had fully supported the ongoing process of European integration, striving for 'a core Europe with one or more European countries, to become in the long term to one federal state' (REP 1983: 11). The party later changed to a more anti-EC course, however, distancing itself increasingly from the existing form of European cooperation. Instead of the alleged 'United States of Europe', a *Bundesstaat* (federal state), it supported a 'Europe of United States', a *Statenbund* (confederal state) (*Rep* 2/87). The ideal type of a future Europe is most often referred to in the famous term of De Gaulle, a 'Europe of Fatherlands' ending at the Ural and the Bosphorus (REP 1993: 3); some authors, most notably Neubauer, preferred the term 'Europe of Ethnic Communities' (Europa der Völker). As none of the authors actually bothered to elaborate the different concepts, the argumentation behind the desired concept(s) of Europe remains vague, although they are all supposed to refer to the same model of Europe, i.e. a limited degree of cooperation on a limited range of policy fields between sovereign nation-states.

Throughout its existence the REP has regularly been accused of racism and anti-Semitism. Despite this, explicit evidence of these features cannot be found in the literature, although the illegal nature and strict monitoring of these features by the German state might well have pressed them 'back-stage'. Nevertheless, even these are hard to find, except perhaps circuitously, and there have been just a few vague indications of a possible racist vision in the paper, which were almost exclusively by one author.

The issue that has raised most dust is the alleged anti-Semitism. Given its past it is understandable that Germans are particularly sensitive to anti-Semitism. Nevertheless, this has led to a climate in which almost any criticism of Israel or Jewish organisations and representatives have led to suspicions of (at least latent) anti-Semitism, especially when the critique comes from alleged right-wing extremists. This was also how Schönhuber defended himself against accusations of anti-Semitism after a public argument with Heinz Galinski, then leader of the Central Council of Jews in Germany. After having listed a number of 'good Jews', he continued: 'However, I do not like to have to like mister Galinski. Next to the Berlin zealot Galinski, who permanently demeans our ethnic community, the Viennese Wiesenthal looks almost like Nathan the Wise' (*Rep* 12/88).

This notwithstanding, there are indications of at least a conspiracy thinking with respect to Jews in the party literature, which is one form of anti-Semitism, and there are regular attacks on Jewish organisations, which are accused of an anti-German attitude. There are also regular references to a very powerful Jewish lobby in the US, as well as to powerful pro-Israeli European and German politicians (mostly of Jewish descent). Regarding Israel the paper paints a picture in which Germany keeps paying the Jewish state, yet will never be forgiven. These themes featured prominently in articles on the Waldheim-affair and the Gulf War. In a discussion on the latter,

Israel was described as *Stichwortgeber* (provider of key words) and world opinion leader (*Rep* 3/91). Overall, there is some evidence of a latent anti-Semitic outlook in the literature, albeit not really prominent and very cautiously expressed.

### Xenophobia

Throughout the years immigration has developed into one of the major topics in the party literature, and most notably in the party paper. Whereas the first programme had addressed the issue relatively calmly, claiming that the 'foreigner issue' had become a 'foreigner problem' (REP 1983: 16), the later programmes spoke of 'the flood of foreigners' (REP 1985: 1) and 'migration of the ethnic communities' (REP 1993: 22). This shift towards a xenophobic view on immigrants and immigration had already been visible in the party paper which under the leadership of Schönhuber and chief editor Neubauer had become more negative and radical. The paper changed its critical though generally constructive style of commenting on (primarily Bavarian) politics for a negative and pessimistic preaching of doom and damnation for future Germany:

> Mass unemployment, problems with a flood of foreigners, left-wing extremism, increasing crime, decay of value-consciousness, and a constitutional state that is on the retreat, build the ingredients of a volatile mix, which could explode around our ears already tomorrow. Kreuzberg [a Berlin area with a lot of immigrants] may not be everywhere yet, though it might already be also there, where it has not burnt – yet. Only the spark is missing. (*Rep* 6/87)

Even though the tone became harsher the paper remained in general quite cautious, using writing tools such as rhetorical questions (e.g. 'Is the FRG becoming oriental?') and including articles in a neutral style which substantiate, on the basis of official figures, a trend which is deemed negative in perspective (e.g. 'More and more asylum seekers').

Xenophobia is most visible in the articles on asylum seekers. Already in the 1980s the REP paid attention to this topic, which at that time was of little importance to the broader political debate in Germany. During the 1990s the number of asylum seekers that came to Germany increased heavily and after several violent attacks on refugee shelters the topic dominated both the public and political debate for months (see Tränhardt 1995). After the major German parties had come to an agreement on a more strict law on asylum in December 1992 (the so-called *Asylkompromiß*), the topic disappeared from the political agenda. The REP tried to keep the issue alive, however, arguing that the new law should be implemented more strictly as still too many *Scheinasylanten* (sham refugees) were coming to Germany. Moreover, the issue was used to prove the political power and success of the REP, which argued that the tightening of the law had always been a key point of its political programme, and that the stricter law was the result of the party's growing support and the consequent fear for electoral defeat by the major parties. It also claimed that the issue proved that all accusations of right-wing extremism and racism against the party were false, since the established parties had actually enforced the programme of the REP.

The issue of the asylum seekers itself has always been presented in a blend of xenophobic, financial, legal and law and order argumentations, and is linked to almost every plague of modern society: crime, drugs, aids, unemployment, etc. (e.g. *Rep* 1/89). Moreover, practically all articles on the issue portray asylum seekers as imposters and criminals. The neutral term *Asylbewerber* (asylum seeker) is used only sporadically and the party favours the more derogative term *Asylant* or even *Scheinasylant* (see Cohn-Bendit and Schmid 1993: 239–40). The general picture that is drawn in the party paper is that of a 'Storm on Europe',[14] i.e. millions of alien, criminal and lazy foreigners that come to Europe (most notably Germany) to enjoy the good life at the expense of the European people (e.g. *Rep* 6/90).

Xenophobia is also directed at particular groups of immigrants, most notably the Muslims. The latter are portrayed as not (willing to be) integrated and fundamentalist, creating their own sub-cultures from which they try to expand all over Europe. Xenophobia is also one of the reasons behind the party's tough stand on naturalisation. A 'subtle' hint to Islam can be found in the elaboration to the demand to integrate, which includes 'also giving up exaggerated national-religious behaviour, which disturbs the peaceful living together within our society' (REP 1993: 23). Moreover, if the law on naturalisation is not toughened Germany could be containing an increasing number of 'Germans' that in case of an emergency would either flee or would defend foreign interests. This is, for instance, suggested by an article on the Gulf war in which the author points to the fact that the Palestinian foreign workers in Kuwait either fled the country or chose the Iraqi side (*Rep* 10/90).

Not only the foreigners that live in the country are seen as a (potential) danger to Germany; So are those living outside the country. The REP considers the international environment particularly hostile to Germany. This is in part a legacy of the Second World War, though the fact that certain limitations to the sovereignty of Germany are still not abolished proves (to the party) that the former allied countries (the US in particular) treat contemporary Germany with hostility too. It even suggests that the Allies had not been concerned that much with Europe's liberation, but rather with fifty years of Germany's occupation (e.g. *Rep* 10/87). A prime example of the international anti-German climate is the so-called 'enemy state clause', articles 53 and 107 of the United Nations (UN) charter, which according to the REP holds that the allied forces may still decide on the destiny of Germany.

---

[14] This was also the title of a book by Manfred Ritter, former CSU member and long-term state prosecutor, to which the paper devoted a series of articles over several issues.

The supposed alliance of the Western Allies with Germany during the cold war has not changed this. According to the party they still limit Germany's sovereignty and are 'practising a partly open, partly hidden occupying law behind the shield of friendly partnership' (REP 1990: 2). The cold war is seen as the other main reason for the country's secondary status in the world.

> We Germans are the muzzled dancing bears of the political world arena, which are one time rewarded with cinnamon bread and then the other time disciplined by the whip. The animal trainers are in New York and Moscow. (*Rep* 2/87)

It is because of this hostile international environment that Germany should take care of its own interests first. 'We Germans can safeguard our right to life only when we think of ourselves again on the principles of the protection of national interests' (REP 1985: 1). This credo is taken furthest in regard to agricultural policy, where the party argues that Germany should be wholly self-reliant in the production of its food. The party states repeatedly that looking out for the interests of one's own ethnic community does not mean threading on those of other countries. It simply means, as Schönhuber stated in his often quoted speech to the Siegburg party congress, '*Andere Völker achten wir, unseres aber lieben wir*' (We respect other ethnic communities, but we love our own; REP 1985: 1).

Since the signing of the Maastricht Treaty opposition to the EU has become one of the main themes of the party literature. The REP uses a wide variety of arguments to express its anti-EU sentiments. In accordance with its belief in a hostile international environment the REP refers to the Maastricht Treaty as 'Versailles without weapons', indicating that the treaty signified another capitulation of Germany. The financial arguments all come down to the big difference in the amount of money Germany pays to and receives from the EU. A strange blend of chauvinist and sanitary argumentation is used in the struggle against the deletion of the German *Reinheitsgebot* (purity injunction) and against the EU policy on environmental protection and food rights, the alleged sole purpose of which is to bring Germany to a lower level in these fields (*Rep-Sonderausgabe* I/89). The anti-EU repertoire of the REP has also been expanded by some mainstream arguments such as, for instance, the democratic deficit, EU centralism, the loss of German sovereignty, and the unequal representation in the EP (e.g. REP 1999).

### Socio-economic policy

A topic on which the REP changed considerably during the years, at least in its rhetoric, is socio-economic policy. The party has taken its policies for a large part from its mother party CSU, supporting the so-called *soziale Marktwirtschaft* (social market economy). Socio-economic policy constitutes one of the most widely elaborated themes in the programmes. Under several different headings the party applauds the advantages of the liberal economy in combination with state protection of special groups (families, persons with a disability, the elderly and pensioners). However, the social market economy can be preserved only by making several budget cuts, primarily limiting the size and thereby the costs of the bureaucracy and state subsidies (*inter alia*, to international organisations). Excluded from these austerity measures are the farmers, as Germany has to remain independent from other countries in its supply of food (REP 1983: 15).

In its early years the party paper devoted much attention to the theme of protecting the interests of the German farmers. Later it also started to champion the protection of the *Mittelstand* (middle class), in part to distinguish itself from (other) right-wing parties, the FDP in particular, which were accused of favouring big corporations. The programme called for the protection of German small businesses against foreign competition (especially from low-wage countries), big corporations and monopolisation (REP 1987: 11). According to the REP, small businesses are the backbone of the economy, providing for the bulk of the employment in Germany (e.g. *Rep* 3/86).

The socio-economic programme further called for a 'social order, which provides the individual with all opportunities for development, in which individual responsibility and self-help are the first commandments and in which communal support for the needy is secured' (REP 1987: 7). This social order will have overcome the class struggle and will result in social peace. However, this can only be realised by a change in consciousness, so that all working people regain the feeling of solidarity, and by the creation of a *Leistungsgemeinschaft* (achievement-oriented society). Finally, employment policy should combine 'the right to a job or state support' with 'the duty to work' (REP 1987: 11).

Throughout the years the REP started to address the interests of the lower classes more and more. At least two factors strengthened this in the 1990s.[15] First, German unification created a pool of socially weak potential voters in the former Eastern states. Second, Klaus Zeitler, a former SPD mayor for twenty-two years in the Bavarian city of Würzburg, joined the REP and quickly became a prominent author in its paper. His articles principally stressed working-class interests, exposed social abuses, and charged the top of the SPD and labour unions with egocentrism at the expense of the working man. The new social image even touched Schönhuber, who argued that the fall of socialism should not mean the triumph of capitalism (*Rep* 6/92), though it nevertheless clashed with the neo-liberal rhetoric, which still existed on many other issues. Hence, in the 1990s the paper's socio-eco-

---

[15] A third factor could have been the many demographic studies on the REP electorate that appeared in the early 1990s and indicated disproportionately large support among the working class (e.g. Roth 1989, 1990; Veen *et al.* 1993).

nomic politics became an amalgam of socialist policies and pleas for budget cuts and state subsidies, presented in a neo-liberal style.

The *Leitmotiv* of the socio-economic policy has become welfare chauvinism: German money should be used for German interests and German jobs should be taken by German workers. Everything non-German, including immigrants, the EU and most notably asylum seekers (not *Aussiedler*), was portrayed as taking much needed money away from the Germans. To protect its own people, especially the working class, the party therefore presented a welfare chauvinist programme in which budget cuts were made with respect to non-German causes and more money was to be invested in upholding a decent level of welfare and employment for the German people.

### Ethical values

One of the favourite topics of Schönhuber has always been the decadence which prevails as a consequence of the ongoing liberalisation of society. In one of the first issues of the paper he named examples of the increasing decadence, such as AIDS, women wrestling and corruption, and then stated: 'We Republicans call for resistance! It concerns the life of us and our children. We demand: Stop any further and deadly liberalisation!' (*RA* 3/84). The general argument is that the process threatens the existence of the German ethnic community by decreasing the birth rate. The only way out is a return to traditional values, most notably family values:

> Dear fellow-countrymen: Thank God wars no longer decide on the future of a nation, but birth rates. We can only restore our national and regional identity when we make the family the centre of our life again, support it morally and materially. (*Rep* 10/90)

The party rarely discusses ethical issues in detail, however, and, although they come up in every issue of the paper, they are mostly part of broader stories on immigration, *Umerziehung* (re-education) or on the established parties. The programmes mainly include demands on the issues of family politics and abortion. Though the number of demands was expanded throughout the years, the party neither changed its position nor radicalised. The basis for its family politics has always been a favouring of state protection of marriage and family (e.g. REP 1998). The concept of the family applies to heterosexual couples and should not be enlarged to include homosexual or lesbian couples (REP 1993: 27). To create a more family friendly climate the state should offer financial incentives. However, more important is a change in mentality, away from the materialist egoism towards communal solidarity (e.g. REP 1993: 68).

A relatively moderate position on ethical values is generally upheld. For instance, the REP calls for the protection of the unborn child through a ban on abortion, though it allows for abortion 'in case of rape (criminological indication), hereditary damage (eugenic indication) and danger for mother or child (clinical indication)' (REP 1993: 29). The section on media politics, which opens with a very liberal agenda (stressing support for freedom of speech and press, plurality, etc.), calls for enforcement of the few restrictions (i.e. contradictions to democracy, human dignity and the values of the ethnic community) mainly through media self-regulation (REP 1993: 79–81).

There are two issues on which the party holds a somewhat ambiguous position: religion and gender relations. Despite the fact that the REP originated as a 'CSU-split' the first two programmes did not once mention the issue of religion. The 1987 programme speaks of a system of upbringing and education that is rooted in German, Christian and *abendländische* (occidental) culture and history and which operates independently of confessional values (REP 1987: 2). The next programme includes a chapter on 'Church and Religion' that starts with the famous idiom of Johann-Gottfried Herder, 'ethnic communities are the thoughts of God' (REP 1990: 30), and calls for 'Christian patriotism', claiming that the preservation of Christian values and tradition is of paramount importance for the future of Germany. The 1993 programme is less explicit on Christian values, which now seem to have become fully integrated into the 'occidental culture' from which the party claims to have taken all its inspiration (REP 1993: 93).

This is not to say that the REP holds a particularly favourable position towards Christian institutions. On the basis of liberal convictions of the separation of Church and state and religious freedom, the party demands the abolition of Church tax (REP 1993: 93). Moreover, it considers the German Churches to have become infiltrated by left-wing and anti-national forces. The fact that various religious leaders have been engaged in actions against the REP has worsened the situation. The programme introduced the demand that '(t)he pulpit should not be misused for political propaganda and for a one-sided influence on religious voters' (REP 1990: 31).

The first programme also included a special section entitled 'Equal Rights for Man and Woman' in which the party pledged to dedicate itself to ensure that the law was put into practice. To send a signal it would award 'an appropriate number of political mandates within the party' to women (REP 1983: 5). The next programme, though more conservative in many respects, upheld the claim of equality and explicitly stated that 'equal work should get equal pay' (REP 1985: 4). In the 1987 programme the support for equal rights for women was combined with a traditional view of the woman as mother.

> Under similar circumstances and demands, woman and man are, despite their difference in essence, of equal competence in life and work. However, it is in particular given to the woman to create by warmth and devotion the safety, in which family and children can prosper. Herein lies the exceptional vocation of the woman, which cannot be fulfilled by any 'househusband' or collective. (REP 1987: 8)

To keep women from getting swamped with responsibilities and work or frustrated from not having a family and children, the REP wants to strengthen the position of the housewife and mother. Among others, the party wants the state to actively support this policy by providing school girls with an education as woman, mother and housewife (REP 1987: 9). This position was later softened, though the REP kept opposing feminism and the *Gleichmacherei* (levelling) of man and woman. In political and social respects, man and woman should be treated equally in terms of rights, not in character. The party does accept working women, claiming equal pay for equal work as well as demanding more part-time jobs, job sharing and business kindergartens (REP 1993: 31). In addition, it calls for the introduction of the job of 'housewife and mother' (REP 1993: 31).

### Strong state

A popular topic in the literature of the party is law and order. Except for the 1987 version, all programmes contain (large) sections on law and order policies. To stress the importance of the topic the 1990 programme stated: 'We Republicans are the party of law and order' (REP 1990: 13). It further includes demands for a better equipped police force, which has to be enlarged in both personnel and powers, and is to be supported openly by politicians. Sentences should be higher, especially for crimes relating to drugs and the environment, and the victim instead of the perpetrator should be at the centre of attention (e.g. REP 1993: 16–22). The party in general, and Schönhuber in particular, has always opposed the death penalty on ethical grounds. It also takes a tough stand on (primarily left-wing) terrorism, which is embedded in the official German state policy of *streitbare Demokratie* (militant democracy). According to the party terrorism is caused in part by the 'general lack of legal security and community spirit' (REP 1987: 15).

Crime always received a lot of attention in the party paper, although over time it became more and more a secondary theme, featuring in articles that dealt primarily with foreigners, asylum seekers or with (critique on) the established parties. In the 1990s the party shifted its focus to a new group, the non-organised left-wing extremists (or so-called *Autonomen*). As they often demonstrated against and even attacked meetings of the REP, the party demanded tough repression of these groups. After left-wing extremists had violently disturbed an official state ceremony, Schönhuber reacted partly with malicious joy, partly misunderstood: 'Now German top politicians have experienced personally what it means to underestimate the left-criminal scene. We have had to suffer this scene for years, and received support of neither the media nor the political establishment' (*Rep* 11/92).

The party position on defense has always been quite moderate. In the few articles on the topic the party showed no signs of a militarist outlook. The REP generally supports the army, arguing specifically for the upgrading of its (low) status, yet at the same time takes a cautious approach to the expansion of weapons and armies. In relation to the Gulf war it rejected war as a means of politics, accusing the allied forces of not having exploited all diplomatic possibilities, and the media of covering the war too positively and clinically (e.g. *Rep* 1/91). Similar reactions were expressed during the wars in Bosnia and Kosovo.[16]

In 1991 the question of a professional army was the topic of the party paper column entitled 'controversy'. Arguing in favour of a professional army was former General Reinhard Uhle-Wettler, while against it vice-chairman Schlierer claimed that the army would no longer be anchored in German society and might become a state-within-the-state (*Rep* 7/91). The REP sees military service as peace service though it has become more favourable to a general year of state service, of which military service is just one possibility (e.g. REP 1993: 10)

The issue of defense features only secondary in the programmes too, where it is linked mainly to the ever-changing position on NATO. In 1983 the programme pleaded for full incorporation of Germany into NATO as well as for more European cooperation in defense politics (albeit with close cooperation with the US). The next programme included no explicit references to either NATO or defense. In 1987 loyalty to NATO was made dependent upon the condition that its interests were similar to those of the German ethnic community (REP 1987: 3), and the 1990 programme added the demand for more German control over its own territory and people. After reunification little support for NATO seems to remain. The REP wants NATO to be converted into an 'all-European security structure, in which Germany keeps its sovereignty' (REP 1993: 9), even though the party is very sceptical about the current attempts at creating such a structure within the EU (REP 1999: 22).

### Populist anti-party sentiment

A theme which clearly combines and guides all ideological themes is that constituted by the critique on the established parties and politicians. The REP criticises political parties extremely harshly, targeting all major parties alike, both government and opposition. However, the party does not reject parties per se and always presents itself as an alternative, which differs from the others in almost all possible ways, but which is nevertheless a political party. That said, the REP does reflect a wide variety of populist anti-party sentiments. Most notably, parties and politicians are portrayed as egocentric, corrupt and anti-national.

In the first years the REP predominantly attacked its Bavarian rival and mother party, the CSU, accusing this all-mighty party in Bavaria of despo-

---

[16] The REP referred to the Kosovo war as 'the bombing war against Serbia that was started without clear thinking' (http://www.rep.de/kosovo1.htm).

tism and corruption. When the party began to contest elections outside of Bavaria, its main target was expanded to include the CDU. Lacking ideas, the CDU/CSU had first incriminated the REP, then stolen its ideas, and finally presented these ideas as their own. In the 1990s the party also increasingly aimed its arrows at the SPD and, to a lesser extent, at the FDP and the Greens. The SPD is portrayed as a party dominated by teachers and social scientists, which has betrayed the German working class. Moreover, its support for the multi-cultural society and the process of European integration is characterised as a betrayal of the legacy of its first post-war leader, Kurt Schumacher, a nationally oriented socialist who is seen as a hero by the REP.

A special place in the anti-party sentiments is reserved for the competitors on the extreme right. From the time when the REP competed with the DVU, this party and especially its leader Frey have been targets of many verbal attacks. Frey is accused of only being nationalist for the money and is referred to with descriptions like 'the Munich-based merchant in NS-devotional objects' and 'the property speculator' (e.g. *Rep* 2/89). In a reaction to the REP's defeat in the Bremen state election of 1987 the paper claimed that Frey's *Spalter-Liste* (splitter list) contested the election with the sole purpose of keeping the REP from success and so protecting the CDU, with the obvious approval of the latter (*Rep* 10/87).

At the beginning of the 1990s state monitoring was becoming more and more a reality for the REP. Consequently, allegations of extremism grew into one of the main issues in the party paper. These allegations were portrayed as part of a conspiracy of the established parties against the REP, out of fear of the latter's inevitable electoral success. It spoke of a 'pogrom mood against the Republicans' and claimed that a plan to morally destroy the party was ready, containing four phases: disinformation, monitoring, alleged proof, and a request for a ban on the party (*Rep* 11/92). However, it always felt assured that the 'decent Germans' would see right through this conspiracy and would support the party even more.

Most anti-party articles are accompanied by or end with a positive reference to the REP, the only viable alternative. Everything the other parties are accused of doing, the REP either does not do or can undo. It portrays itself as the only party that has the ideas and the people to govern the country through these ominous times and, more importantly, that has the confidence of the people. This is not that surprising, it argues, as most disasters are a consequence of the fact that the old parties have ignored the warnings of the REP. This line of reasoning was used particularly in its defense against allegations of providing ideological fuel to the arsonists of refugee homes in villages like Hoyerswerda in the early 1990s.

> We Republicans are the only party in the new states which can master the historical task of keeping deluded young people from slipping to the radical and

violent scene. The established parties have lost their credit over there. Hoyer-swerda is an alarm signal. (*Rep* 10/91)

The paper also features many articles that exclusively contain (positive) references to the REP. Usually these articles are (based on) the quotations of outsiders, such as politicians of other parties and journalists, which state that the REP is not an extremist party. One of the most stunning aspects of the pro-REP articles are the many predictions of its bright future, again generally based on external sources.[17] The party went furthest in blowing its own trumpet where (then party leader) Schönhuber was concerned. Numerous headlines and articles cheered his rhetorical talents and the fascination of the masses with his speeches. In fairness, many of these were (verbatim) citations from other newspapers, ranging from the left-wing *Frankfurter Rundschau* to the right-wing *Frankfurter Allgemeine Zeitung*, though the party paper itself was by far the most jubilant. On his sixty-fifth birthday, it wrote:

> Schönhuber has kept standing where others fell or left. What would kill the weaker was confirmation and reinforcement to him. There are no pauses for the man who runs from appointment to appointment, and as a rhetorical locomotive pulls whole election trains. (*Rep* 1/88)

The central tenet of the party's anti-party sentiments is the anti-national behaviour of German politicians, most notably the way they are seen to misuse German history against Germany and its people, but primarily against Schönhuber. In this respect, he still fights a war over the reactions to his book. A general feature of the many articles on this topic, most often written by Schönhuber, is the outing of the 'brown [Nazi] past' of people who have in the eyes of the party indulged in anti-national behaviour. They are generally not attacked because of their past actions, as they only did their duty, but because of their present denial or concealment of them. Two of his main targets were the then German President Richard Von Weizsäcker and the then Austrian President Kurt Waldheim. The articles are presented as a fight of the little man against the establishment: whereas the former has been punished too harshly during the process of denazification (like Schönhuber himself), the latter has escaped punishment. Schönhuber's favourite remark is related to the hypocrisy of the elite and holds that it is impossible that from 80 per cent of National Socialists under Hitler came 90 per cent of resistance fighters after Hitler.

---

[17] Before almost every contested election the paper predicts extremely positive results, which are even higher than the best score they polled. One reason is that the party is convinced that the polls consistently and willingly present a lower support for the REP than is actually measured. The alleged reason behind this is that the polling agencies are financally dependent upon support from the established parties.

## Democracy

Several authors have claimed that the REP is anti-democratic according to the German constitution (e.g. Jaschke 1994; Pfahl-Traughber 1993). This claim is difficult to substantiate on the basis of the party literature. Nowhere in the party paper, for example, can one find an open rejection of (German) democracy or fundamental aspects of it. One of the few possible indications of a surpressed extremist character is a remark by Schönhuber that contrary to sectarians like Neubauer and the NPD the REP 'has to consider the existence of a certain political environment, however, without thereby allowing that programmatic basic principles are abandoned. The Bureau for the Protection of the Constitution is – however one may judge its actions – a reality' (*Rep* 1/91). Still, this is hardly evidence to prove the party's extremist character. On top of that, the whole party literature is larded with statements in which the REP counters allegations of extremism and radicalism. A favourite slogan in this respect is 'We are radicals only in one aspect: In the defense against extremism of both left and right' (e.g. *Rep* 7/85). There are two examples that the party never fails to mention to prove its democratic credentials. First, double-membership of the REP and any extremist organisation, i.e. organisations officially listed as extremist by the *Bundesverfassungsschutz*, is illegal according to the party statute. Second, the REP has been purged of all extremists at the Ruhsdorf party meeting of 1990 – by which they refer to the expulsion of the Neubauer group.

The democratic credentials can, however, best be taken from the various concrete measures the party supports. Over and over again the REP stresses its democratic character in articles in the party paper and sections and introductions of the party programmes. The first thesis of the 1983 programme, entitled democracy, states:

> We Republicans trace back our existence to the old-Roman 'res publica'. We want to serve the state and not to make money out of it. All thinking and actions are to be directed at a society of emancipated citizens in a republic, in which conservative and liberal principles complete each other. (REP 1983: 3)

All election programmes further include a variety of demands to strengthen the rights to political cooperation of the citizenry, such as the popular election of the Federal President and the introduction of referendums of different kinds, especially on topics concerning the sovereignty of the German state, i.e. German reunification and European integration (REP 1993: 5). The 1990 programme, which opens with an avowal to all aspects of the official definition of German democracy (as mentioned in the constitution), includes the new demand for a strict separation between private and public means and positions for politicians (REP 1990: 6). Moreover, the REP has always been favourable to compromises and power sharing, calling it a democratic virtue, not a sin: 'Our goal has to be and remain, to take part in the parliamentary expression of the will' (*Rep* 8/91).

## Revisionism

One of the topics that regularly features in the party literature, most often in columns of Schönhuber, is the so-called *Umerziehung* (literally re-education) and *Vergangenheitsbewältigung*, the official dealing with the German Nazi past. According to the party these are aimed at keeping Germany small and silent, so that the superpowers can continue to dominate world politics. Even in the post-Schönhuber era the REP considered the issue important enough to address it in the introduction of the party programme. Linking past and present, the party proclaimed

> The mental Babylonian imprisonment of the established parties and large parts of the society as a consequence of the stigmatisation and criminalisation of the German history has led to the situation that many important law proposals were not accepted or existing laws were not implemented. (REP 1998)

In the early years the last page of the party paper contained an overview of books recommended by Schönhuber (and available through the party), which mainly dealt with German history, the Second World War, and the 'lost territories'. In articles and book reviews the party presented a moderate and circuitous revisionist view on the Second World War. It rejects Germany's *Alleinschuld* (sole guilt), claiming that France and mainly the Soviet Union had forced the country to war. Believing that the latter country had been at the verge of invading Germany, the REP considers the German invasion of the Soviet-Union a *Präventivschlag* (preemptive strike) (e.g. *Rep* 7/91). It further vehemently rejects the thesis of the *Kollektivschuld* (collective guilt) of the German people, claiming that the typical German could not have known of the Nazi's atrocities. The fall of the Berlin wall and the consequent unification of Germany have strengthened the REP in demanding an immediate stop of the (legal) *Vergangenheitsbewältigung* (e.g. REP 1990).

The favourite topic of Schönhuber in this respect has always been the defence of the German soldiers that served in the Second World War, particularly those of the Waffen-SS, like himself. Quoting several (former) politicians of the main parties Schönhuber argued over and over again that the Waffen-SS had been more similar to the regular German army, the *Wehrmacht*, than to the Nazi-loyal SS. Though in general condemning the NS regime and confirming its atrocities, Schönhuber at times sounded obligatory or reluctant. This notwithstanding, there are no indications that he (or the party) supports the NS regime or fundamental aspects of its ideology and actions. The only exception to this is perhaps the ideal of a Europe of Nations, which he claims to have experienced in the Waffen-SS (see also Schönhuber 1989).

Though Schönhuber was the main author of the moderately revisionist articles, he was certainly not the only high-ranking member of the REP that held these views. The earlier programmes had been very cautious in this respect, explicitly stating that the end of the legal *Vergangenheitsbewältigung* would not mean that war criminals would no longer be punished (REP 1983: 12). The 1987 programme, however, openly rejected 'the absurd thesis of the "collective guilt" of the German people over generations' and demanded the complete opening of all archives 'to clear the "single guilt"-thesis' (REP 1987: 3). And the party deemed the (past) treatment of former German soldiers important enough to be addressed in the 1990 programme: 'We demand the rehabilitation of 27,000 German soldiers, who were unjustly convicted as prisoners of war in short trials in the Soviet Union in 1949/50 (!)' (REP 1990: 12). The underlying sentiment seems to be personal rather than political and can best be summarised as: 'Our fathers were no criminals' (*Rep* 7/91).

## Conclusion

The REP originated as a conservative party, ideologically close to its mother party CSU. Its first programme contains a moderate nationalist outlook, allowing room for support of the EC, NATO and Third World countries. Its socio-economic policy entailed full support of the social market economy, combining a fairly open economy with the protection of specific groups (most notably farmers and elderly people). The programme is generally set in a very moderate and general tone and even the policy towards foreigners, though restrictive, is not presented in a xenophobic style.

The party radicalised shortly afterwards, with the take-over of Schönhuber as party leader and Neubauer as chief editor, expressing an increasingly nationalist and xenophobic outlook. However, both cautiousness and superficiality kept the party from a clear and elaborated ideology. Instead, the REP literature contains parts and often starts of a (mainly ethnic) nationalist ideology that is exclusively applied to the own situation. At the core is the nationalist demand for an independent and culturally homogeneous German state. This state is neither inhabited with only 'ethnic' Germans (as assimilation is accepted) nor all Germans (as some 'ethnic' Germans live in other countries, like Austria).

Xenophobic nationalism is at the core of almost all themes that are discussed regularly in the party literature. Its socio-economic outlook, for example, has the two ideological features combined in a welfare chauvinist programme, stating that the German state should take care of (the socio-economic needs of) its own people. Nationally this means work for the own people and internationally it means cooperation but without the loss of much sovereignty. The party holds an extremely xenophobic view on the world in which foreigners within and outside of the country are seen as a hostile threat. This is closely linked to the struggle for national revival and pride, leading to (moderate) revisionism and (intense) populist anti-party sentiments. Though the REP puts a lot of attention on the ongoing process of degeneration, its views on ethical values are moderately conservative.

Finally, the REP is a democratic party, in that it supports parliamentarianism, and even militant democracy, and strives for acceptance and power within the current German political system.

# 3

# Deutsche Volksunion

### The whims of an extreme right business man

One of the most influential people in the German post-war extreme right scene is Gerhard Frey, the multi-millionaire media czar who owns and publishes several newspapers (see Müller 1989: 66–74; Backes and Jesse 1993: 295–7; Mecklenburg 1999b). Born in 1933 into a traditional national-conservative merchant family, Frey first worked for the *Deutsche Soldaten-zeitung* (German Soldiers Newspaper, *DSZ*) and later bought 50 per cent of its stock. During the 1960s his publishing company acquired the rest of the stock and Frey became both publisher and chief editor of the newspaper (Mayer 1998: 185). He bought several other right-wing newspapers and journals, among them several journals of the *Vertriebenen* (expellees), and shares of various others, among them the influential nationalist monthly *Nation [und] Europa* (Sippel 1989).

Under his management the *DSZ* was renamed several times before getting its current name *Deutsche National-Zeitung* (German National Newspaper, *DNZ*) in 1968 (Sippel 1989; Virechow 1999). It grew from an almost bankrupt monthly with about 9,000 readers into a flourishing weekly with around 80,000 readers. With it Frey's own position rose to that of a powerful voice within extreme right Germany. In 1971 he enlarged his media empire even further by buying the *Deutscher Anzeiger* (German Informant, *DA*) and founding a new publishing company, owned by his wife. The *FZ-Verlag* publishes several 'revelation' books, often edited by Gerhard Frey himself or his son Gerhard Frey Jr. In 1985 the company was expanded by a book service, the *Deutscher Buchdienst*, and a year later by a travel agency, the *Deutsche Reisen* (Sippel 1989; Linke 1994). The same year Frey acquired the *Deutsche Wochen-Zeitung* (German Weekly Newspaper, *DWZ*), which at the end of 1990 absorbed the *DA*.

In January 1971 Frey founded the *Deutsche Volksunion e.V.* (German People's Union, DV), a registered association without a party licence, as a successor to the already diminishing *Aktion Neue Rechte* (ANR). Among the thirteen co-founders of the DV were leading members of various nationalist and expellee organisations, as well as local leaders from right-wing parties, such as the CDU and the *Bayernpartei* (Braasch 1996). The organisation described itself as a 'supra-party political collection of freedom-loving and law abiding citizens'. A year later Frey founded the *Freiheitlicher Rat* (Freedom Council, FR), an umbrella organisation of several extreme right (and revisionist) groups under his own leadership. The FR organised the anti-*Ostpolitik* 'March on Bonn' of April 1972, which was attended by some 5,000 people (Stöss 1991: 194). It was also supposed to prepare the foundation of a new party, the *Deutsche Nationalpartei* (German National Party), which, however, never materialised (Sippel 1989).

During the 1970s Frey founded several specialised 'action groups', which were able to absorb a substantial part of the rapidly diminishing NPD membership. The various groups worked together in the FR and called themselves *Vereinigte Freiheitliche* (United-Freedom Loving), after 1976 *National-Freiheitliche*. In the beginning of the 1980s Frey restructured his organisation: the various groups (and their members) became part of the umbrella organisation DV.[1] In the mid 1990s the Frey imperium was restructured once again, and this time only four organisations remained: the political party DVU, the political organisation DV, and the 'action groups' *Initiative für Ausländer-Begrenzung* (Initiative to Limit Foreign Immigration) and *Ehrenbund Rudel – Gemeinschaft zum Schutz der Frontsoldaten* (Rudel League – Society to Protect Front-Line Soldiers). Although these organisations engage in virtually no activities, the umbrella organisation DV has been the biggest (officially registered) right-wing extremist movement in Germany since 1980. That year the membership doubled from 6,400 in 1979 to 13,500.[2] The next year it decreased somewhat, but until 1986 it fluctuated around 12,000.

After the short and unsuccessful flirtation with the NPD in the mid 1970s, Frey stayed away of party politics for almost ten years, devoting his time primarily to the development of his media empire and political movement. At the end of 1986, however, he decided to found his own political party, the *Deutsche Liste* (German List). Surprisingly, he was helped by his old rivals, the now sectarian NPD. After having used the name *Deutsche Volksliste* (German People's List) for a short time, Frey renamed his party *Deutsche*

---

[1] In the early 1990s this included the following organisations: *Volksbewegung gegen anti-deutsche Propaganda* (People's Movement against Anti-German Propaganda); *Aktion Deutsche Einheit* (Action German Unity); *Initiative für Ausländer-Begrenzung* (Initiative to Limit Foreign Immigration); *Aktion deutsches Radio und Fernsehen* (Action German Radio and Broadcasting); *Ehrenbund Rudel – Gemeinschaft zum Schutz der Frontsoldaten* (Rudel League – Society to Protect Front-Line Soldiers); and *Deutscher Schutzbund für Volk und Kultur* (German Protection League for Ethnic Community and Culture).
[2] Unless indicated differently all membership figures and election results are based on Backes and Moreau (1994: 59–76).

*Volksunion-Liste D* (German People's Union – List D) on 6 March 1987, in which D stands for *Deutschland*. In February 1991 it dropped the appendix 'Liste D', which was hardly noticed by the outside world, as the party was generally referred to as DVU or *Deutsche Volksunion*.

The *DNZ* of 6 March 1987 opened with the headline: 'New party to the right of the CDU. The union of the nationals [Nationalen].' Frey explained his step into party politics as a reaction to the fact that the *Wende* (turning back), promised by the newly elected CDU/CSU-FDP government in 1983, had failed to materialise, and to the failings of the government in the areas of *Deutschlandpolitik* (the politics of the FRG towards the GDR), internal security and the immigration issue.

The DVU began its activities in Bremen and Bremerhaven with a 'citizens' request to limit foreign immigration'. In 1987 it also made an electoral pact with the NPD leadership, despite fierce internal opposition within the latter party (Sippel 1989). It was agreed that only one of the two parties would stand in each election. For example, the DVU would contest the 1989 European election, whereas the NPD would contest the parliamentary election a year later. They further agreed that the party that contested the election would put candidates of the other party on its list. Everything considered the agreement was primarily an alliance of two weak parties against a stronger third party (the REP). It was also an alliance of money and cadre: the NPD had cadre but no money, the DVU had money but no cadre.

Between 1987 and 1990 both parties profited from the alliance. In its first ever election, the *Bürgerschaftswahl* (city state election) in Bremen of September 1987, the DVU gained 3.4 per cent. Because of the 5.4 per cent in the constituency of Bremerhaven the party not only got two seats in the city council, but was also the first (officially registered) right-wing extremist party in twenty years that gained a seat in a state parliament. The electoral success of the DVU had been preceded by a massive campaign, in which Frey was said to have invested two million DM, more than SPD and CDU together, and received only sixty-five thousand DM *Wahlkampfkostenrück-erstattung* (Assheuer and Sarkowicz 1990: 36–7). Nevertheless, it had been a successful dress rehearsal for the 1989 European election.

The DVU's 1989 European election campaign was one of the most expensive in German history. Frey paid no less than seventeen million DM, mostly his own money, primarily for three national door-to-door deliveries of pamphlets with a total circulation of seventy million (Assheuer and Sarkowicz 1990: 37). This notwithstanding the DVU was completely overshadowed by the REP in the election: the parties won 1.6 and 7.1 per cent respectively. This political and financial fiasco, involving a loss of fourteen million DM, led Frey to terminate the alliance prematurely. Despite the electoral misfortunes the membership of the DV(U) grew from 18,600 in 1988 to 25,000 in 1989. In September 1991 the party returned from the dead, being re-elected into the Bremen state council with six seats. The 6.2 per cent it gained made the DVU the third largest party in the council. In April of the following year, the DVU repeated its success in Schleswig-Holstein, gaining 6.3 per cent of the votes and six seats (against the REP's 1.2 per cent). At the Hamburg state council election in September 1993 the DVU was not able to continue its success in the northern part of Germany. It gained 2.8 per cent, far less than the 4.8 per cent of the REP, yet enough to keep the latter out of the council.

Surprisingly, the DVU did not contest any elections in the *Superwahljahr* 1994. The main reasons for the party's abstention were the disappointing results in the prior elections and the poor financial situation of the party (primarily as a result of the first). The DVU was said to have debts of around nine million DM, which were covered by the personal capital of the Frey family (VSB 1995: 128). In addition, and following NPD leader Mußgnug's succession by former Frey rival Günter Deckert, the relationship between the DVU and the NPD deteriorated into open hostility. Together with the hopeless situation of the DVU, this led to the rapprochement with the old enemy, the REP. Even though Frey had often attacked Schönhuber in his newspapers, he had always kept open the possibility for cooperation. However, the consequent publicity led to the expulsion of Schönhuber as REP leader, and his successor Schlierer immediately terminated the cooperation.

The inactivity of the party in 1994 cost the party dearly: its membership decreased by almost one quarter to 15,000 the next year (VSB 1996: 153). This notwithstanding, the DVU contested the May 1995 election in Bremen with a costly campaign of, according to the party itself, some two million DM (Mayer 1998: 196). The results were another setback, as the DVU lost its representation in the state council, dropping to just 2.5 per cent. The next year it was also voted out of the state parliament in Schleswig-Holstein, gaining 4.3 per cent (Jesse 1997). In September 1997 the party was close to a stunning comeback, failing the 5 per cent hurdle in the Hamburg state election by only 190 votes (Stahl 1997; VSB 1998). The result of 4.97 per cent did bring the DVU back into the spotlight though (see Mayer 1998). Moreover, it revived the debate on party political cooperation within the extreme right camp. Frey targeted particularly the REP, hoping to come to some kind of non-aggression pact with its leader, while at the same time wooing his internal opponents. However, Schlierer did not budge and Frey found himself still isolated – the 'moderates' (e.g. REP) rejected his extremism, while the 'extremists' (e.g. NPD) despised his pragmatism (and his businesses).

The next year the party knew both setbacks and successes. Regarding the former, two of its state branches (Berlin and Brandenburg) left the party in March, bringing the total number of state branches back to sixteen (VSB 1999). This notwithstanding, on 26 April 1998 the DVU celebrated its biggest electoral victory so far, winning 12.9 per cent and sixteen seats in the Saxony-Anhalt state election (Mayer 1998). This was the first time an officially registered extreme right party made it into parliament in a 'new' (i.e. Eastern) state. The victory brought the party huge publicity as well as a true flood of new members (some 3,000). The period of euphoria lasted only a short time though: on 27 September the party scored just 2.9 per cent in the Mecklenburg-Vorpommern state election and got stuck at a mere 1.2 per cent in the parliamentary election – despite the fact that the former REP figureheads Schönhuber and Krause headed the DVU lists as independents in Bavaria and Saxony respectively (VSB 1999). In November 1998 Frey and Schlierer finally met and the two agreed upon forming a strategic pact not to compete in the Hesse and Bremen elections the next year. This narrowly paid off in Bremen, where the DVU scored 3.0 per cent overall, but because of the 6.0 per cent in Bremerhaven, it is for the third time represented in the state coucil (with one seat; see Ohne 1999). On 13 June 1999 the DVU did not contest the European election – these were left for the (unsuccessful) REP.

Even though the DVU has had several (surprising) electoral successes in its short existence, these were obtained with an existing but not functioning organisational structure (see Mecklenburg 1999a). The party is and has always been a ghost party. This is at first sight contradictory to the fact that it is at the same time Germany's biggest right-wing extremist party in membership figures. The membership figures peaked in 1992 at 26,734 to drop to some 15,000 in the late 1990s (see the annual VSB). The high membership is due to the fact that, since December 1988, all members of the 'action groups' and movement DV have been automatically registered as members of the party DVU. The membership is primarily built upon the readership of the two extreme right newspapers though. Moreover, its membership is ageing, as most members are believed to be older than sixty-five (Moreau and Backes 1998: 153). More importantly, both papers, and in a sense also the party and movement, are part of Frey's business empire. This is also why the party has always had major difficulties in finding (suitable) candidates for elections and why it worked together with the more activist-oriented NPD. The lack of cadre in combination with the authoritarian leadership of Frey from his Munich headquarters has led to a desolate situation among party delegates (Butterwege et al. 1997; Löblich 1998). From the six people who were elected on the DVU ticket in Schleswig-Holstein in April 1992, for example, only one was still a member a year later, while four of the other five formed a DLVH faction (Backes and Moreau 1994: 62ff). In the Bremen state council the situation was much the same (see Hoffmann and Lepszy 1998), while in Saxony Anhalt one quarter of the parliamentary faction had defected within the first year (Löblich 1999).

Except for the occasional election campaign, often primarily fought by mail, the DVU is at its most visible during its annual meeting in Passau, at the border of Germany and Austria. There the party fights (and defeats) the city council every year in a lawsuit to win the right to keep its so-called *Großkundgebung* (big demonstration). The traditional meeting at the end of

September is one of the biggest 'extreme right' meetings in Western Europe, drawing between 2,000 and 3,000 visitors annually.[3] Except for the party leader and some other prominent members, there are always foreign speakers, among them have been the Russian right-wing extremist politician Vladimir Zhirinovski and the English revisionist David Irving (both of whom have been banned from entering Germany since 1993). The speakers are in general little known right-wing extremists though, such as (in 1994) Robert Brock (leader of an obscure US black-nationalist movement) and Hubert Verhelst (low-key delegate of the VB).

## Profiling the literature

### Externally oriented: party programmes

The party programme of the DVU is probably one of the shortest of all German parties today. In addition, it is little more than a selection of points from the programme of the non-party political DV, itself a collection of parts of the programmes of its various actions groups. The party programme is not only short, it is also unchanging. Since the foundation of the party in 1987, the *Programm der DVU-Liste D* (DVU 1987) has consisted of twelve points on a total of eight very small or five small unpaged pages, and during this time its content has undergone no substantial alteration. Even the fall of the Berlin wall, which forced political parties throughout Europe to rethink their positions, had little effect on the DVU programme. Though the party accepted a new *Partei-Programm* (DVU 1993) in August 1993, the few actual changes in the programme were more reactions to the ongoing process of European integration, most notably to the signing of the Maastricht Treaty, rather than to the end of the cold war. The party has not changed its programme since.

Nor has the party been very divergent in the content of its election propaganda. In general the party programme functions as an election programme, although the party used special election programmes in some instances, most notably the 1989 European election. The core programme for these elections, *Schwerpunkt-Programm der DVU zur Europa-Wahl am 18. Juni 1989* (DVU 1989), was almost an exact copy of the party programme, though with a particular focus on the European Community. Even though the party often used the same slogans and material for different elections, its campaigns were certainly not cheaply run, and far more money was spent than was received back from the state (see Haller and Deiters 1989: 270). As the party had only money and no activists, its election campaigns

---

[3] This figure is based primarily upon the annual *Verfassungsschutzberichte* (VSB), which speak of 'some 2,000' and my own observations; the DVU itself claims about 6,000 visitors annually.

were primarily capital rather than labour intensive. The party often just bombarded (special sections of) eligible voters with pamphlets (see Müller 1989: 75–9).

### Internally oriented: Frey's newspapers

As the DVU never published an official party paper, the newspapers of Frey have served as the effective party press. Originally Frey published three newspapers, but with the merger of 1991 only two remained: the *Deutsche National-Zeitung* (*DNZ*), with the subtitle 'freedom-loving, independent and above parties', and the *Deutsche Wochen-Zeitung* (*DWZ*), with the subtitle 'for national politics, culture and economy'. The two papers are almost identical in style and content and are published weekly; the main difference is in the timing and wording of the stories. They can be bought at newspaper stands, especially in railway stations, though the large majority of its readership is by subscription.[4] Until 1990, the *DNZ* and *DWZ* together had a total circulation of well over 100,000 (Backes and Moreau 1994: 68). This made them (together) the third best-selling weekly in Germany (Pfahl-Traughber 1993). In the 1990s, however, the circulation seems to be in a free fall, fluctuating between 55,000 and 60,000 at the end of the decade (see the annual VSB). In 1999 the two papers merged.

Because of the similarity of content (and style) the two newspapers are treated as one and the same in this analysis.[5] The lay-out of both papers is based on the German tabloids, especially its most popular representative *Bild-Zeitung*. The papers generally contain twelve pages and are professionally made with big headlines in red ink and a lot of pictures, tables and figures. The make-up of the papers is clear and consistent: the stories are organised per issue on a page, there are regular features and several serials. The papers are further filled with advertisements for (items of) the various businesses of Frey: the last two pages are always reserved for the *Deutscher Buchdienst*, which advertises a broad assortment of books, video's, cassettes, flags, medals, coins and maps. Moreover, many articles in the paper are based on these books or are ended with a reference of 'further reading' to one of these books (or to join one of the action groups within the DV).

---

[4] The subscribers are bombarded by letters and offers of Frey's other businesses, especially its book service. Approximately every two months they receive a letter in which they are asked to support the 'just cause' by ordering books, medals or cassettes, or by giving a friend a subscription to one of the papers. The advertisements are always presented as a struggle of good against evil; one of the advertisement slogans for the newspapers is: 'subscribe to the truth'.

[5] The similarity of the newspapers was established on the basis of both secondary literature (Assheuer and Sarkowicz 1990; Lange 1993) and own research. As the amount of 'party' literature was too vast both practically and in comparison to the other parties in the study, only one issue per month of one of the two newspapers has been analysed. The main criterion for the choice of the newspaper (*DA, DNZ* or *DWZ*) was its availability: the choice of issues was random.

The style of writing in the newspapers is generally very cautious and suggestive. Some of the more often used figures of speech are insinuations and rhetorical questions: e.g. 'Do foreigners have more rights than Germans?' (*DNZ* 12/87). Frey and his papers have been prosecuted over 120 times and yet have not once been convicted (Lange 1993: 73). The papers are primarily concerned with the past instead of the present, even though they try to relate the two. Most articles do not contain much ideological elaboration. The papers present 'facts' and comment on them. The ideology is hidden in the selection of topics.[6] Many articles reappear in different issues throughout the years and citations (often from books edited and sold by Frey himself) are used endlessly in both articles and issues.

## Deutschland über alles!

Though a certain difference in content and style between the externally oriented programmes and the internally oriented papers will be present with all political parties, specific circumstances cause a particular difference in the case of the DVU. The programme is the only genuine literature of the party and is very concise but at the same time deals with various themes. The newspapers, on the other hand, are extensive in number of issues and pages, yet mainly address a few limited topics. Moreover, they are directed at their own readership of which only a part are (also) members of the DVU. Hence, the content of the party programmes will be at the centre of the description of the party ideology.

### Nationalism

The DVU is first and foremost a nationalist party. The struggle for a German Germany is the only prominent feature in both sources of literature. Whether the party is state or ethnic nationalist is impossible to decipher from the literature. Though the party claims the right to a German Germany it does not explicate the basis for this claim. Nor does it address the issue of 'who is a German'. In general the language fits the ethnic nationalist discourse, with terms like *Volksgemeinschaft* (ethnic community), but the party never elaborates on the meaning of the concept. It considers national sovereignty a *Lebensrecht* (right of life) and consequently argues:

> Germany should remain the country of the Germans. The German ethnic community should receive the same rights as all other ethnic communities. This includes the right to hereditary land, national identity and full sovereignty. (DVU 1993)

---

[6] A lot of these short factual presentations deal with scandals or failures in politics or negative aspects of Jewish businessmen and Israel.

With the term 'hereditary land' the party refers to the territories to the East of the Oder-Neiße border, including parts of Poland, Russia, Ukraine and the Czech Republic. Though the terminology seems to indicate a clearly ethnic nationalist argument, based on the feature of *external exclusiveness*, the DVU employs almost solely legal arguments. It claims that the annexations of these territories are in violation of international law and sees itself thereby supported by (the preamble of) the German constitution. In line with the legal argument it wishes to arrange for the return of the territory exclusively by peaceful means, i.e. through negotiations rather than war. In open contrast to the nationalist argument of external exclusiveness is the fact that, like the REP, the DVU feels closely related to the Austrians, which it considers to be a part of the German *Kulturnation*, yet accepts the Austrian state (not the Austrian nation). It does express the hope that the two states will one day rejoin.

The rights to national identity and full sovereignty are based on the notion of *internal homogenisation*. The party wants the German state to be both inhabited and governed exclusively by members of the German ethnic community. This means that the (few) foreigners that are allowed to live in Germany should not be allowed to interfere in German politics. This is why the party forcefully rejects the extension of the right to vote to foreigners, not only for non-European guest workers but also for the citizens of the Western allies, particularly of the three former occupying countries (France, the United Kingdom and the United States). Again the argument is primarily voiced in legal terms: according to the German constitution the German people are sovereign and this should 'thus' not be changed.

The Maastricht Treaty has pushed opposition to the EU to the fore in the party literature. This is particularly visible in the programme; where the 1987 version addressed the issue of European integration solely in relation to agriculture, the 1993 version relates it to several fields. The EU is mainly opposed on nationalist grounds. Though the party claims to support cooperation between European countries, it does not want this to be at the cost of a loss of sovereignty on the part of the individual countries, most particularly Germany. In this respect the DVU seems to have given up on its desire for a European alternative to NATO (DVU 1993).

### Patriotism

The second most important ideological feature of the party literature is patriotism: Germany first! At the core of several sections is the belief that German interests, which means the interests of the German people, ethnic community and state, should be the prime (and in fact only) interest of the (West-)German government. This was expressed most clearly by Frey himself:

> For us it is Germany that matters in the first place, it is Germany that matters in the second place, and it is Germany that matters in the third place. Then there

is for a long time nothing, and then we can talk about the interests of ethnic communities that live 10,000 km away from us. (Sippel 1989: 176)

The patriotic policy is applied chiefly to foreign policy, and according to the party all countries should follow such a policy. Germany should not interfere in matters pertaining to other countries and other countries should not interfere in German matters. This is the only way the Germans can win back their full sovereignty, especially since the party believes that the country is still treated as hostile by the outside world, and particularly by the UN which is dominated by the anti-German Americans (see below). Financial transfers to foreign countries, both Third World and European Union, should be linked to the condition that the recipient countries are pro-German, i.e. support the right to an independent German state. Furthermore, German soldiers should not take part in UN missions or support foreign actions that do not primarily lead to the good of Germany. This was argued forcefully during the Gulf war, where the party distanced itself from the official German policy of support for the UN and argued that Germany should support Iraq, as it is part of the Arab nation, the only true friend of Germany in the post-war period.[7]

Except for articles that deal with attacks on anti-national people and countries, there are a variety of positively formulated examples of patriotism. Several articles on German accomplishments are even outright chauvinist. Virtually every German success in a major sporting event, for instance, is mentioned on the front page of the papers (e.g. the world championship in soccer in 1990 or the all-German victory at Wimbledon in 1992). There are also various small (neutrally formulated) articles on positive performances of German companies and quotations of (often foreign) leading persons that are positive about (some aspect of) Germany. This notwithstanding, the papers are always careful not to downgrade other countries or explicitly to claim superiority of the Germans. In essence, the fact is simply that the party is not really interested in anything other than Germany and the German ethnic community.

### Exclusionism

Although it is clear that matters of inclusion and exclusion in the German nation are very important to the DVU there is virtually no reference to the desired criterion for this process. For example, whether foreigners are believed to be able and allowed to integrate (assimilate) into the German community remains unknown, as this question is never addressed. Only very occasionally does the party portray some signs of an ethnopluralist conviction, as in a book review of Roland Tichy's *Ausländer rein* (Foreigners In) in

---

[7] A similar argument was used in relation to the war in the former Yugoslavia, where the party advocated open and unconditional support for the Croats and Bosnians against the Serbs, as these two ethnic communities had fought with the Germans in 'previous wars'.

which the reviewer almost desperately remarks: 'Does Tichy fail to see that nature created people of different ethnic communities, and that those, who want to change this inflict severe harm to the ethnic communities.' However, the reviewer knows the aim of Tichy: 'the destabilisation of these ethnic communities, so that the plan to de-Germanise [entdeutschen] Germany and to lead it into a multicultural society still succeeds' (DNZ 20/7/90). The main cause for the 'destabilisation' is generally voiced in cultural rather than ethnopluralist terms, pointing to the lack (or destruction) of 'natural' traditions and bonds.

Another example, pointing to the totally different approach of the party towards *Aussiedler* and foreigners, is in the rhetorical question: 'Do we want a storm of millions of foreigners from often totally different cultures or the reinforcement of people of German descent?' (DNZ 11/5/90). This quote aptly shows the style of writing and particular use of language in the papers: first, it speaks of a negatively formulated *Ansturm* (storm) of foreigners, which is then contrasted to a positively formulated *Zuzug* (reinforcement) of the *Aussiedler*. Though not openly stated, it is clear that the fact that the latter group is 'of German descent' and the former are 'from totally different cultures' is the basis of the divergence in treatment: difference (of culture) means problems.

There have been even fewer hints at racism, and these appeared exclusively in side stories, especially in reports of readers on trips to Namibia (described by its German colonial name Southwest Africa) which are organised by Frey's travel agency. In one report various remarks were made about the inefficiency and stupidity in agriculture of the black population compared to the white (DNZ 15/5/87). Another report, which wallows in nostalgia over the colonial past, states that '(i)n almost no black African state does a functioning parliamentary democracy exist, because this is alien to the African mentality and will also remain alien' (DNZ 14/4/89).

### Revisionism

While open revisionism is primarily visible in the newspapers, the first programme also included a call for a general pardon for all war criminals and a rehabilitation of all front-line soldiers (DVU 1987). Though this point did not return in this radical form in later versions, the few minor changes in the programme were primarily directed at a passage which deals with the issue of rehabilitation. The text originally contained the sentence: 'We oppose any discrimination and outlawing of front-line soldiers, *particularly of the Waffen-SS*, and any defamation of their fallen' (DVU 1987: my italics).[8] In

---

[8] In the version of 2 May 1990 the part marked above in italics was changed into 'including the Waffen-SS'. In the versions after 28 December 1992 the marked area was crossed out with a felt-tip – the dates refer to the dates that the programme was requested by the *Bundeswahlleiter* and might differ (slightly) from the dates on which the corrections were made by the party itself.

the 1993 version the marked area was deleted, and the passage was also enhanced and modernised:

> We oppose any discrimination and outlawing of front-line soldiers and any defamation of their fallen. They did their difficult duty without being responsible for the actions of the political leadership. (DVU 1993)

The party wants the Germans to be proud (again) of their people and heritage. It wants to do away with the 'anti-national' *Vergangenheitsbewältigung* (the official dealing with the Nazi-past by the German state), so that Germany can again be seen by both Germans and the rest of the world as a country like any other, with good and bad sides. Referring to Hitler's aspiration for a German Reich the paper writes: 'The Thousand-Year Reign will become reality after all: 12 years of practice and 988 years of Vergangenheitsbewältigung' (*DNZ* 23/9/88).

Prominent Germans that according to the party indulge in anti-national behaviour are attacked endlessly in the paper. They are denounced as communists and anti-national left-wingers, or their 'brown past' is revealed. The prime target of the paper was for a long time the then German president Richard von Weiszäcker, famous for his warnings against nationalistic sentiments in Germany. Various articles dealt with the past of the president himself as *Wehrmacht* officer on the Eastern front, but especially with that of his father, assistant secretary of foreign affairs in the Nazi regime.

The critiques on Von Weiszäcker and his father were also used to attack the thesis of the collective guilt of the Germans. The DVU denounces this thesis as a plot to keep Germany small and humble. It believes that the common German was innocent and that the (few) crimes that were committed by the Nazi regime were the work and responsibility of a small group of people around (and including) Hitler. The party argues that it was impossible for ordinary Germans to know of the atrocities of the Nazi regime, but that Von Weiszäcker himself could have known as his father was part of the elite. This is not to say that the party explicitly rejects the actions of Von Weiszäcker (or his father) during the war. It mainly rejects his actions *after* the war. On top of that the party wants to show that the fierce anti-nationalists of the post-war period have dirty hands themselves, and have become anti-national as a consequence of either blackmail or opportunism.

The bulk of the articles in the papers deal with topics that are directly related to the Second World War. Probably the most prominent is the role of Germany. Almost every issue covers at least one article in which this role is revised. This is done directly, e.g. by 'proving' that crimes generally ascribed to Nazi Germany were not as bad as is claimed. Several articles deal with the question of 'How many Jews really died?' (*DNZ* 7/6/91). In these articles the crimes against the Jews are not denied, but the number of (possible) victims is considerably reduced. Other articles try to prove that Germany did not start the war but was forced to react to the aggressive and unjust actions of others (most notably France and Poland). In the same spirit the attack on the Soviet Union in 1941 (Operation Barbarossa) is described as a preemptive strike on the eve of a Russian invasion of Germany. Sometimes the papers try to prove that various crimes were not committed by the Nazis at all. In this case, the crimes are acknowledged in all their horror, but they are simply ascribed to others. Many of these articles are excerpts from books edited, published and sold by Frey, with titles like 'The True Guilty of the Second World War', 'Concealed Documents' and 'Acquittal for Germany'.

Another way to get Germany acquitted is by comparison, that is, by putting war crimes of other countries at the same level of those of Nazi Germany. In this respect it is interesting to see how the papers use the term 'holocaust'. Under this heading articles are published that deal with the bombardment of Dresden, while no word is spoken about the genocide of the Jews (e.g. *DNZ* 23/10/92). The term holocaust is further used in the many articles that deal with the expulsion of Germans from the Eastern territories shortly after the war. A related strategy is the so-called *Aufrechnung*, meaning both 'guilt comparison' and 'addition' in the German language. This is primarily achieved by comparing the number of people killed by the Nazi regime with the number of victims of the communist regime of the Soviet Union. A lot of attention is also given to the number of wars that have been fought since the Second World War, especially by former allied forces, and the number of people that died in these wars.

Even though the papers always devote a few condemnatory words to the Nazi regime and never openly endorse its politics, their description of the events and the classifications used often paint a rather favourable picture. For instance, in an article on the trial of war criminal Klaus Barbie, the author speaks on the one hand of the 'terror' and 'murder gangs' of the *Maquis* (the French resistance), and on the other hand of the 'phenomenal abilities' of Barbie, who allegedly has been put on the war criminal list 'because of a thirst for revenge of the resistance' (*DNZ* 5/87). No indelicate word is spoken about Barbie, infamous in the rest of the world as 'the butcher of Lyon'. Another example is a review of a book that deals with the German annexation of Sudetenland (the western part of the Czech Republic) in 1938, in which the author speaks on the one hand of the 'overheated nationalism' of the Czechs and on the other hand of the 'liberation of the Sudetenländer' (*DNZ* 24/6/87).

### Anti-semitism

A topic that is present in almost every issue of the newspapers is that of the Jews in general and of Israel in particular. Even though anti-Semitism is nowhere openly present, there are so many implicit remarks and indications that the party can be called anti-Semitic without any hesitation. For one, (individual) Jews are only mentioned in a negative way. Several neutral short articles deal with fraudulent businessmen, in which it is explicitly written that they are Jewish (even though it is not relevant). This is also true for articles on Israel, which always refer to Israel as the *Judenstaat* (Jewish state). Disproportionate attention is devoted to negative aspects of the Israeli state, particularly its aggression in the occupied territories. The only time that Jews are mentioned in a positive way is when they support the revisionism of the DVU, as this is believed to add strength to the own argument.

The party is more open in its many insinuations of a Jewish conspiracy. In general Jews outside of Israel are seen as first and foremost loyal to Israel and only secondarily to the country in which they live (and often are born and raised). For instance, the German Jew Michael Friedman, who is active in both the Jewish community and local politics in Frankfurt, is described not only as 'Frankfurter CDU-politician' but also as 'Israeli functionary' (*DNZ* 24/11/89). A classic example of anti-Semitic conspiracy thinking is present in an article on the *Alija* (the Jewish exodus from Russia), which extensively covers the alleged disproportionate presence of Jews in the leadership of the communist party (*DNZ* 20/7/90). There is also much speculation on 'Israel's true power' in the papers; they even had a seven-part series on this topic. Another good example of anti-Semitic conspiracy thinking is taken from an article on a Jewish anti-fascist living in Germany, who is suspected of working for the Israeli secret service:

> In addition, interested circles in the Federal Republic need to speak and write about an alleged hatred of foreigners by the Germans, to divert in that way the attention from the hatred of Palestinians by the Israeli state. (*DNZ* 19/5/89)

Frey has always denied allegations of anti-Semitism, claiming that he never said or wrote that all Jews are bad and that he should have the right to call some of them bad. According to Frey, the fact that everyone is attacking him only proves that Germany is still not free from its past, and that Jews have a special position in Germany. As proof of his good behaviour, he points to the fact that the father of the late famous Jewish violinist Yehudi Menuhin worked for years as chief of the cultural-political section of the *DNZ*. In 1967 Moshe Menuhin resigned because, contrary to Frey, he supported the *Ostpolitik* and thought the paper was not militant enough towards Israel and Zionism.

Though the most prominent, Jews and Israel are not seen as the only 'dark forces' in the world. The usual shady enemies of extreme right conspiracies are present in the party literature: the trilaterals, the Bilderberg group and the Council for Foreign Relations. Most articles on these organisations and the people in them are based on the book 'Leaders without Masks – International', edited by Gerhard Frey himself. The book provides the reader with information on 'the truly powerful and the puppet-master [Drahtzieher] of world politics'. It should come as no surprise that many of the leaders are … Jews.

## Xenophobia

A feature that has become one of the most prominent in the papers in the 1990s is xenophobia. It is directed at two subgroups of foreigners: immigrants and asylum seekers. The picture that is usually painted of the multicultural society is an ominous one in which chaos is the only rule, and the paper always displays the US, and the city of Chicago in particular, as the spectre of this degenerated, criminal, violent society.

Asylum seekers became the major issue in German politics in the early 1990s, after their number had increased dramatically. The DVU was well prepared for this issue, as it had always opposed immigration and had discovered the issue of asylum seekers already at the beginning of the 1980s. The issue is mostly debated in legal and economic terms. The main argument is that the large majority are not genuine asylum seekers, which is proven by the very low percentage that are officially recognised by the German state. This is combined with the issue of the high costs of the asylum seekers for Germany, primarily in financial but sometimes also in personal and ecological terms. The DVU does not always address the subject only in 'objective' terms and the screaming headlines of the papers are used to enhance the existing fears within the readership for an *Überfremdung* (a flood of foreigners). The paper devotes much attention to scandals in which asylum seekers are involved: for instance, in articles with telling titles such as 'Sham asylum seekers exposed as criminals. Clear way for foreign swindlers' (*DNZ* 10/6/88) and 'What gypsies cost us. Asylum seekers cash in' (*DNZ* 16/8/91).

The DVU does not consider itself to be xenophobic and even claims to help to prevent its (further) widespread outbursts within German society. After the (obligatory) remark that genuine asylum seekers should be accepted a Bremen DVU delegate stated:

> Throw the swindlers out, the imposters, the criminals of multinational descent, the heroine Turks and cocaine Negroes, Gipsy plunderers and Polish smugglers and car thieves, because by tolerating them we breed hate against foreigners! (*DNZ* 11/9/92)

This type of argument has always been the party's main defense against allegations that its alleged anti-foreigner propaganda provides ammunition for those fire-bombing refugee homes. In reaction to the many campaigns for *Ausländerfreundlichkeit* (kindness towards foreigners) and against *Ausländerfeindlichkeit* (hostility against foreigners), which were launched in the beginning of the 1990s and were supported by all main political parties, the DVU started a campaign in support of its own organisations with the slogan: 'In name of the law: deport sham asylum seekers – fight hate against foreigners!'

Even though the issue of immigration is a separate issue, it is generally discussed in the same terms. Originally guest workers had more credit than asylum seekers. Despite the fact that the party and its papers often pointed to the high crime figures of the foreign population in Germany, they did not fail to mention (though less regularly) that still only a minority is criminal:

> Hereby one has to consider: the majority of foreigners living here have no more to do with crime than that they themselves are threatened by imposters with a German or foreign passport. Certainly, the majority of the decent foreigners that live here wish for decisive action against native and foreign gangster as much as this is the wish of the decent Germans. (*DNZ* 24/5/91)

After the 1992 compromise of the major German parties on a more strict law on asylum, the DVU toughened its stand on other foreigners. This is probably tactically motivated as the issue of asylum seekers proved successful for the party and it hopes to sustain this success with similar campaigns against other foreigners.

### Socio-economic policy

Socio-economic policy is dealt with rather extensively in the party programme, yet is almost non-existent in the newspapers. The programme entails a combination of socialist and liberal policies, which the party (in imitation of the CSU/CDU) describe as the 'free social market economy' (DVU 1987). It is primarily based upon the capitalist system and the freedom of property, but tries to overcome its negative aspects by (sometimes massive) state intervention. For instance, German tradespeople should be helped by granting them public contracts in preference to foreign multinationals. Similarly, German farmers should be protected against EU mass production. Though the DVU claims that this should (and can) be done within the free market, it is quite clear that it involves protectionist measures: 'through subsidies the state should keep the coal-mine, shipbuilding and steel industry alive and competitive, as is also done abroad, as we should not become even more dependent on foreign interests' (*DNZ* 12/2/88).

The papers increasingly express concern over the possible extinction of German industrial branches as a consequence of the free market. The original attacks on the EC are expanded with attacks on the free world market. More attention is given to what the party considers as its negative aspects, such as poverty and unemployment (in Germany), international competition and pollution. This notwithstanding, most articles on socio-economic policy serve mainly the purpose of proving either the strength of Germany or the mismanagement of others (most notably the EU). As a consequence of the latter, as well as because of its welfare chauvinist policy, the party wants to cut back on Germany's spending on foreign countries and international organisations (most are anti-German anyway), and use the money which is thereby saved to ensure the pensions and social benefits of the German people (e.g. REP 1993).

## The strong state

Though the issue of the strong state is present in the party literature, it does not feature prominently. The section in the programme entitled 'protection from criminals' entails a classic collection of *law and order* demands. It calls for higher sentences for serious crimes, smuggling (of people and goods) and drug dealing in particular, which have to be served fully. It believes that the proposed law and order policy can only be executed by a police force that is capable, well equipped and no longer the *Prügelknabe* (scapegoats) of a failed policy (DVU 1993). Moreover, more attention should be given to the victim instead of the perpetrator. Both the programme and the papers devote special attention to crimes of left-wing activists. To put a stop to the misuse of the right to demonstrate, it calls for a law against *Landfriedens-bruch* and disguise (DVU 1993). In the papers the issue is mainly linked to that of foreigners and drugs, which are themselves interlinked. In general, the papers call for higher punishment and, contrary to the programme, the introduction of the death penalty.

The party's *militarism* is strongly related to revisionism and national revival. For years the *DNZ* ran a series under the heading 'our immortal fallen' (in Gothic letters) in which pictures of memorials for fallen German soldiers were printed. Another series cheered 'great German soldiers'. In both cases a large number of the soldiers in question were (high ranking) members of the (Waffen-) SS. The programme wants the state to play an active role in rehabilitating German soldiers of the present and the past, including 'putting the standing and honour of German soldiers under legal protection' (DVU 1987). It further demands a well-equipped and sovereign German army, which is commanded by Germans and not by foreigners (i.e. NATO). German soldiers are not allowed to be deployed for foreign interests or in a far away war and crisis areas (DVU 1993). The party is also sceptical about a leading role for civilians within the army. For instance, the social scientific institute of the army in Munich is described as 'a civilian *Fremdkörper* within the army' (*DNZ* 10/4/87).

## Ethical values

The theme of (the loss of) ethical values is primarily related to that of abortion, while the party's position on the theme is predominantly based on its nationalism. The DVU strongly opposes the liberalisation of abortion and attacks prominent supporters of this view (especially those in the CDU like Rita Süssmuth). The issue of abortion is itself related to the drop in the birth rate in Germany, which when combined with immigration, draws into question the issue of the survival of the German ethnic community.[9] The DVU claims that the established parties use immigration to counter the declining

[9] This is nicely illustrated in the *DNZ* headline: 'Can the German ethnic community survive? The results of the decreasing birth rate and the flood by aliens' (*DNZ* 29/4/88).

birth rate of the Germans, which will lead to the extinction of the German ethnic community. Against this disastrous policy the party puts forward its own family friendly policy which is based on 'generous state support for German families and mothers' (DVU 1993). Except for tax measures and a ban on abortion this would include better possibilities for care outside of the family and a general recognition of the impressive achievements of mothers.

Other dangers to traditional values and thereby to the survival of the German ethnic community that feature in the literature are divorces, homosexuality, drugs, pornography and individualism. The programme calls for better health protection and an effective fight against epidemics, including a report duty of AIDS (DVU 1987). However, the main value that the party defends are national(ist) values, i.e. love for the *Heimat* and the German ethnic community. In this context the programme argues for an educational system that is in favour of equal chances but against 'levelling' and teaches 'respect for the values of humans and for religious conviction, courage, sense of responsibility, spirit of democracy and the sympathy for nations, love of the fatherland and of the German ethnic community' (DVU 1993).

### Populist anti-party sentiment

Particularly in the 1990s, critique on (most) established parties is clearly gaining prominence in the party literature. The major bone of contention is the extensive state financing of the (established) political parties and their delegates, and every suggestion for an increase of these subsidies is met with fierce critique and resistance. When confronted with the issue, the party delegates voted against such plans in their respective state parliaments. Despite the often harsh language the populist anti-party sentiments are quite moderate in content and do not cross the line into extremist anti-party sentiments. In most instances the behaviour and politics of specific parties are attacked and criticised in relation to one of the issues mentioned above. The criticism is mostly directed against left-wing parties, which are accused of anti-national or even of extremist and terrorist behaviour (in the case of the *Grünen* and the 'post-communist' PDS). In the case of the SPD, the main critique concerns its alleged betrayal of the nationalist legacy of Kurt Schumacher. Overall, the papers are quite friendly towards the CSU (especially politicians like Theo Waigel and Friedrich Zimmermann) and to a lesser extent the CDU.[10] Most criticism against the traditional right-wing parties is directed at the liberal FDP and factions within the CDU – especially 'left-wing' or 'liberal' prominent members like Norbert Blum, Rita Süssmuth and Heinrich Geißler, because of their support for the liberalisation of abortion and their support of the multi-cultural society.

The most fierce criticism is reserved for the REP. The main reason for the

---

[10] This is in line with the fact that, before he founded his own political party, Frey generally called upon his readership to vote for the Union parties.

critique has always been the outspoken distancing of that party from 'the extreme right'. Schönhuber explicitly included the DVU, which he accused of an anti-democratic ideology (see chapter 2). For its part, the DVU describes Schönhuber as an opportunist and a destructive force within the *nationales Lager* (national camp). Because of his vanity and his lust for power, he is used as a pawn by the anti-national forces. Typical of this argument is the reaction to its loss in the 1989 European election, which also marked the breakthrough of the REP. In an editorial the paper wrote that the REP had reaped what the DVU had sown, because the whole media had led the right-wing protest down this 'harmless road' (*DNZ* 23/6/89).

This touches on another sentiment that is often voiced in the paper: the unjust way in which the DVU is treated by the outside world. Especially in regard to election campaigns and the annual meeting in Passau the party complains about the way political enemies ('left-wing terrorists') attack its members and the fact that the other parties and media either ignore this or, even worse, encourage it. In addition, the party forcefully rejects its description as right-wing extremist by the German state. It has always claimed to be the most democratic party in Germany, as it takes the German constitution, its preamble in particular, to be its highest authority. According to the DVU the 1990 unification proved that it had always been right, as it had always strived for the unification of the FRG and its 'lost territories'. The party also argued that the other parties should recognise its right of existence, among others by striking the DVU from the official list of right-wing extremist organisations.

## Conclusion

The DVU is in many ways an unusual political party, having a rare combination of many members and no real cadre. It has won a relatively large number of seats in regional elections without maintaining functioning regional branches. The literature of the DVU is quite singular as well. On the one hand, it entails one of the shortest party programmes in Germany (and possibly in Europe), a limited range of election material, and strictly speaking no party paper. On the other hand, it has fought very expensive election campaigns and has two weekly newspapers at its disposal with a total circulation of more than five times its membership. This is the result of the specific character of the party and its leader. The DVU is first and foremost the instrument of a wealthy German businessman, who one day decided to add a political party to his strange blend of nationalist businesses.

Even though the party programme is very short, it includes a broader range of ideological themes than do the various papers. There is in fact a rather big difference in (secondary) features presented in the externally and internally oriented literature. Issues like social and economic politics or ecology have a prominent place in the programme, yet are hardly touched upon in the party papers. On the other hand, the party papers devote much attention and space to anti-Semitism and anti-Americanism, whereas these are absent from the party programme. Though a certain degree of discrepancy between the two will be present in all parties (resulting from the different tasks and audiences of the two sources), the situation of the DVU differs from that of other parties in the fact that the programme is the only genuine piece of literature that the party as such distributes. The two newspapers, though owned by the party leader and openly supportive of the party, are at best officious and not official party papers. They are (semi-)independent organs, which preceded the political party (and will probably also outlive it).

Not withstanding the particular situation of the DVU, the two sources of party literature together constitute a lot of propaganda material based on a very limited though clear ideology. The DVU ideology is built upon three main features: nationalism (Germany for the Germans!) patriotism (Germany first!), and xenophobia (alien equals anti-German). The party aspires to a completely sovereign German state, which contains only German citizens. However, it remains silent on the important question of 'who is a German'. This German state should take care of its own people and should not interfere with the business of other states. International cooperation is only accepted when it is to the good of the German people and any membership of supranational organisations like NATO and EU is 'thus' rejected. This negative attitude towards international cooperation is not only the result of the party's nationalism but also of its xenophobic, if not paranoid view on the world. The DVU sees the world as full of anti-German conspiracies, which is in part the result and the cause of its (open) anti-Americanism and (more hidden) anti-Semitism. A final feature of the party ideology is chauvinism, which is expressed mainly through the demand for a national revival entailing a moral revision of Germany's role in the Second World War and the demand for a renewal of national pride.

# Part II

# Flanders:
# 'Eigen volk eerst!'

## The extreme right in Flanders, 1917–80

Until the beginning of the First World War, the heterogenous *Vlaamse Beweging* (Flemish Movement) was primarily cultural in orientation (see Willemsen 1969: 10–27). Its principal goal was the emancipation of the Dutch language (i.e. Flemish) and culture from the dominance of French speaking Belgium, and its supporters looked favourably upon a multinational Belgian state. The First World War led to a split in the movement: a small section collaborated with the Germans and, led by the *Raad van Vlaanderen* (Council of Flanders), proclaimed the independence of Flanders on 22 December 1917; the majority of the movement remained loyal to Belgium (Willemsen 1969). Indignant at being linguistically discriminated against by French speaking officers, Flemish soldiers in the Belgian army founded the so-called *Frontbeweging* (Front Movement), which later gave rise to the *Frontpartij*.

The Flemish Movement was, by the end of the war, discredited, and it soon split into two distinct camps: a patriotic, culturally nationalistic camp that wanted to see a Dutch Flanders within a federal Belgium; and an anti-Belgian, politically nationalist camp that sought political autonomy for Flanders and the destruction of Belgium (Vos 1992). During the first post-war years the former was the sole political representative, in the form of the *Frontpartij*, which called for the establishment of a federalist Belgian state. Initially, it gained moderate successes in the Belgian elections: five seats in 1919, four in 1921 and six in 1925 (Fitzmaurice 1983: 37). However, by the end of the 1930s the Flemish Movement had changed in three respects: its Flemish identity had grown (if initially only in a cultural sense); its leaders had become almost exclusively Catholic; and its ideology had become more extreme, having shifted in favour of the anti-Belgian, politically nationalist camp (Goedbloed 1991: 400–1). In the 1920s and 1930s many Catholic, Flemish nationalist intellectuals, mostly active in the *Algemeen Katholiek Vlaams Studentenverbond* (General Catholic Flemish Students' Association) and in the *Katholiek Vlaams Hoogstudentenverbond* (Catholic Flemish University Students' Association), encouraged an osmosis between Flemish nationalism and the 'new order ideologies' (Vos 1992). This process culminated in 1933 in the foundation of the *Vlaams Nationaal Verbond* (Flemish National Union, VNV) under the leadership of Staf De Clercq (later Hendrik Elias).

The VNV wished to see the creation of a Greater Netherlands or *Dietsland*, i.e. a 're-unification' of the Netherlands with North and South Flanders,[1] within a Europe structured along the lines favoured by Nazi ideology. After having absorbed the extreme wing of the deteriorating *Frontpartij* and other small Flemish nationalist groups (De Wever 1992), it was left with only one principal rival prior to the Second World War: the *Verbond van Dietse Nationaal-Solidaristen* (Association of Diets National Solidarists, Verdinaso), founded in 1931 by Joris Van Severen. This was a para-military movement that originally had an almost similar goal as the VNV, i.e. a corporatist, authoritarian and 'organic' Greater Netherlands. However, in the mid 1930s it changed its goal into a 'Diets Empire', including Luxembourg, Belgium, the Netherlands and their colonies (Willemsen 1969).

At the end of the 1930s, the VNV scored some electoral successes after entering into various strategic pacts with other political groups. Under different names the Flemish nationalist pacts secured approximately 13 per cent of the votes (in Flanders and Brussels) in 1936, and 15 per cent in 1939 (Willemsen 1969: 414, 464; Gijsels 1992: 26). During the Second World War a substantive minority of the Flemish Movement collaborated with the Nazis; the VNV members thereby hoped to achieve their goal of completely uniting the Flemish nation(-state) under the VNV banner (De Wever 1992). However, the Germans played the VNV off against other groups, including its main competitor, *De Vlag* (The Flag or German–Flemish Working Community), which prior to the war had called for an autonomous Flanders but had abandoned this line during the German occupation in favour of a Greater Germany. During the war, *De Vlag* was completely absorbed by the General (later 'Germanic') Flemish SS, which fought 'the Bolshevik enemy' on the Eastern Front.

Flemish nationalism emerged from the Second World War in an even more feeble state than following the First World War. The collaborators were exposed to all sorts of repressive measures (the same was true for the many Walloon collaborators) and, although these so-called 'catacomb days' only lasted five years, calls for their amnesty or rehabilitation became major issues for the post-war Flemish Movement (Seberechts 1992). In 1954 some 1,500 collaborators were still in prison and roughly 150,000 Belgians, the so-called *incivieken* (those unworthy of citizenship), did not enjoy civil rights – including the right to vote or to be elected to public office (Gijsels

[1] North Flanders refers to the Dutch speaking part of Belgium (i.e. Flanders), South Flanders to a small part in the Northwestern region of France (around cities like Dunkirk and Lille).

1992: 41). In the first few years after the war, most of the former collaborators confined their activities to charitable pursuits, especially on behalf of former soldiers who had served on the Eastern Front, for example in the *Vlaams Verbond der Oud-Oostfrontstrijders* (Flemish Association of Former Eastern Front Fighters). Within the Flemish Movement, the moderate wing exercised the most influence, particularly in the christian democratic *Christelijke Volkspartij* (Christian People's Party, CVP), and claimed the traditional 'holy' sites of Flemish nationalism as its own. This stirred up ill-feeling among the radicals of the movement, although for a considerable time they continued to remain isolated and marginalised.

As of 1949 several radical Flemish nationalist organisations were set up again, including the anti-repression party *Vlaamse Concentratie* (Flemish Concentration), and the direct-action group, *Vlaamse Militanten Orde* (Order of Flemish Militants, VMO).[2] All these organisations remained marginal until the *Christelijke Vlaamse Volksunie* (Christian Flemish People's Union) was launched as an electoral alliance to contest the 1954 parliamentary election, in which it won 3.9 per cent of the Flemish vote and one seat (Dewinter and Van Overmeire 1993: 26). This success led, on 21 November 1954, to the foundation of the *Volksunie* (People's Union, VU) as its official successor. The new political party secured 6 per cent of the Flemish vote in 1961, giving it five seats in the Chamber of Deputies, and two in the Senate (Vander Velpen 1989: 43). This constituted a significant comeback for Flemish nationalism in Belgian politics.

The movement was fuelled further in the 1960s by the smouldering dispute between Dutch and French speaking Belgians over the national language, a dispute that led to rioting and to the first steps towards inaugurating a federalist structure in Belgium. This federalisation soon developed a momentum of its own, causing a split within the Belgian political party structure (see Huyse 1986; Deschouwer 1991). The three important political currents (christian democracy, social democracy and liberalism) split into separate Dutch speaking and French speaking parties. In this climate, the VU, with its Poujadist-like manifesto and style, scored several electoral victories, gaining a record 18.8 per cent of the Flemish vote (and 21 seats) in the 1971 parliamentary election (Fitzmaurice 1983: 177).

Although the VU was the only political representative of the Flemish Movement, and proved to be relatively successful, criticism was nevertheless forthcoming from within its ranks. From the outset, the federalist party was regarded with suspicion by the separatists. These suspicions grew when the VU, under the sway of the democratisation movement of May 1968, increasingly assumed the shape of a left-liberal, moderate nationalist party. Under the leadership of Hugo Schiltz, Nelly Maes, Maurits Coppieters, and others

---

[2] The VMO was originally called *Vlaamse Militanten Organisatie* (Organisation of Flemish Militants), but renamed into 'Order' only shortly afterwards.

the party attempted to ensure that it was regarded as a respectable coalition partner, incurring the wrath of the radical wing which saw itself as the 'whip' of the CVP (see Dewinter and Van Overmeire 1993). Relations between the moderate leadership and the radical membership, most notably the activists of the VMO (who had since the party's inception staffed its stewarding and propaganda service), became ever more strained. After protracted debates, on 12 June 1971, the problems finally seemed to have been resolved when VMO leader Bob Maes was made a member of the Belgian Senate and allowed his organisation to be absorbed by the VU. However, only a short time elapsed before, on 2 July, Bert Eriksson founded a new VMO. In subsequent years this new VMO became a violent, neo-Nazi, direct-action group, and on 4 May 1981 it was outlawed by the Antwerp high court for being a private militia (see Gijsels 1992: 54–68).

By the mid 1970s, dissatisfaction with the left-liberal stance taken by the VU had already prompted several radical members to leave the party. They initially worked together in non-party political organisations, such as the (new) VMO, the *Verbond van Nederlandse Werkgemeenschappen Were Di* (Association of Dutch Working Groups Protect Yourself, Were Di) and the direct-action group *Voorpost* (Outpost), which splintered off from Were Di in 1976.[3] In 1973, twenty-seven of these organisations joined ranks in the *Vlaams National Raad* (Flemish National Council), which had as its main objective to be(come) a thorn in the side of the VU (Gijsels 1992). There were, however, radicals who wanted to found a new party. Although circumstances were soon to change, the time was not yet ripe for such a move.

On 24 May 1977 the leaders of the VU signed the so-called Egmont Pact, which envisioned the federalisation of Belgium.[4] Three days later, the VU party conference adopted the Pact by 62 votes to 31 and joined the second government of Leo Tindemans. The Egmont Pact provoked heated debates, and not only in the VU; the whole Flemish Movement was divided over it and found itself caught up in the worst crisis it had known in the post-war period. Federalisation, so both the pro-democratic and anti-democratic separatists believed, did not go far enough and in September 1977 they joined forces in the *Egmontkomitee* (Egmont Committee).[5] The Committee was united in rejection of the Egmont Pact, but internally divided on how best to oppose it, whether from inside or from outside the VU (see Dewinter and Van Overmeire 1993).

[3] For (short) descriptions of these organisations, see Gijsels (1992: 38–81), Vander Velpen (1989: 39–57, 1992: 127–31), Verlinden (1979, 1981) and Verstraete (1992).

[4] According to the Egmont Pact, Belgium was divided into three *gewesten* (autonomous regions), i.e. Flanders, Walloon and Brussels, as well as into two *gemeenschappen* (communities), the Dutch and the French speaking. Both communities could implement their own policies (on education, culture, welfare) in the Brussels region (see Fitzmaurice 1983: 115–17)

[5] Another main problem of the Flemish nationalists was the fact that Brussels had become an autonomous region of its own, instead of being an integral part of Flanders.

The group in favour of opposing from within the VU – led by Edwin Truyens, founder and leader of the *Nationalistische Studentenvereniging* (Nationalist Students' Association, NSV), and Were Di leader Bert Van Boghout – joined forces in the *Vlaams Nationaal Directorium* (Flemish National Directorate). Despite exerting great pressure, this group did not manage to unite all the anti-Egmont forces under its banner. Two former prominent members of the VU wished to found their own political party: former senator Lode Claes, and former leader of the Antwerp *Volksunie Jongeren* (People's Union Youth), Karel Dillen. Although the two held several sets of talks, they could not reach agreement on a joint party. Claes was interested in a broad, national and liberal popular party, whereas Dillen was planning a small, radical-nationalist, 'solidarist' direct-action party (see Gijsels 1992: 83–8; Dewinter and Van Overmeire 1993: 63–84).

On 2 October 1977, after a brief but hectic period characterised by mutual distrust and confusion, the *Vlaams Nationale Partij* (Flemish National Party, VNP) saw the light of day. Its founders included Dillen, Gerard Slegers, Leo Wouters (the latter two were former VU senators) and Wim Verreycken, leader of the tiny *Vlaams Republikeinse Partij* (Flemish Republican Party) that was immediately absorbed by the VNP (Dewinter and Van Overmeire 1993). Surprised and indignant, Claes proceeded to found his own party, the *Vlaamse Volkspartij* (Flemish People's Party, VVP) on 19 November. Immediately after these two parties were established, they were urged to come to a merger by prominent outsiders, such as Truyens and Van Boghout as well as Jan Brans, former chief editor of the VNV newspaper *Volk en Staat* (People and State).

The fall of the government fuelled this effort as the parliamentary election was brought forward to December 1978. The VVP was prepared to enter into such a merger, for the duration of the election only, but laid claim to a dominant role in the election list. This was, in fact, what happened, and in December the two anti-Egmont parties campaigned for a joint list of candidates under the name *Vlaams Blok*. The list was dominated by the VVP both in terms of ideology and candidates, but to everyone's surprise only Dillen, whose followers had persuaded him to stand for the list in Antwerp, managed to win a seat in Parliament. Claes failed in his bid to become a senator, dissolved the alliance and unsuccessfully went it alone with the VVP in the 1979 European election. As he gained less than 1 per cent of the vote, this marked the end of the political road for both Claes and his VVP (see Gijsels 1992; Dewinter and Van Overmeire 1993).

# 4

# Vlaams Blok

## The establishment of an anti-Establishment party

On 28 May 1979 the VNP was disbanded and the political party *Vlaams Blok* (Flemish Block, VB) was founded as a fusion of the VNP and the nationalist wing of the VVP (Gijsels 1992: 88; Dewinter and Van Overmeire 1993: 91–3). Dillen (VNP) became party leader and Piet Bocken (VVP) deputy leader. Shortly thereafter Bocken was replaced by Roeland Raes (VVP), who continues to fill this post in 1999. For the first few years the VB remained a small splinter party that drew its strength almost exclusively from the efforts and reputation of Dillen, Raes and party secretary Jaak Peeters. The party recruited its members from the ranks of activists in Flemish nationalist organisations with which VB was in close contact, such as the *Taal Aktie Komitee* (Language Action Committee), Voorpost, Were Di, and VMO. Moreover, the various local branches of these organisations often doubled up as local party branches of the VB.

From the beginning the party (and in particular Dillen himself) received support from veterans of the radical wing of the Flemish Movement, many of whom had a history as collaborators and/or were in the VU. When the Egmont Pact collapsed together with the second Tindemans government, the anti-Egmont party seemed to have outlived its purpose. In 1981 Dillen was re-elected to parliament, but with a smaller share of the vote than in 1978 (1.8 as opposed to 2.1 per cent).[1] The VB had concentrated its activities almost completely on the city of Antwerp, standing candidates in less than thirty of the over 300 Flemish communities (Gijsels 1992: 89; Dewinter and Van Overmeire 1993: 118). As a consequence of the small scale electoral success the party was continually pressured to merge with the VU in the first decade of its existence.

In the mid 1980s, the VB began to change. New members entered the party cadre and some of the veterans left. This change did not take place

---

[1] All election results of the VB are based on the Flemish vote and taken from the Belgian political science journal *Res Publica*.

without some (minor) blood-letting. For example, Truyens, the party ideol-
ogist, was expelled from the party in 1983 after he had called on Dillen to
muck out the 'immoral stables' – referring to some of the prominent VB
members (Verstraete 1992: 125). Moreover, prompted in part by the electoral successes of like-minded parties in the surrounding countries (the
French FN and the Dutch CP), the VB revamped its propaganda. It grew
more and more from an anti-Egmont VU split into a broad and modern
extreme right party. This did not, however, immediately result in rewards at
the polls. In 1984 the VB won 2.1 per cent in the European election, thereby
failing to gain entry into the European parliament. A year later Dillen was
again re-elected, this time with 2.2 per cent.

The results were met with disappointment, to which Dillen reacted with
the so-called 'Operation Rejuvenation' (Dewinter and Van Overmeire 1993:
138), which involved an across-the-board change in the party leadership.
Various young VB members, most of them (former) leaders of nationalist
youth and student organisations, were integrated into the party council. In
1987 Gerolf Annemans, a twenty-nine-year-old, took Dillen's seat in Parliament. At the same time, serious efforts were undertaken to set up an independent party organisation and to make the VB less dependent upon the
resources of its friendly movements. An official youth organisation, *Vlaams
Blok Jongeren* (Flemish Block Youth, VBJ), was founded in 1987 by former
prominent members of the NSV – notably Filip Dewinter and Frank Vanhecke.

In April 1987 a group around Roger Frankinouille, co-chairman of the
right-wing anti-tax party *Respect voor Arbeid en Democratie* (Respect for
Labour and Democracy), switched to the VB, partly out of dissatisfaction
with its Walloon sister party, and partly owing to the VB's emphasis on the
immigration issue (Dewinter and Van Overmeire 1993). In this manner, the
party's only remaining competitor on the right was eradicated. At the same
time, the VB won increased media attention. It had conducted a sharp and
vociferous campaign in the 1987 parliamentary election. Under the new
slogan *Eigen volk eerst!* (Own people first!) the party had doubled its seats
in parliament (3.0 per cent) and, for the first time in its history, had won a
seat in the Belgian Senate. Dillen moved to the Senate and Dewinter, only
twenty-five years old at the time, entered parliament alongside Annemans,
thereby becoming the youngest MP in Belgian history.

In the 1988 local election the VB won twenty-three seats in ten local councils. It scored its greatest success in Antwerp, where it secured 17.7 per cent
of the vote and ten of the fifty-five seats (Van Eycken and Schoeters 1988:
22ff). The success attracted a great deal of publicity and opponents began to
take the VB seriously. On 10 May 1989 the leaders of the five largest Flemish parties signed an agreement stipulating, among other things, that they
would neither negotiate with the VB nor make immigration a political issue
(Gijsels 1992: 103). This so-called *cordon sanitaire* was torn apart seven

weeks later and only the *Socialistische Partij* (Socialist Party, SP) and the green party *Agalev* remained loyal to the 'anti-Bloc' agreement (Damen 1998: 15–16). The other parties resumed their ambivalent stance towards the VB: a great deal of anti-VB rhetoric together with conciliatory gestures whenever it proved opportune.

In December 1988 the first major split in the VB occurred. Having smouldered beneath the surface for years, dissatisfaction with 'Operation Rejuvenation' finally came out into the open. A group of long-standing prominent members of the VB – including party council chairman Geert Wouters and party secretary Peeters – attempted to squeeze the VBJ-group around Dewinter out of the ranks of the party leadership. In an 'Address to Karel Dillen' they were accused of being 'Lepenists' (supporters of FN leader Le Pen) and of sidelining the Flemish question in favour of the anti-immigrant issue (see Gijsels 1992: 141–2; Dewinter and Van Overmeire 1993: 161-2). When the Wouters group realised that Dillen was siding with Dewinter, the members left the VB and founded the nationalist pressure group *Nationalistisch Verbond-Nederlandse Volksbeweging* (Nationalist Association-Dutch People's Movement).

The VB was able to continue to win elections even after the split. In 1989 it won one seat on the Brussels city council and one in the European parliament, polling 6.3 per cent. Dillen took the seat in Strasbourg and, on the evening of the election, he proclaimed that cooperation with the FN was considered a possibility.[2] During negotiations with his fellow extreme right MEPs, Dillen first sealed a pact with the REP and subsequently refused to make any ideological concessions to the FN (Dewinter and Van Overmeire 1993). This resulted in the final organisational structure of a 'Technical Group' of the European Right, which was not organised on the basis of an ideological programme, but rather on pragmatic principles (i.e. financial arrangements).

The real breakthrough did not come until the parliamentary election of 24 November 1991. On what was afterwards referred to as 'Black Sunday', the VB more than trebled its 1987 share of the vote, gaining 10.3 per cent. This yielded a total of eighteen parliamentary seats, twelve in the Lower House (parliament) and six in the Upper House (Senate). Antwerp again was the stronghold; every fourth voter supported the VB, making it the strongest political force in the city. Yet, the VB also put in a vigorous showing outside of its traditional stronghold. Even in villages with no foreign inhabitants the

---

[2] Dillen had for a long time been very cautious about cooperation with Le Pen, a state nationalist and therefore, by extension, a Belgian nationalist (Verstraete 1992: 144). In his first official visit to Belgium, invited by the French speaking mayor (Nols) of the Brussels area Schaarbeek, Le Pen argued for the foundation of a *Front National Belge* and supported a form of Belgian nationalism (or 'Belgicism'). In reaction, Dillen wrote: 'He should know that he hereby makes himself impossible in Flanders, also in right-wing circles where he can count on sympathy' (*VLB* 8/84).

VB picked up roughly 2 per cent of the vote (Swyngedouw 1992: 83). Immediately after the election the VB attracted attention by refusing, after a brief
inner-party discussion, to take up its seat in the Flemish government to
which it was entitled by law (Dewinter and Van Overmeire 1993).

The electoral success of the VB prompted an enormous shock-effect and
consequent reaction within the 'democratic camp' (e.g. Piryns 1992).
Numerous new organisations were founded, ranging from broadly supported anti-racist pressure groups like *Objectief 479.417* and *Charta '91* to
small and violent anti-fascist groups like the *Blokbusters* (see Gijsels 1994;
Damen 1998). Despite the hostile climate the VB was able to receive a good
press on two occasions the following year. In July a VB motion was for the
first time accepted in the *Vlaamse Raad* (Flemish parliament); the motion
opposed the right of French speaking inhabitants of Flemish Brabant and
Voeren to vote for Walloon institutions (Dewinter and Van Overmeire
1993). In the autumn of 1992, the party organised a press conference where
it announced that Staf Neel, for twenty-two years a popular SP city council-
lor in Antwerp, was crossing the floor to the VB. His change of allegiance
caused the CVP and SP to lose their majority in the Antwerp city council
(Van den Brink 1994).

In the following years the social and political pressure on the VB increased
even further, leading to a new *cordon sanitaire*, which was signed by over a
thousand local, regional and national delegates of all major parties (see
Gijsels 1994; Damen 1998). This notwithstanding, the party succeeded in
establishing itself as a solid force in the Flemish party system. In the 1991
parliamentary election it had become the fourth largest political party in
Flanders, overtaking old rivals the VU (which scored 9.3 per cent). At the
1994 European election the VB managed to increase its share to 12.6 per
cent, thereby doubling its number of seats in Strasbourg. A small setback was
that the two-man VB contingent – Dillen was joined by his former
spokesman Vanhecke – could not be part of an official Group of the European Right, due to a lack of cooperation and seats.[3]

On 9 October 1994 the VB scored a major victory in the local election,
winning a total of 199 seats in eighty-two local councils. As always, it was
again the city of Antwerp where the party did best. With 28 per cent of the
votes it became the largest political party in the local council, increasing its
total number of seats to eighteen. The Antwerp result was the main focus of
media attention inside and outside Belgium, as was the issue whether the
party would be invited to play a part in the city's administration. The VB had
unequivocally stated that it would be willing to assume responsibility for the
city of Antwerp; it had even formed a shadow cabinet under Dewinter. Nevertheless, the VB remained excluded from power for the next six years,

---

[3] The REP did not pass the 5 per cent threshold required in Germany, and disappeared from
the EP; the AN and LN refused to join a Euroright group.

owing to the renewed *cordon sanitaire* instituted by all other parties (which together formed the new city council).

The next year brought a premiere to Belgian politics: for the first time the population could directly elect their regional parliament. This meant that on 21 May 1995 the Flemings had to vote for the two federal chambers (i.e. parliament and Senate) and for the *Vlaamse Raad* (Flemish parliament). Despite the fact that the pre-election period was dominated by political scandals, most notably the Augusta affair, the election results showed hardly any significant difference compared to the 1991 election. The two major parties, CVP and SP, remained fairly stable, although the latter had been deeply involved in the Augusta affair. The VB gained 12.1 per cent of the vote for the Belgian parliament and a slightly higher 12.3 per cent for the Flemish parliament. This was almost 2 per cent higher than the 1991 parliamentary result, though just under the 1994 European result. Nevertheless, it meant that the VB sent more representatives to the various parliaments than ever before: eleven to the Belgian parliament, three to the (Belgian) Senate, and fifteen to the Flemish parliament (as well as two to the Brussels city council).

During the next years the VB became increasingly isolated; the other parties kept their distance, while various anti-racist organisations increased their 'resistance'. Moreover, the party came into open conflict with leaders of the Flemish Movement, most notably the organising committee of the *Ijzerbedevaart*. This led to endless accusations back and forth and to confusing parallel manifestations in a fierce struggle over the hegemony within the Flemish Movement. Moreover, the VB was confronted with an increasingly hostile state; for example, a law banning negationism (i.e. the denail of the Holocaust) was introduced, while a law linking state funding of political parties to their commitment to human rights was discussed. In both cases the discussion was for the most part kept in general terms, though it was clear who was the target. In addition, the VB was more and more curbed in its actions; as in the surrounding countries, the party had to deal with an obstructive (local) government, which refused to allow demonstrations or to rent out facilities.

In this hostile political and public climate, the VB went through the most perilous stage in its existence, the change in leadership. On 8 June 1996 seventy-year-old Karel Dillen stepped down as party chairman and appointed his fellow MEP, thirty-seven-year-old Frank Vanhecke, his successor. With this strategic move Dillen prevented a much anticipated internal fight between the Flemish nationalist wing around Annemans and the Lepenist wing around Dewinter (e.g. Swyngedouw 1998). As Vanhecke was acceptable to both, and had the explicit backing of honourary chairman Dillen, the VB overcame its first leadership change without any major upsets.

At the same time, and more than ever before, Belgian politics became riddled with scandals. The affair that dominated Belgian politics and society in the late 1990s was the so-called Dutroux affair. The investigation into

Dutroux' pedofile murders uncovered various judicial failures, and, as always in Belgium, led to a stream of rumours concerning political involvement. So-called 'white marches' were organised throughout Belgium, protesting the crimes, their sloppy investigations, and, the alleged political cover up of the perpetraters. The VB was well prepared for this situation, having for years attacked the Belgian Establishment in general, and the allegedly weak law and order policies in particular. Moreover, Gerolf Annemans boosted the party's image by being one of the most visible members of the parliamentary committee investigating the Dutroux affair.

On 15 June 1999 the Flemings had to vote for the Flemish (or Brussels), Belgian and European parliaments. As was prophesied by most opinion polls, the elections became a true waterloo for the Flemish governmental parties. The CVP lost its position as largest party to the liberal VLD, while the VB overtook the SP to become Flanders' third largest party. In all three elections the VB scored over 15 per cent, while it became the largest Flemish party in the Brussels city council with 4.5 per cent of the overall vote. The latter result was nevertheless somewhat disappointing, as the party had campaigned for almost three years in a self-proclaimed 'Battle of Brussels', distributing hundreds of thousands of bilingual pamphlets, and also using the popular Johan Demol – the (French speaking) former police chief of the Brussels area of Schaarbeek who was fired because of his (concealed) membership in an extreme right youth group – to attract votes from French speakers (see Abramowicz and Haelsterman 1998: 62–3). This notwithstanding, the 1999 elections were a clear success for the VB, which brought it a total number of forty-five parliamentarians: two in the European Parliament, fifteen in the Belgian parliament, four in the Belgian Senate, twenty in the Flemish parliament and four in the Brussels city council.

The various electoral successes have brought the VB extensive funds (see Swyngedouw 1998: 62), which it used, among other things, to build a solid party organisation. By 1996 the party had over 180 local branches and thirteen permanently opened secretariats throughout Flanders (Spruyt 1996: 39). The province of Antwerp has always been the stronghold in terms of party membership, a long way ahead of East Flanders, Brabant, West Flanders and Limburg, traditionally a region of very weak VB support (e.g. *Kaderblad* 4/94). The local party branches are often highly active in political education, propaganda and demonstrations.

The VB has a strict hierarchical structure, rather similar to that of a communist party (Gijsels 1992; Spruyt 1995). Regional and local party organisations do not have the right to appoint their own heads or preferred candidates. They can only put forward nominations, which the party council has to approve; the same applies to all party decisions. The various cadres at the upper and middle management levels receive their ideological and political training from one central organisation, the *Nationalistisch Vorm-*

*ingsinstituut* (Nationalist Educational Institute, NVI), founded in 1987. Like all other party organisations the NVI comes under the jurisdiction of the party executive; it not only publishes a fortnightly cadre bulletin, but also numerous brochures on various topics (see Spruyt 1995). Other important sub-structures within the VB are the propaganda service, the study service, the *Vereniging van Vlaams Blok Mandatarissen* (Association of Vlaams Blok Delegates), and the *Nationalistische Omroepstichting* (Nationalist Broadcast Foundation, NOS). The NOS was established in 1983 and is responsible for radio and television programmes, providing the material for the air-time the state grants all parliamentary parties.

It is uncertain how many members the VB precisely has. According to one source, the VB had 1,231 members in 1980, 3,698 in 1985 and 6,500 in 1990 (Deschouwer in Spruyt 1995: 53). Vanhecke stated in April 1992 that the VB had 7,639 members, or an increase of 500 over the figure published prior to the election victory of 1991. Dewinter, on the other hand, spoke at that time of between 8,000 and 9,000. In January 1995 deputy chairman Raes spoke of 'some 9,000' members, which will probably have gone up to 10,000 by 1999 (Spruyt 1996: 39). However, despite the relatively small membership, the party is able to mobilise a substantial number of activists, who often double as (active) members of other Flemish nationalist organisations.

In addition to virtually all more or less radical Flemish nationalist organisations, the VB holds also good contacts with many nationalist parties throughout Europe. Traditionally, the closest contacts have been with (members of) Dutch and South African extreme right organisations, such as the CP'86, Voorpost and *Boerestaatparty* (Boer State Party). Since the mid 1980s, the party also has a very close relationship with the French FN, and its youth wing, as well as with several German parties and youth movements (including the DVU, REP, NPD and JN). The VB has also always been very supportive of nationalist parties that are generally not considered to be part of the extreme right, such as the Scottish National Party, the Irish *Sinn Fein* (Ourselves Alone) or the Basque *Herri Batasuna* (People's Unity), though without keeping official contacts at the party level. Ever since the fall of the Berlin Wall, the VB has been extremely active in establishing contacts with nationalist parties in Eastern Europe. Among others, VB delegations have visited the *Hrvatska Stranka Prava* (Croatian Party of Rights), the *Slovenska národná Strana* (Slovak National Party) and the Bulgarian *Vutreshna makedonska revolyutsionna organizatsia* (Internal Macedonian Revolutionary Movement).

## Profiling the literature

### *Externally oriented: programmes and brochures*
In 1980 the VB published its first party programme entitled *Grondbeginselen* (Principles, VB 1980). Both the labelling and the programme, albeit in a

slightly different form, had already been used by the predecessor party VNP (Spruyt 1995). At the end of 1999 the programme is still, with a few minor emendations, its 'manifesto of right-wing Flemish nationalism' (as has been the subtitle since 1990). It closely resembled the *Were Di* programme, entitled *Grondslagen* (Principles), published in 1973 (Gijsels 1992). This is not that surprising, given that the lion's share of the Were Di programme was written by the present VB deputy chairman, Raes.

The original programme, which, because of its colour, was also called the 'Orange Booklet', included sixteen A5 pages and has a professional appearance. It started with some quotes – hailing (Flemish) nationalism, hierarchy and fighting spirit – and a two-page introduction by party leader Dillen, who addressed the question of, 'Why a new political party?'. The answer was simple: the Egmont Pact had brought an end to the nationalistic character of the VU and hence the 'fighting Flemish nationalist Movement' needed a new representative political party (VB 1980: 4). The rest of the programme contained five sections, three dealing with particular ideological features and two providing summaries. The republished 1990 version is almost identical in both format and substance (VB 1990). The only extensive revision has been made in the introduction, which now deals with the how and why of the VB.

During its first decade the VB never published separate election programmes, fighting the various elections with special issues of the party paper (which were distributed in far greater quantities than the normal issues). The breakthrough election of 1991 featured the first professional election campaign of the VB. The party presented a widely circulated election programme with the title *Uit Zelfverdediging* (Out of Self-Defence, VB 1991).[4] The belligerent connotation of the slogan was strengthened by the image of two boxing gloves. The election programme counted twenty-eight A5 pages, opened with a large general introduction by Dillen and a small specific introduction by Annemans, chairman of the programme commission, and further contained five major thematic sections and a miscellaneous final section. The campaign for the European election of June 1994 was organised around the main slogan *Grote kuis* (Clean sweep), supported by a picture of a broom. This combination 'fully voices the wish of the voter to make a clean sweep for one time, but also charges that these old, decayed political structures have to be replaced by new fresh ideas' (*Kaderblad* 47/94). The parliamentary election the next year was fought with the similar slogan *Nu afrekenen!* (Pay now!). The professionally styled election programme counted no less than 160 A5 pages, by and large a collection of the main conclusions of the various thematic brochures of the preceding years (VB 1995).

The 1999 elections were contested with the general slogan *Baas in eigen land* (Boss in Own Country). The campaign was focused first and foremost

---

[4] The campaign further introduced the unofficial party name 'Vlaams Blok Eigen Volk Eerst'.

on the issue of crime, for which the party had created the slogan *Recht op veiligheid* (Right to security). Already in 1997 the VB presented its comprehensive programme, entitled *Een Programma voor de Toekomst van Vlaanderen* (A Programme for the Future of Flanders, VB 1997), counting a record 225 pages. The party published also a separate summary version, entitled *Toekomstplan* (Plan for the Future, VB 1999a), as well as a *Veiligheidsplan* (Security Plan, VB 1999b), bundling the law and order policies of the party (programme).

Throughout its existence but increasingly since the late 1980s, the VB has produced a wide variety of thematic brochures. In general these were elaborations, and only occasionally innovations or changes, of the relative sections in the party programme. They were written by leading members, Annemans and Dewinter in particular, and published by the responsible party organisation, the NVI. Some were based on a thematic party conference, summarising the party's elaborated position on a specific theme. Others were written as a consequence of an existing feeling within the party that an elaboration of the specific point was needed, often triggered by the increasing salience of the issue in day-to-day politics. In addition, general brochures were published to function either as an introduction to the party in membership campaigns, or as a general review of the past, present and future of the party (e.g. Dillen 1992). Finally, both Dillen and Dewinter have published books of their own (for an overview of the different items, see Spruyt 1995).

### Internally oriented: party paper

The party paper is the elaborated successor to that of the VNP. Since December 1977 this latter party had published a 'journal of the VNP' entitled *De Vlaams Nationalist* (The Flemish Nationalist, *VLN*). It initially appeared twice a month, but was reduced to a monthly already in 1979. As its official sub-title Dillen had chosen 'and that's why we stand here [to] rebel'; in memory of Reimond Tollenaere, the former propaganda leader of the VNV who fell at the Eastern Front (Spruyt 1995: 29–30). The VNP paper had always contained four A4 pages, of which the last page had been devoted at least half to advertisements and announcements. The circulation of the paper was later claimed to have been around 1,200 (*VLB* 8/90).

With the transformation of the VNP into the VB, the paper was transformed into 'the journal of the Vlaams Blok'. The renewed *VLN* was identical to the old paper, except for the fact that it now generally contained generally eight (later twelve) pages. In September 1981 the paper was renamed *Vlaams Blok* (*VLB*), sub-title 'The Flemish Nationalist Party'. The format was changed to eight A3 pages and the lay-out was altered. The counting, however, was consecutive to that of the *VLN*. In November 1982 the paper claimed a circulation of 10,000, among members, sympathisers and others. Except for the monthly issues the party published several special

issues, some devoted to national or local (Antwerp) elections, some to political issues (e.g. the Flemish state). In May 1988 the paper got a new lay-out,
which was again changed one and a half years later. Since then, the party
paper kept more or less the same lay-out until 1997, containing sixteen A3
pages, and being printed in only three colours: black, white and orange. It
contained various regular features, such as 'In de kijker' (In the spotlight),
which included short interviews with (local) VB delegates, and 'Rapport
Buitenland' (Foreign Report), discussing the (mis)fortunes of 'like-minded
right-wing nationalist' parties abroad.[5] In August 1990, the *VLB* claimed a
circulation of 25,000, which had increased by just one thousand by December 1995. In November 1997 the paper went through a complete make-
over, being transformed into the rather glossy *Vlaams Blok Magazine* (*VBM*)
with the remarkable sub-title 'monthly of the Flemish National Party'. The
new magazine is very professionally styled; it is printed in colour, counts
thirty-one A4 pages, and includes various regular features, pictures and
advertisements (also by commercial companies). The only aspects that
stayed the same were the counting, which is consecutive to that of the *VLB*,
the circulation, which is still at 26,000 (*VBM* 6/99), and the goal: 'This paper
is and remains the mouthpiece of the Vlaams Blok, which looks at the current affairs through nationalist glasses' (*VBM* 11/97).

## For a free and Flemish Flanders!

### Ethnic nationalism

Flemish independence is and always has been the most prominent topic in
the VB's literature, both externally and internally oriented. Moreover,
(Flemish) nationalism has always been the most important ideological feature. According to its party programme ethnic nationalism (volksnational-
isme) is 'based on the ethnic community being a naturally occurring entity
whose cultural, material, ethical and intellectual interests need to be preserved' (VB 1990: 5). As is typical for ethnic nationalists, the ethnic community is placed over the state: the state should serve the interests of the
ethnic community and not the other way around (e.g. *VLN* 4/80).

In the short run, the party wants the Flemings to become the dominant
ethnic community within the Belgian state, as they compose the majority of
the Belgian population. Further, an active state policy is demanded to undo
the Frenchification of the Flemings that live in the areas now dominated by
French speakers. In the long run the VB strives for an independent Flemish
state, including all places that ever were Flemish (such as, for example,

---

[5] Originally Vanhecke (and sometimes Raes) used to discuss primarily the atrocities of communist regimes, and only secondarily the positive developments of like-minded foreign parties
and right-wing heroes like British prime-minister Thatcher, American president Reagan and
Chilean dictator Pinochet.

Voeren and Brussels). As a model for the split of the Belgian state, the party
has taken up the 'velvet split' of Czechoslovakia in 1993 (see VB 1997: 11;
also Annemans *et al.* 1998).

The independent Flemish state was for a long time considered but a first
step in the process of creating a Dutch Federation, described as a 'federalism
within the frame of the Low Countries at the sea' (VB 1990: 7).

> In the coming Europe, twenty million Northern-Dutchmen and Flemings have
> to again experience their unity as language, culture, people to take their own,
> independent place in Europe and so to maintain their own character. (VB 1990:
> 7)

This Dutch federation was to do everything possible to ensure that the Flemings living in South Flanders, a small region in northwestern France with
Lille at its centre, should also be able to live 'according to their own nature'
(VB 1990: 7). In line with the party's *external exclusiveness*, it would follow
that they can only accomplish this within the Dutch federation, and not
within the French state they currently belong to. However, this is never
openly stated. Throughout the years, the party paper addressed this issue less
and less; even the solidarity with the Dutch people, contrary to that with the
Afrikaner people, was voiced only occasionally. Indeed, the Dutch were regularly attacked for their impartiality in the Flemish struggle – an old
reproach within the Flemish Movement. Also, the Netherlands was increasingly presented as a country which has fallen prey to left-wing decadence.
This notwithstanding the ideal of a reunification has not died, but is just
rephrased: 'The Vlaams Blok strives for a unity of North and South Netherlands, with a healthy suspicion for the ethical and societal evolution in North
Netherlands' (*VLB* 6/94; also VB 1997).

The feature of *internal homogenisation* features in almost every issue of
the party paper. It used to be primarily linked to the Belgian problem, but
increasingly became connected to the theme of the 'immigration problem'.
Though immigration had regularly featured as a topic in the party paper and
has been omnipresent since 1987, it received only little attention in the two
party programmes. However, since its last version in 1990, the party has
issued almost one brochure per year on it, primarily written by Dewinter
(Spruyt 1995: 147–8).

Already in its first programme the VB identified 'the ever more acute problem of guest workers' and called for their prohibition from entering Belgium
and for the gradual reduction in their numbers (VB 1980: 14). Since then,
the problem of the 'mass invasion of foreigners' has grown into 'perhaps the
largest threat to our ethnic community' (Annemans and Dewinter 1988: 5).
The various proposals that the party developed throughout the years were
collected and published in the seventy-point programme (Dewinter 1992),
which was 'updated' four years later (Dewinter 1996). Should this programme be implemented, the future Flemish state will be free of non-Euro-

pean immigrants and will include only assimilated European immigrants. Moreover, as the party believes that people should be received in their own cultural environment, and they recognise political refugees only in the most strict sense, only European asylum seekers from closely related cultures will be accepted into the country (see also De Man and Dewinter 1991).

The seventy-point programme is only marginally concerned with the long-term vision of a Flemish Flanders. First and foremost it presents a plan for the 'guided repatriation of non-European foreigners to their countries of origin', which is 'operational and immediately performable' (Dewinter 1992: 3). Among the points that can be implemented in the short-term are the complete closure of the borders for non-European immigrants, the abolition of the promotion of a multi-cultural society in both words and means (e.g. subsidising pro-foreigner organisations), and the application of the 'own people first'-principle in all policy fields. Most of the programme, however, deals with the (middle-range) period of transition between present-day Belgium and future Flanders. These policies are aimed at creating a dual society, or a state of social apartheid, in which immigrants and Flemings will live completely separated. During this stage, all non-European immigrants are to be prepared for their repatriation. A separate system of social security as well as a special tax on the employment of non-European immigrants will be created and the money generated by these measures will go to a so-called 'repatriation fund', which will pay for the repatriation and 'repatriation premiums' of the immigrants. To ensure that they will repatriate 'voluntarily' the VB proposes a 'deterrent policy' containing, for instance, a limitation of the right to ownership, a reduction of child support and social security, and the obligatory repatriation after three months of unemployment (Dewinter 1992: 27-8; also Annemans and Dewinter 1988: 25–7). In the revised version of the plan, the for the party revolutionary option of assimilation of non-European immigrants is introduced (Dewinter 1996). However, this seems to be mainly a token of good will, as it hardly features in other party literature and goes against the ethnic nationalist ideology of the party.

Against these radical policies on non-European immigrants, the proposed policies of assimilation for European immigrants look quite moderate. This is not to say that the VB does not consider the European immigrants a problem. For the party the sizable group of European immigrants in Flanders, especially the thousands of 'Eurocrats', are one of the most important threats to the (restoration of the) Flemish character of Brussels and its neighbouring rural areas. Whereas the non-European immigrants are primarily inhabiting the inner city areas of Brussels, the Eurocrats inhabit the richer areas in and around the city. There they integrate into the French speaking sub-culture, for example by sending their children to French schools, which strengthens their dreaded 'facilities'. Even worse, they have been given the right to vote at local elections from the year 2000, according to European legislation, and the VB is convinced that the majority will vote for parties of

French speakers. Hence, the VB emphatically campaigns against 'Euro voting right', i.e. the right of EU-citizens to vote in Belgian local elections (e.g. *VBM* 10/98), and against 'Euro-Brussels' (e.g. *VLB* 6/94).

## Exclusionism

The ethnopluralist world view of the VB is based on the belief that the ethnic community is the core unit for organising large groups of human beings. Combining liberalism and nationalism, the party argues that its only goal is 'the maximum self-fulfilment of all members of the ethnic community' (*VLB* 2/83). To achieve this people need, and have the right, to develop within their own ethnic community. After all, '(o)utside of the group he can neither exist nor even grow up and live. It is natural groups like the family, the ethnic community, which in their turn, like man himself, are equal and different' (*VLB* 7/83).

Ethnopluralism is at the heart of the party position on Europe (e.g. Verreycken 1994). The VB has always been very supportive towards European cooperation, though not towards the current European Union. It considers the EU both too limited (in territory) and too extended (in power), but it also sees in European cooperation the chance for Flanders to break away from the dreaded Belgian state. This is only possible if the current road of integration is abandoned though, and a new 'Europa der volkeren' (Europe of Ethnic Communities) is created (e.g. VB 1997: 138–9). This Europe will not be based on artificially constructed states, but on natural ethnic communities. In addition, it will be based on the respect for the sovereignty and individual character of every individual ethnic community instead of a supranational (and thus imperialist) goal.

Ethnopluralism is also one of the core arguments in the party's solution to the immigration problem. The Flemish ethnic community should remain untouched by alien elements and must defend itself against the ongoing invasion of 'elements from alien cultures'. According to Annemans, the right to cultural identity includes the right to one's own culturally homogeneous territory (*VLB* 12/92). In this manner the VB claims not only to protect the identity of its own people, but also that of the immigrants. Given that each ethnic community has the right to a strong and protected identity, the party opposes any attempt at integration. It defines integration as genocide, since it transforms independent ethnic communities into an 'inferior mixture' (*VLB* 7/83). Its ethnopluralism is moderated to the extent that the VB distinguishes between European and non-European ethnic communities. The first are believed to be related to the Flemings, as they share a (higher-order) European culture. This would enable Europeans to assimilate, whereas non-Europeans miss this communality and are (thus) seen as incapable of assimilating into the Flemish community.

Opponents have condemned this distinction between European and non-European immigrants as racist. This view is believed to have been strengthened by the party's explicit reference to different 'races' and its exclusion of Turks from the 'Occident' (Avondland). The VB always sharply rejected any suggestion of racism; Annemans even called upon his colleagues to press legal charges against people that call them racist (*VLB* 6/87). The party insists that it never speaks in terms of 'superiority' and that it even explicitly states that Flemings are no better than people of any other ethnic community. It merely states that just as Flemings would have difficulties living in the desert, so too would North Africans (Muslims) have difficulties living in a complex modern society such as Flanders. Moreover, having been uprooted from their own culture, they find themselves embroiled in all sorts of problems, such as drug addiction, crime, etc. Since this is a natural process, the immigrants themselves are not responsible, but rather the Belgian and Flemish politicians. They have torn them out of their own cultures by false promises and stripped them of their own identity by a policy of integration. The immigrants are therefore 'deracinated' which, in the party propaganda, is tantamount to saying 'murdered'. Consequently, the VB concludes that it is the established parties that are the *real* racists (*VLB* 11/82).

Notwithstanding the dominance of ethnopluralism the party paper is not completely free from claiming the inferiority of other cultures. For instance, in its protest against ritual slaughter the VB claims that '(i)t is wrong that more and more foreign cultures, and that more and more foreign customs and traditions, which often involve a centuries-old civil and cultural degeneration, would be getting protection with us' (*VLB* 8/87). This kind of ethnocentrist reasoning is quite recurrent in the party paper. Outright racism, on the other hand, is not.[6] Even though the party does distinguish between different races and ascribes certain hereditary features to them, it does not place them in a hierarchical order. In accordance with the ethnopluralist vision, it speaks of 'different but equal'.

The party has only rarely been accused of anti-Semitism. The first time it happened, Dillen reacted furiously. He compared the accusing journal to the defamatory (and rabidly anti-Semitic) pre-war German journal *Der Stürmer* (The Stormtrooper) and dared them to find one anti-Semitic remark in all his (many) writings. As far as the party literature is concerned, no evidence of, or even hint at, anti-Semitism could be found. The few times that Jews are mentioned in the paper, they are cited as examples of a nationalism that is accepted by the media and the left-wing, in sharp contrast to the nationalism of the Flemings.

---

[6] A rare exhibition of colonial racism is given in an article on independent Surinam: 'The sweet innocent savages, so adored and glorified by the red media, churches, literature and other lucrative organisations, have in a natural manner beheaded at least 17 opponents. Whether they have eaten their prey, we do not know. They did have a large banquet, so they say, and the heads were put on the table. Because we do not know French, we say: Chase away the whites, and the savages will come back at a gallop' (*VLB* 1/83).

## Xenophobia

In the early years the VB aimed its xenophobia mainly, though not exclusively, at the French speaking part of the country. Even in the 1990s, every issue of the party paper contains at least one article in which the Belgian abuses against the Flemish people were raised. In the vision of the party Belgium is a 'historical mistake', founded against the wish of the (Flemish) people by French speaking 'mutineers'. With reference to its 150th anniversary, the Belgian state was described as: 'The absurdity that has enslaved, crushed, derided, hit, hurt and oppressed our ethnic community – with the deliberate intent to destroy Flanders and the Flemish ethnic community – and this is the truth' (*VLN* 2/80).

By French speaking Belgians the party refers to both Walloons and 'Belgicists', i.e. people that consider themselves first and foremost Belgians instead of Walloons or Flemings. Though the Walloons are attacked at least as often as the Belgicists, they are treated with (slightly) more respect and understanding. The VB accuses the Walloons, most importantly, of imperialistic and expansionist behaviour by not honouring the 'facilities' of the Flemish minority in Walloon, while at the same time misusing their own facilities in Flanders. Belgicists are seen primarily as immoral entrepreneurs, who act solely out of egocentric materialist motives. Its personification is the Belgian royal family, which only supports the Belgian state because its life of luxury depends on it. Even more detested are the pro-Belgian Frenchified Flemings, referred to as *franskiljons*, who are not only hedonists, but also traitors to the own ethnic community – the most serious crime for nationalists. However, as most of them are perceived as victims of actions of earlier generations or simply weak characters, the VB is prepared to take them back. After all they remain (inextricably linked) members of the Flemish ethnic community and can thus again find their natural place after a proper process of 're-Flemification'.

The VB is fairly critical of the Flemish people. The 'Flemish Sancho Panza' (Vlaamse Lamme Goedzak) is regularly described as passive and easily appeased by promises of the 'wallingants' and Belgicists. In an exceptionally harsh criticism, it once wrote: 'Already a long time ago our party has come to the conclusion that the reason that an independent Flanders still does not exist is the character of the Flemish people rather than the obstinacy of the French speakers in this country' (*VLB* 5/87). All in all, the party paints a remarkably negative picture of the *cohabitation* of the two main ethnic communities in Belgium: 'A cheat (Walloon) and a dope (Fleming) cannot play cards together' (*VLN* 10/80). Hence it should come as little surprise that the VB is not chauvinist, often considered a core feature of nationalist parties.

Originally, the 'immigration problem' was addressed entirely as part of the Belgian problem. Already the first issue of the paper featured a large article in which the guest workers were pictured as playthings of higher and darker forces. In a later article the conspiracy was unfolded further: the guest workers were brought to Flanders by Belgicist big business to replace the Flemish workers, so that the wages would not have to be raised. This was supported by Walloon politicians, as they were either servants of big business or saw the guest workers as a way of enlarging their political power. This latter motivation also explained the support of the labour unions, which saw the foreign workers as potential supporters.[7] The party claims a historical analogy in its opposition to the settlement of immigrants in Flanders.

> For years Flanders has fought for its own existence, for self-government without interference of others. After years we more or less succeeded in silencing those other foreigners, the French speakers, in a large part of Flanders. We do not at all like having to start another battle against other influences in our territory that are alien to our ethnic community. (VLN 7/79)

Though the first Belgian political party to address the issue of immigration as a problem, the VB saw it primarily as an issue for the future at that time.[8] However, the immigration problem became more pressing for the party over time. Already one year later the party congress decided that a start should be made on 'making the over abundant foreigners redundant, especially the non-European' (VLN 4/81). That same year the party began to address immigration in a xenophobic manner; suggesting, for instance, that the day 'that the guest workers will – literally – face us with drawn knives is really not that far away' (VLN 6/81). Since the mid 1980s, under the influence most notably of Dewinter, opposition to immigration was voiced not only more prominently, but also differently.[9]

Most importantly, the standpoint on immigrants toughened considerably. The separation between Europeans and non-Europeans became decisive in the choice between repatriation and assimilation. Originally the propaganda had been directed primarily at Italians and Portuguese and their repatriation. Under the (perceived) pressure of the growing number of non-Europeans,

---

[7] This strange coalition of big business and labour unions was seen to be the result of their shared Belgicist ideology, which, like the immigration policy, was anti-Flemish.

[8] 'The extremely complex problem of the politics on foreigners also came up. This problem will have to be elaborated further. However, we must not bury our heads in the sand here, if we want to avoid that in due time the immigrants will dictate the law. A clear end to immigration forces itself upon us. Also the repatriation of those elements that are not willing to work or that are criminal' (VLN 10/80).

[9] This is not to say that this issue had not featured within the party propaganda before that time. The 1981 parliamentary election was contested with the slogan: '400,000 unemployed, so why then guest workers?'. The next year, the VB fought the local election in the Antwerp region primarily on the issue of immigration. Nor is it correct to suggest that the VB's sixth party congress of 1984, which was devoted solely to the issue of guest workers, was the starting point of its xenophobic propaganda (as does Gijsels 1992). In fact, it was not until 1987 that it became a central issue in all party literature, both externally and internally directed. It was also in this year that the unofficial sub-title of the party was changed from 'the Flemish nationalist party' to 'Our own people first'.

European immigrants were allowed to remain if they assimilated. This was accompanied by the uprooting of two new groups as prime targets of the xenophobic propaganda: first and foremost the Muslims (predominantly immigrants from Morocco and Turkey), and second (non-European) asylum seekers. While the guest workers had originally been portrayed primarily as naive slaves at the hands of big business, they featured increasingly as the cause of all problems. The term 'guest worker' was more and more replaced by the term 'immigrant', which indicated that they had come out of their own free will and had come to stay. The immigrants were more and more portrayed as a financial burden ('guest unemployed') and as a threat ('guest terrorists').

The most important aspect of the party's xenophobic propaganda, however, is Islamophobia. Fundamentalism is seen as the logical consequence of Islam: 'a doctrine, which preaches holy war, assassination, forced conversions, oppression of women, slavery and extermination of "infidels", will automatically lead to what we now call fundamentalism' (VLB 6/93). Muslims are portrayed as the fifth column of a cruel and expansionist religion. As a consequence of the Gulf war, for instance, the VB called upon the government to immediately make a list of repressive measures which it considered necessary to keep Belgium (and thus Flanders) from being Islamicised and Brussels from becoming 'the most Northern town of the Magreb' (VLB 2/91). As a prime example of the ongoing Islamisation of Flanders, the VB usually points to the Antwerp district of Borgerhout, which it refers to as 'Borgerocco'.

Though less prominent, asylum seekers have also grown into a target of the xenophobic propaganda. In general, the VB portrays them as either 'gold diggers' or cowards. The first term is used to describe the economic refugees, who according to the party constitute the vast majority of all asylum seekers. The genuine political refugees, on the other hand, are often accused of cowardice, as their political struggle is in their own country (VLB 10/86).[10] More and more, refugees are integrated into the xenophobic picture of the 'time bomb', which has different applications: on the one hand, the threat of Islamic fundamentalism and terrorism in Western Europe, and, on the other hand, the demographic time bomb, i.e. as a consequence of birth figures Flanders will be inhabited primarily by immigrants in the not too distant future (e.g. De Man 1991).

---

[10] This argument seems to apply only to political refugees from non-European countries, as the party had always been extremely sympathetic towards refugees from (European) communist regimes; referring to them as 'driftwood of collapsing political systems, of which they bear no guilt' (VLB 5/91).

### Socio-economic policy

One of the few topics on which the VB expresses a somewhat ambiguous position is socio-economic policy. Whereas the party paper, and to a lesser extent the election programmes, mainly features neo-liberal rhetoric and preoccupations, the party programme seeks its inspiration in so-called soli-darism.[11] Solidarism is an ideology composed of a 'social-ethical triptych': the idea of solidarity, the principle of subsidiarity and tolerance (VB 1990: 9). A solidarist system is an organic structure of smaller and larger commu-nities that blend into one harmonious entity. Without using the term the VB seems to aspire to a 'third way', i.e. an alternative societal system to 'both the liberalistic capitalism of exploitation [and] the Marxist and communist systems of compulsion' (VB 1990: 10). However, it is not able to provide a concrete description of this alternative system: 'A solidarist community is an achievement-oriented community, which the Vlaams Blok sets consciously against the delusion and blurring of the modern welfare state' (VB 1990: 10).

In contrast to the party programme, socio-economic policy has for a long time played an almost negligible role in the party paper. Originally the topic had the interest of only a few authors, most notably Truyens and Smout, who tried to elaborate an 'ethnic economy' (volkse economie) based on solidarist principles. One of its central principles is the duty to work. Social security is seen as an emergency situation for those members of the ethnic community that, through no fault of their own, are willing but unable to perform their task towards that same community (VLN 6/81). Indeed, those that are phys-ically able to work but cannot find a job will have to do compulsory com-munity service in return for unemployment benefits (VLB 3/87). Another solidarist trait is the stress on the role of the family within the socio-eco-nomic system. 'In our current neo-capitalist society the problem of unem-ployment is considered a problem of the individual: the unemployed. However, as the family is the smallest organic cell in the society, one can safely say that unemployment is a family problem' (VLB 1/87). In line with this vision the party's call for full employment does not mean that every indi-vidual should have a job, but rather that within every family at least one member should have a job.

Throughout the years, socio-economic policy was increasingly presented in a neo-liberal style. The VB now primarily demands less state involvement in the economy, arguing for the privatisation of certain state tasks or at least a limitation of the role of the state. Real jobs can be created only by a climate of investment that is friendly to businesses, not by 'artificial injections of the

---

[11] Solidarism has its roots in the Papal Encyclical of 1931, the *Quadragesimo anno*, and the 'new order' movements that preceded the Second World War (in the case of Flanders, the VNV and Verdinaso).

state' (VLB 6/93). It further wants a reduction of the welfare state, including a 'reasonable financial hurdle' on all medical performances (VLB 2/93) and more individual responsibility for pensions (VLB 3/93). The party favours free transfer of goods within the EU, though rejecting the 'European Moloch' with its excessive body of restrictive rules (e.g. VLB 3/93). Rather, it seeks salvation in reducing social expenses, easing the economic structures and promoting technological innovation. In typical neo-liberal discourse, the VB wants to give the 'European genius' its breathing space back by replacing the 'Eurocratic palaces and their extravagant lackeys' (VLB 6/94).

In the early 1990s the VB started working on a more social image, taking up issues such as employment and poverty. In December 1993 the VB organised the thematic conference 'Poor Flanders' which was considered a first step in 'building the natural bridge between nationalism and social revival', which socialism has always prevented (VLB 1/94). This led to an increase in attention to socio-economic policies within the party paper, as well as in brochures and election programmes. Under the guidance of Jan Penris, the VB has tried to modernise its solidarism. In November 1996 the party organised a special conference under the title 'Flanders works' to elaborate its socio-economic programme (VB 1/97). In addition, in an attempt to consolidate its strong support among workers, the party started to organise large celebrations on Labor Day – to the embarrassment of the SP and the trade unions (e.g. VBM 4/99). In line with the new position, the election programmes proclaim that 'social security is much needed' and include the (costly) goal 'to save and even increase the pensions' (VB 1997).

This notwithstanding, socio-economic policy has always held and had a clear and dominant nationalist and welfare chauvinist component. On the one hand, the party uses nationalist arguments to proclaim that the policies have to benefit (exclusively) their own ethnic community. On the other hand, economic arguments are used to corroborate the claim for an independent Flemish Flanders. The party criticises the so-called 'North–South transfers in Belgium', claiming that Flanders (including Brussels!) transferred 418 billion BF to Walloon in 1992; which means that each Walloon received almost 130.000 BF from Flanders (Annemans and Smout 1993: 15). Consequently, the party calls for Flemish independence to overcome this injustice. In preparation for Flemish independence the VB wants a split of the Belgian social security system into an independent Walloon and a Flemish system.

In a somewhat similar vein the party presents economic arguments against the presence of immigrants (e.g. Annemans and Dewinter 1991; Dewinter and Penris 1993). Given the high unemployment Belgium/Flanders cannot afford (illegal) guest workers. The VB has expressed this belief since the 1981 election in its slogan '400,000 unemployed, why then guest workers?'. It wants the guest workers to get a golden handshake and to go home: 'Work in the own area!' (*VLN* 6/79).[12] At the same time, however, the VB points to the high percentage of unemployed immigrants ('guest unemployed'), stressing the high welfare costs of this group. According to the party immigration costs the Belgians annually over 120 billion BF (Dewinter, Huybrechts and Penris 1992: 3).

### Ethical values

A theme that plays an important role in the whole party literature is that of ethical values. This theme has always featured prominently in the party paper and, especially in the early 1990s, the VB devoted several brochures to it. The core of the party's view on ethical values is its vision of man, which is purely ethnic nationalist: man cannot be separated from tradition, which 'reflects the true nature of an ethnic community' (VB 1990: 11). This indicates an organic vision on the ethnic community, made explicit in the remark that 'the dead live on in future generations' (VB 1990: II).

There are three topics on which the VB has expressed its ethical views most prominently: abortion, the family and AIDS. In 1989 the party issued its first brochure on abortion, in reaction to the ongoing debate on its liberalisation (Annemans 1989). The VB explicitly portrays itself as the only defender of the unborn child against the onslaught of the left-wing pro-abortion lobby. It believes that human life starts with conception and that abortion is permitted only when the life of the mother is in danger. In addition to the complete rejection of *abortus provocatus*, it calls also for the cultivation of a new mentality towards the unborn life, for making the adoption of Flemish children both easier and cheaper, and for a renewed and radical family policy to fight (the need for) abortion (Anhemans 1989: 26). The party holds similar views on euthanasia, which it links to the position of the National Socialists (Annemans 1992: 5), but the topic is addressed far less frequently.

In May 1991 the VB organised a thematic conference on the family, which led to the brochure 'The Family Party' (Annemans *et al.* 1991). The foundation of the VB family policy is sketched as follows: 'The family, as it exists in our European civilisation, emerges as a highly developed and stable basic cell, within which the responsibility (towards the next of kin and towards the ethnic community) is central' (Annemans 1991: 12). The 'European family model' is based on the marriage between man and woman and a particular sexual ethos (i.e. monogamy, loyalty, equivalence of man and woman, respect for physical integrity). This combination is explicitly opposed to

---

[12] With the slogan 'Work in the own area' the party tries to set its struggle against foreign labour into the tradition of the historical struggle of the Flemish Movement, which had used the same slogan to oppose the nineteenth-century situation, in which the Flemings had to find work in Walloon and even France, because Flanders was an underdeveloped, primarily rural area (and was kept that way by the Belgicists).

non-European models, such as to Arabian polygamy, and to (European) anomalies like homosexuality and, to a lesser extent, living together and divorce (referred to as serial polygamy).

All topics within the ethical value discourse are seen as proof of the claim that Flanders, as well as the whole of (Western) Europe, is in a process of moral decay. The 'progressives' have created 'a world in which the tearing into pieces of millions of children is legal' (Annemans 1989: 4). To overcome moral decay the VB wishes the state to play 'an ethical educational role' in the promotion of traditional values (Annemans 1989: 19). The state has to provide a favourable environment for families, though without interfering with(in) the family itself. Hence, it should support organisations and educational programmes that are pro-family and anti-abortion, and help to create a family friendly economy, chiefly through tax reductions for (large) families and through a split of the Belgian system of social security. The VB considers attention to the issues of AIDS and drugs, which feature prominently in the more recent party literature (e.g. De Man 1993), as the means of reaching the youth with its call for a new morality. Both are linked to immigration and the general process of moral decay and can be overcome only by a change in morals, not by more permissiveness.

Within this moral order the woman is expected to perform first and foremost the traditional role of mother, and only secondarily that of worker. Though the VB does its best not to limit the role of educator to the woman and has certainly become less traditional in this respect after the rejuvenation of the party leadership, it nevertheless tends to equate the two. This is clearly demonstrated in the otherwise quite progressive plea for career breaks:

> One of the parents with one or more children of three years old or younger has to have the legal right to career breaks. During this period this *woman* will enjoy an educators fee in accordance with *her* family situation and with the retention of pension rights. (*VLB* 5/81; my italics)

The party further wants the state to be more vigilant against the influence of Anglo-Saxon culture and language. Many articles point to the 'Cocacolonisation' of Flanders (and the West), which stands for materialism, consumerism, hedonism and multi-culturalism (e.g. *VLB* 5/94).

### The strong state

A core aspect of the party ideology is the belief that human life is possible only in a well-ordered community. However, strong authority should never become tyranny, but should remain between the two extremes of an omnipresent collectivist state and an anarchic profligacy (e.g. VB 1990: 14). To ensure this the VB has always called for a strong level of law and order. With the increasing salience of the immigration problem crime was linked more and more to that problem and, consequently, has become a major issue in the party literature. Many articles deal with the increase in crime and the fact that the true figures are hidden by the government to mask its failure (e.g. *VLB* 3/94). Moreover, the occasional honest researcher (read the VB) 'comes up against a wall of resistance and refusals' in the quest for the truth (Dewinter *et al.* 1992: 3).

In April 1993 the VB organised a thematic conference entitled 'Crime: The Tough Approach' to develop its programme on this topic (e.g. *VLB* 5/93). In its resolutions the party calls for various law and order measures to prevent and punish crime (De Man 1993). In 1999 the issue of crime was put at the centre of the VB's election campaign. New figure-head Demol, illegally wearing his police chief uniform, demanded on posters the 'right to security'. In addition, the VB had elaborated upon its law and order programme, bundling the demands in a special 'Security Plan' (VB 1999b), and calling for a 'zero-tolerance plan' on the basis of the American (i.e. New York) example. The programme is fully in line with earlier convictions of the party. Both crime and drug abuse (always linked in the literature) are considered first and foremost the outcome of the ongoing process of moral decay, and thus the VB calls for a stronger sense of values. And since the moral decay among immigrants is the direct result of their being uprooted, the party calls for their repatriation as part of its crime prevention plan.

Another main feature of its law and order policies is the demand for vigilance on the part of both the state and the population. The VB calls for meting out harsher punishments and easier possibilities for investigation (especially regarding drugs dealers), increased funding for the police and gendarmes, the immediate deportation of foreign criminals, and the abolition of the Lejeune act on the reduction of sentences (e.g. VB 1991). This can only be accomplished if the judicial system is purged of all progressive people, who hold the 'perverse position that the perpetrator is the victim of society' (*VLB* 5/93). For the VB the real victim should be at the centre and should be given a far better position in both the legal and help system.

Originally the VB opposed the death penalty, probably as a consequence of the legacy of the post-war 'repression' (the period of 'denazification' directly after the end of the Second World War). It was mainly party leader Dillen who had held the party back in this respect.[13] It was therefore surprising that in 1987 the party (through Annemans) proposed a parliamentary bill in which the introduction of the death penalty for drug dealers was demanded. Even though the party later stated that such sentences would not be carried out, it looks like the death penalty can count on a more favourable

---

[13] In a reaction to the sentencing of African National Congress members to the death penalty in South Africa the party paper wrote: 'The people who know Karel Dillen know that he is a conscientious objector to the death penalty, indiscriminately of where it is applied' (*VLB* 9/84).

response from the younger party leaders (e.g. *VBM* 3/99).[14] Nevertheless, the call for the death penalty has not yet found its way into the party programme: the most recent election programme speaks vaguely of toughening the sentences 'up to the most severe sentences', which mean life-long imprisonment without the possibility of parole (VB 1997: 26).

In contrast to the position on law and order, the VB's standpoints on *defense* are quite moderate. Military matters feature very scantily in the party literature, and, even then, the party shows no signs of glorification of either the army or martial values. Nevertheless, the VB believes that '(p)eace is unthinkable without vigilance' (*VLB* 2/85). Hence it supports the institution of a well-trained and equipped army, though with a relatively small personnel of some 40,000 people including 5,000 civilians (*VLB* 1/93). The main task of this army was for a long time to keep Flanders and Europe free from both 'totalitarian Soviet imperialism' and 'omnipresent American dollar-imperialism' (*VLB* 7/81). As long as Europe is not able to defend itself, the party accepts NATO as the lesser of two evils. With the downfall of communism the VB saw a new task for NATO in defending against the threat of Islam (e.g. *VLB* 8/90). At the same time it became more and more anti-American, claiming that US presidents use foreign wars (like the Gulf war and the invasion of Somalia) for internal political benefits. European leaders were accused of slavishly following the US instead of creating an independent and strong European force (within the structure of the WEU). Moreover it wants to limit the deployment of European forces to the European continent. The only exceptions to this rule are when European interests are very seriously threatened or when countrymen are in danger (e.g. *VLB* 9/93).

Rather than a vigilant army the party is concerned with creating a vigilant 'state of mind', which it considers to be one of the cornerstones of its nationalism (*VLB* 7/81). This is also at the heart of the party's opposition to conscientious objection to military service. Dillen's first speech to the European Parliament was devoted to this topic, in which he described it as a result of left-wing decay, though accepting the odd exception of a genuine conscientious objector. His opposition was primarily argued on the basis of the nationalist belief that members of the ethnic community are obliged to defend their community. Moreover, when people are not prepared to perform all duties, they should also not be allowed to enjoy all rights (e.g. *VLB* 2/85).

---

[14] In the internal brochure *100 Vragen* the party writes: 'On the matter of the death penalty no agreement exists within the Vlaams Blok. There are arguments pro and con. The Vlaams Blok is known for the fact that its party standpoints are always forceful and unified, therefore, we plea in the first instance for a more stringent approach of crime, but not as such in favor of the death penalty' (pp.126–7).

## Populist anti-party sentiments

Another important strand in the party literature is constituted by the criticism of the established parties. Originally the VB primarily attacked the party it derived from, the VU. This 'enemy number one' was accused of having squandered its legacy of Flemish nationalism in order to be accepted by the established parties and subsequently to profit from the Belgian flesh-pots. Throughout the years, the VB became more and more detached from its VU past, and was able to create an identity of its own, only partially linked to the VU. One of the results of this development was that the party increasingly directed its anti-party sentiments towards all other parties.

The main point of criticism of the established parties is their alleged anti-Flemish character. This is linked, on the one hand, with 'old-fashioned' Flemish nationalist propaganda, in which the established Flemish parties are presented as the lackeys of Walloon parties – particularly the all-powerful *Parti Socialiste* (Socialist Party, PS). Flemish parties are accused of ignoring Flemish interests and serving only Belgian, that is Walloon, interests. On the other hand the critique is connected to the immigration problem, whereby the established parties are charged with discriminating against Flemings in favour of (Muslim) immigrants. Thereby they degrade them to third-rate citizens, behind French speaking Belgians and immigrants.

According to the party, the 'mass invasion' is caused by a sinister interplay of big business, political parties and trade unions: the first wanted cheap labour, the second have acted as 'water-carriers' of the first, and the third hoped to either destabilise the system or to win new members, thereby increasing their own power (Annemans and Dewinter 1989: 8). To cover up their own failure the established parties were accused of having launched a massive propaganda offensive with a torrent of falsified information through the loyal press. In addition, any opposition to the official gospel is silenced by accusations of racism, neo-Nazism or fascism (e.g. Annemans and Dewinter 1988). Throughout the years, the topic of the 'witch hunt' against the VB has received more and more attention in the party paper (e.g. *VBM* 1/99); the VB even created a 'media cell' which reports on anti-VB features in the Belgian media. Most articles carry reactions to recent events in which the party is 'opposed' by the 'Establishment' and its helpers (e.g. Ceder and Dieudonné, 1994).

Ever since its foundation the VB has attacked the alleged immoral behaviour of the established Flemish parties. It accuses them of only furthering their own interests and of betraying the interests of the Flemish people, using epithets such as 'Gang of Four', 'political banditry' or 'political Mafia'. No distinction is made between the various Flemish parties; all have 'dirt on their hands' and all are inimical to the VB.[15] The direct competitor, the VU,

---

[15] Dillen once voiced this opinion clearly and simply: 'The Vlaams Blok have it on for all parties, even though there is bad, worse and worst' (*Kaderblad* 29/91).

comes in for extra heavy flak, as it used to be a good and clean political party. The 'decline of politics', the VB suggests, can be halted only by an honourable and idealist party. In this context the party pursues a strategy of polarising the electorate along the lines of 'one against all'. While the other parties purportedly pursue only their own egocentric interests by making all sorts of compromises, the VB puts the interests of the Flemish ethnic community above those of the party.

In the 1990s the party changed its self-definition. As the political arm of the (radical wing of the) Flemish Movement, the VB had seen itself as simply a tool of others. Consequently, it could not compromise itself by becoming part of the (Belgian) political establishment, as that would compromise the whole Movement. The VB therefore operated as a *zweeppartij* (literally 'whip party'): 'a party that puts the other parties under electoral pressure to adjust their policies to the wishes of the people, to the citizen' (Vlaams Blok 1992: 12). However, under the pressure of its own electoral success, the VB has moderated this position. Its electorate might no longer expect only words but also actions. Yet, at the same time, it also holds deep grudges against the established parties and politics. This has led the VB to change its strategy in those cities where it has (or probably will) become the biggest political party. There the party will

> on the basis of a clear and profound programme have to prove that it is not only willing, but also able to take its responsibility. The other parties that say they choose for 'renewal' have to be given the choice: either with the Vlaams Blok or together with the other traditional parties against the Vlaams Blok. (*VLB* 4/93)

According to the party, politics should be withdrawn from 'the climate of petty-mindedness, the spirit of cliques and of base calculation' (VB 1990: 18). This can only be accomplished by the VB as this party is 'different in programme, actions and attitude from the shameful business of the current traditional political parties' (VB 1990: 18).

While the VB is clear and explicit in its populist anti-party sentiments, it is nevertheless ambivalent towards party politics *per se*. On the one hand, it seeks to bring about a 'clean sweep' in politics; in its literature the VB is almost exclusively negative about (other) political parties (and organised interest groups). Yet, on the other hand, the VB presents itself as a true political party and considers itself part of the same political system as the other parties. All in all, therefore, it is impossible to find truly extremist anti-party sentiments in the party paper. Even though the party wants to limit the power of political parties considerably, particularly by abolishing the system of political appointments in the civil service and state-owned organisations, it does not actually attack the institution of the political party itself. Moreover, it fiercely rejects the label of being simply a single-issue party, claiming instead to be 'a party of full value' (*VLB* 10/93).

## Democracy

The literature hold many derogatory references to the political system, such as 'the hopeless Belgian political mess' and 'the Belgian nest of vipers' (Belgische adderkluwen). The party programme even states that '(a)s a solidarist party the VB demands the restoration of a constitutional state in place of the dictatorship of political parties, pressure groups and individuals' (VB 1990: 10). Condemnation is also directed at parliament, described as a 'talk shop' full of incompetents who sacrifice the interests of the people 'on party orders' (VLB 7/81). At times the comments seemed to indicate a rejection of not only the practice of parliamentarianism, but also its theory. The party programme, for instance, speaks of 'false democratisation and the poisoning of parliamentarianism' (VB 1990: 18).

Especially in early publications leading party members had propagated highly elitist views, devoid of any faith in the judgement of the ordinary citizen. The most active writer in this respect, Eric de Lobel, wrote several articles in opposition to compulsory voting, disclaiming it as a Trojan horse in which the 'intellectual proletariat' is bought off by drinks in order to bring certain parties to power (VLB 6/83). In a more 'academic' style, he wrote:

> On the one hand, our residual freedom is limited by having to vote, while, on the other hand, the community falls prey to the decisions of a totally unqualified, manipulable mass, which is forced to vote. That way the democracy will bring itself down, in the words of Plato, by... a surplus of democracy. (VLB 1/85)

Except for the abolishment of compulsory voting, he also proposed 'the introduction of a minimum level of competence for the aspiration to political responsibilities (and voting is one of them)' (VLB 6/83). This elitism was shared by others, for instance at that time party secretary Jaak Peeters, who wrote: 'We reject being guided by "the average man", by Mr Average. The rights that are defended by the average equal the right to decay' (VLB 2/84). In a similar vein the VB rejected the plea for a referendum on the deployment of cruise missiles in Belgium, arguing that the people 'are blinded by the one-sided pacifist hysteria, especially by radio and television' (VLB 9–10/83).

Under the influence of the 'Dewinter group', the party literature has presented a more populist image. Since 1990 the VB no longer presents itself as the voice of a specific group, but as the vox populi, caught aptly in the slogans 'We say what you think' and 'The VB: that is you!' (e.g. VLB 9/90). The newly defined party goal is, in the words of Staf Neel, 'to express the voice of the small man' (VLB 10/92). This does not mean that the party maintains to follow the man in the street indiscriminately. It merely claims to say things that the man in the street also thinks (though often does not dare to voice).[16]

---

[16] Van Nieuwenhuysen writes on the relationship between the VB and the people: 'The Vlaams Blok says what a lot of the Flemings think. Fortunately that does not mean that we play up to the voters. As, in some cases, it requires a lot of arguments and persuasive power to convince the population that we are right' (VVBM-Nieuwsbrief 8/92).

This has also led to a revaluation of the instruments of direct democracy. In 1993 the party proposed the introduction of a decisive referendum, thereby explicitly disclaiming the argument that the people would not be able to judge in difficult matters (*VLB* 10/93).

One of the most interesting publications of the VB to date is the 'Proposal for a Constitution of the Republic of Flanders' (Verreycken 1991: 106–32). The first section of the 'constitution' addresses the basic rights of the future Republic, entailing a largely familiar plea for a liberal constitutional state. The only major deviation from most other West European constitutions is the choice for a strict *jus sanguinis* over a *jus soli*: 'A Fleming is someone who has been born of a Flemish pair of parents' (Verreycken 1991: 108). In the commentary the author already nuances this point by stating that a special workgroup will have to add a formulation to include the possibility of children of one Flemish and one Dutch parent, 'to name but one example' (Verreycken 1991: 108). The sections on the different organs of the future Flemish state contain few new ideas.[17] Even though the whole constitution is based on the democratic ideal – article 24 explicitly states that '(t)he Flemish republic is a democratic state' (Verreycken 1991: 115) – the VB remains sceptical towards the way this ideal has been put in practice. 'Democracy should not be confused with endless talking, without saying sensible things' (Verreycken 1991: 115); a traditional form of anti-parliamentarism. According to the proposal, '(d)emocracy should lead to the situation in which the whole ethnic community can control and sanction the government' (Verreycken 1991: 115). This is also why political parties will have to be incorporated. Yet, on the other hand, it stipulates: 'The founding of political parties is free. These contribute to the people expressing its political will ... exclusion of political parties should be impossible' (Verreycken 1991: 115).

The most radical change that the party wants to make to the regular model of parliamentary democracy, however, which has not found its way into the constitution proposal, is the representation of children. The VB argues that the democratic principle of 'one man, one vote' is not upheld in present-day democracies, as children are not represented. Hence, it proposes that children will be represented by their parents until they are themselves eligible to vote: the mother gets an additional vote for the first child, the father for the second, etc. (Annemans 1991: 25). The party believes that this will give the family a distinct impact in the political arena and, moreover, will encourage parents to vote more consciously as parents, thereby promoting the family (Annemans 1991: 22).

---

[17] The political system of the future Flemish state will differ in four major respects from that of the current Belgian state: (1) it is to be a republic instead of a monarchy; (2) it is to be a unicameral system instead of a bicameral system; (3) double mandates are to be prohibited (as they are considered to be at the root of the Belgian political corruption); (4) the right to vote is to replace the current compulsory voting.

## Revisionism

Amnesty has always been a core issue for post-war Flemish nationalists, and not only those of the extreme right. The early issues of the paper in particular featured bitter articles on the way the Flemings were treated by the Belgian state during the post-war 'repression'. Originally it had been the VU that almost annually submitted bills to parliament calling for amnesty. After 1978 the VB took over this highly symbolic task. The party has always devoted attention to the topic, especially in relation to specific occurrences and dates, and even in the 1990s deemed it important enough to publish a special brochure (see Verreycken 1993).

The most interesting quality of the brochure is the insight it provides into the reasons for the plea for amnesty, i.e. the way the VB evaluates the Second World War and the controversial role of the Flemish Movement during that period in particular. According to the party there are too many different, and even opposed, forms of collaboration and resistance to speak of 'the' collaboration or 'the' resistance. Moreover, good and bad were on 'both sides of the barricades' (Verreycken 1993: 5). The sole criterion for the VB to decide between good and bad was and still is whether one acted in the interest of Flanders (or the Low Countries).

> What mattered was the declaration of solidarity with all those, who, coming from the Flemish Movement, acted for the sake of Flanders and were punished because of Flanders. Again, that means no approval or disapproval of what has happened on the Flemish side during the Second World War. (*VLN* 5/81)

Collaboration and the post-war 'repression' are judged from a purely nationalistic perspective by the VB. On the one hand, the party speaks of 'those who, for the good of the population, have held a political or administrative office during the Second World War' (Verreycken 1993: 16), and refers to the former Eastern Front combatants as 'soldiers ... who, fifty years ago, driven through idealism, wanted to fight the madness of communism' (Verreycken 1993: 8). On the other hand, it portrays the repression as 'blind persecution [by] anti-Flemish magistrates', who wished to defend their Belgicist views (Verreycken 1993: 9).

Another indication of its revisionist view on the collaboration of Flemings in both World Wars can be taken from the self-definition of the VB. The party sets itself up as the latest political representative of the Flemish Movement, placing itself in a long tradition of Flemish nationalist 'heroes', including leading members of the *Raad van Vlaanderen* (such as Dillen's personal hero August Borms) during the First World War, as well as Cyriel Verschaeve (poet and priest) and Verdinaso leader, Joris Van Severen, who both collaborated with the Germans during the Second World War.

## Conclusion

The VB is a party with an elaborated ideological programme built around the core of Flemish nationalism. It considers the ethnic community as the main organisational unit of groups of people. Each ethnic community should live according to its own nature, that is, they should live separately in their own states. Regarding their own country this means that the multinational state Belgium is rejected. The Flemings should get their own Flemish state, which will become part of some form of federation with the Netherlands, as the Flemings are considered part of the Dutch ethnic community. In line with the party's ethnic nationalism, it demands the return of Flemish territory and people that have been Frenchified by the Belgian state. Foreigners are perceived in a xenophobic way, i.e. as a threat. They are to repatriate to their own countries, though an exception is made for European immigrants, which are believed to be related to the Dutch culture and have the option of assimilation. A belief in collective order, either through the family or ethnic community, is at the core of the party's view on socio-economic policy and ethnic values. The economy should support the whole community and the whole community should support the economy. In general, rights are only granted if duties (to the ethnic community) are performed. The strong emphasis on ethical values and law and order are also in accordance with the nationalist belief: the rejection of abortion and euthanasia, the support for the family, and the tough law and order policies are all to ensure the healthy development and future of the ethnic community. Finally, ethnic nationalism is at the core of the VB's anti-party sentiments, view on democracy and revisionism. What matters first and foremost is loyalty to the (Flemish) ethnic community.

# Part III

# The Netherlands: 'Nederland voor de Nederlanders!'

## The extreme right in the Netherlands, 1945–84

Following the end of the Second World War the Dutch process of denazification began with the internment of some 100,000 collaborators. Several former members of the *Nationaal Socialistische Beweging in Nederland* (National Socialist Movement in the Netherlands, NSB), the only legal Dutch political party during the German occupation, and of the *(Waffen-) SS* lost their political rights, mostly for several years (see Bank 1998). The 'Besluit Ontbinding Landverraderlijke Organisaties' (Resolution concerning the Dissolution of Treasonable Organisations), which was signed by Queen Wilhelmina in London on 17 September 1944, led to the ban on the NSB and some thirty other (National Socialist) organisations (Van Donselaar 1993: 88). The decree was also supposed to keep the country free from the extreme right by explicitly stating that future organisations which sought to promote the goals of the banned organisations would also be banned (Bank 1998).

Attempts to build extreme right groups were not completely prevented (see Iddekinge and Paape 1970; Van Donselaar 1991, 1993). In 1951 some 100 former internees organised themselves in the *Stichting Oud Politieke Delinquenten* (Foundation of Former Political Delinquents, SOPD), a support movement for those who felt harmed in the post-war years. Though the SOPD did not have any political ambitions, it served as a test case for leaders of later extreme right parties in respect of the validity of the government decree. One of them, former *Waffen-SS Untersturmführer* Paul van Tienen, was a member of the party executive of the Malmö-based European Social Movement, an international extreme right organisation led by the Swede Per Engdahl, which despite its notoriety was never politically active or important. In 1951 Van Tienen founded a Dutch section, the *Werkgemeenschap Europa in de Lage Landen* (Working Community Europe in the Low Countries, WELL), which never extended beyond a dozen of activists. Two years later the WELL and the SOPD merged into the first post-war extreme right party in the Netherlands: the *Nationaal Europese Sociale Beweging*

(National European Social Movement). Originally, Van Tienen had favoured the name *Nederlandse Sociale Beweging* (Dutch Social Movement), but this resembled the NSB of the pre-war era too much, especially in name and acronym. The small adjustment did not rescue the small party (between 100 and 400 members, primarily 'alte Kameraden'), which was banned in 1955 on the basis of the 1944 decree (see Van Donselaar 1991: 51–79).

The ban led to the development of a new strategy by the old extreme right. Since it had become clear to them that the authorities would never tolerate a right-wing extremist party in which former members of the NSB and SS would play a leading role, Van Tienen and his comrades decided to ally themselves with people of the non-discredited political right. In 1956 they joined the *Nationale Oppositie Unie* (National Opposition Union, NOU), an electoral list of right-wing and extreme right individuals and (splinter) parties, which received a mere 0.34 per cent of the votes in the parliamentary election of that year. This result meant the political end of both the NOU and Van Tienen, who spent his later life in his 'Dutch Archive of the Conservative Revolution', a revisionist book shop with a related study centre.

In 1958 the *Boerenpartij* (Farmers Party, BP) was founded as the party political representative of a sub-culture of dissatisfied so-called *Vrije Boeren* (Free Farmers), which had developed in protest against the forced introduction of a corporatist structure in Dutch agriculture in 1950 (see Nooij 1969; Van Donselaar 1991: 121–33). The movement as well as the later party were led by Hendrik Koekoek, who became (in)famous as Boer (Farmer) Koekoek, and who had also been part of the NOU. Where the latter had remained unsuccessful, the BP was one of the most successful newcomers in Dutch postwar politics (see Lucardie 1996). After a failed attempt in 1959 and some initial positive results in the provincial election of 1962, the BP entered Parliament with three (out of a total of 150) seats in 1963, increasing to seven four years later. Although the BP was not an extreme right party, its diffuse national-conservative programme exercised a strong pull toward not only free farmers but also other groups of dissatisfied people. Among them were former members of the NSB, some of whom fought elections for the party, leading to fierce internal debates. The BP was stigmatised in the media through parallels with the German NPD and the French *Poujadists*. After 1968 the party was plagued by internal splits, which led to its rapid demise – though Koekoek was able to retain his parliamentary seat until 1981, when he competed unsuccessfully under the name *Rechtse Volkspartij* (Right-Wing People's Party). At the end of the 1960s the BP had also lost its attraction to extreme right activists, and the connections between the right-wing and extreme right came to an end.

In the 1970s the *Nederlandse Volks-Unie* (Dutch People's Union, NVU) dominated the extreme right spectre in the Netherlands (Bouw *et al.* 1981; Van Donselaar 1991: 142–71; Bank 1998). The NVU had been founded on 27 March 1971 by former members of the NSB, although it tried to present a modern outlook. In the first three years of its existence the party was virtually unknown to the general public and was preoccupied with internal struggles. This changed in 1974, when Joop Glimmerveen entered the scene and put the NVU on the political map. His openly racist campaign for the local election in the Hague of that year, under the slogan 'The Hague should remain white and safe', won him and the party substantial publicity. The NVU did not win a seat in the local council, but its name was established as was the position of Glimmerveen as the new party leader.

Johann Georg Glimmerveen, born in 1928, was a rabid anti-communist veteran of the Korean War, who afterwards worked as a clerk at a NATO office in the Netherlands (see Bouw *et al.* 1981). Though too young to have a 'brown past', his open admiration of Hitler and National Socialism went beyond what several of the 'alte Kameraden' within the NVU deemed acceptable. However, by combining his admiration of the past with the modern theme of mass immigration, Glimmerveen made the NVU into a reservoir of both new and old right-wing extremist persons and ideas, though it always remained a small political party with probably only a few hundred members in its heyday. It never achieved an electoral breakthrough, its best electoral result in a parliamentary election being 0.4 per cent in May 1977. This notwithstanding, the NVU was to some extent an influential political party in the Netherlands. Through carefully directed actions of distributing pamphlets, it spurred already slumbering tensions between different ethnic groups within the population and gained extensive media coverage.

Both Glimmerveen and the NVU had to pay a price for their radical, aggressive campaigns and provocative actions. Several anti-racist organisations were founded in the 1970s, predominately as a reaction to the NVU's openly racist propaganda. These groups fought a fierce battle with Glimmerveen and the NVU, both verbally and, once in a while, violently. Even more destructive to the party, in political terms, was the increasing legal threat. After several years of discussions and preparations, the NVU was finally characterised as a criminal association by the Amsterdam court in March 1978. Because of legal technicalities and flaws, this meant that the party was excluded from the local election of 1978, though without being banned (see Van Donselaar 1993: 95). Thus the NVU still existed as a legal political party, but was at the same time characterised as a criminal association and excluded from openly functioning as a political party. This schizophrenic situation was ended by the Dutch Supreme Court one year later, when it decided that as long as the NVU was not banned, the party could not and should not be obstructed from functioning as a political party in any way. The exclusion from the local election was ruled unlawful, even though this did not have any practical consequences for the party. Moreover, the legal rehabilitation could not save the NVU from a rapid demise.

The radicalisation in both ideology and style of the NVU went too far for several members. Already in the 1970s it had led to internal conflicts, even leading to the temporary ousting of Glimmerveen as party leader. After his return, and the consequent legal troubles, several of the 'moderate' members left the NVU and founded other, more or less moderate extreme right parties. One of these was the *Nationale Centrumpartij* (National Centre Party, NCP), founded on 28 December 1979. The NCP lived a short life: after a meeting in February 1980 – the first meeting of the party after its foundation – some of the youth that had attended the meeting (among whom some leading members of the party) attacked 'illegal' foreigners who took shelter against expulsion in an Amsterdam church. One week later the NCP dissolved itself. Already the next day, on 11 March 1980, the *Centrumpartij* (Centre Party, CP) was founded by one of the NCP-founders: Henry Brookman, a social scientist at the Free University of Amsterdam, who had been a prominent member of the NVU.

The CP was the first 'successful' party of what was to become the so-called *centrumstroming* (centre movement), the collective term used for the CP and its successor parties (see below), in which several former members of the NVU would find a new political home (see Brants and Hogendoorn 1983; Hirl 1987; Van Donselaar 1991). The party presented a manifesto, similar to that of the NCP, marked 'not left, not right'. It contained ten points which were a remarkable combination of right-wing (law and order), left-wing (protection of social benefits), and green (protection of the environment and animals) standpoints (see Mudde 1998). It was the tenth point, however, that would be the centre of attention in the following years: 'The Netherlands is not an immigration country, so put a stop to the stream of foreigners.' This, together with the political history of some of its early members, was the main reason that the media portrayed the CP from the outset and consistently as an extreme right party, despite the party's fierce rejection of any accusations of racism and fascism.

At the parliamentary election of 1981 both the CP and NVU gained a mere 0.1 per cent of the votes. It seemed that both parties were destined to disappear into oblivion. As a consequence of the fast fall of the government, both parties could contest another parliamentary election one year later. For the NVU the 1,632 votes (0.0 per cent) it received signalled the end of its electoral existence; it disappeared completely from the political scene, though it was not disbanded officially until 1991 (and refounded in 1998). The CP, on the other hand, gained 0.8 per cent of the votes and thereby one seat in the Second Chamber. It was the first parliamentary seat won in the post-war period by a party that was generally considered to be right-wing extremist. Party leader Hans Janmaat became the Member of Parliament for the CP.

Johannes Gerardus Hendrikus Janmaat, born in 1934 and a political scientist by training, had a history of various short-lived and failed professional and political careers (see Van Ginneken 1994; Van Holsteyn 1998). In earlier days he had been a (active) member of the *Katholieke Volkspartij* (Catholic People's Party) and the *Democratische Socialisten '70* (Democratic Socialists '70) – he might also have been a member of the left-wing liberal *Democraten'66* (Democrats'66) and the right-wing liberal *Volkspartij voor Vrijheid en Democratie* (People's Party for Freedom and Democracy). After reading an interview with Brookman, he joined the CP (allegedly as its seventh member) and within a short time had taken over the leadership of the party. This was largely facilitated by the small membership, his 'clean' (i.e. non-extreme right) political history, and the fact that Brookman had to move more into the political background after pressure from his employer.

During the first years following its electoral success of 1982 the CP grew steadily, claiming some 3,500 members in 1984. During that time it had some remarkable electoral results, of which the most significant were the almost 10 per cent in the local election in the new city of Almere in 1983 and the (nationwide) 2.5 per cent in the European election of 1984. As the NVU before, the CP received its highest scores in the urbanised western part of the country, the so-called *Randstad*, especially in the four main cities of Amsterdam, Rotterdam, the Hague and Utrecht. Consequently, its electoral success was primarily seen as a protest against the presence of foreigners, and some commentators even spoke of a 'racist electorate' (Van Donselaar 1982: 134; Brants and Hogendoorn 1983: 42).

The success led to serious conflicts between the party leadership, led by chairman Nico Konst and vice-chairman Henk de Wijer, and the 'parliamentary party', i.e. Janmaat and his assistants (see Schikhof 1997). The fighting factions were given much space in the media to slander each other. There followed weeks of public counter-accusations in which the party leadership accused Janmaat of financial and personal improprieties and in which Janmaat reacted by accusing the party leadership of neo-Nazi sympathies and political and organisational incompetence. In the autumn of 1984 the party leadership decided to expel Janmaat (and a few of his followers). Janmaat refused to give up his seat in the Second Chamber and stayed on as an independent MP. The end of the CP was but a matter of time.

# 5

# Centrumdemocraten

## Janmaat – right or wrong!

At ten o'clock in the morning of 7 November 1984 four people walked into a notary office in The Hague. Eleven minutes later they left again, having created the *Centrumdemocraten* (Centre Democrats, CD). Three of the founders were former (low-key) members of the CP. The same evening the party gained two more members, yet it would take four weeks before the seventh member, Hans Janmaat, would join the party. On 5 December 1984 Janmaat announced his new affiliation to the chairman of the Second Chamber. Because of legal technicalities Janmaat remained officially an independent MP.

From the moment Janmaat joined, the CD was identified as *his* party. Most journalists and scholars even (incorrectly) mention him as the founder of the CD. But even though the new party received extensive media coverage during its first years, mainly as a consequence of Janmaat's reputation, its membership remained well below 100. The party contested its first election in May 1986, trying to defend Janmaat's seat in the Second Chamber. It used the name *Lijst Janmaat/Centrumdemocraten* to profit from Janmaat's profile, which was far higher than that of the virtually unknown CD. However, the 1.5 million pamphlets that the party had claimed to have distributed prior to the election could not undo the damage of the years of internal fights in the 'centre movement'. The CD gained a disappointing 0.1 per cent of the votes, partly as a result of the competition with the old CP, which gained 0.4 per cent. It appeared that the CD was to finish like most new parties, particularly splinters of (small) parties, in political oblivion. This expectation was strengthened by the results at the provincial election the next year, where the CD unsuccessfully stood candidates in the three provinces of the Randstad, i.e. North and South Holland and Utrecht.

During this time the CD had received large media attention on two occasions. The first and most widely covered story was an 'anti-fascist' attack on a hotel in Kedichem, in which members of the CP and CD had convened, in March 1986. Within extreme left circles it was believed that they were planning a fusion of the two parties. Some anti-fascists thought that this should be stopped by all means necessary, including fire bombing the hotel. In the consequent panic CD party secretary Schuurman lost one of her legs after jumping out of a window of the burning hotel. The second occasion was Janmaat's attempt to win reinstatement as a teacher at his old school. The school did not want to take him back for fear of his reputation as a racist (as some students and parents had protested). Janmaat claimed his right to return to his old job after having served as MP, a claim supported by the Dutch court. However, the court also acknowledged the school's claim that the relations between Janmaat and the school had become unworkable, and Janmaat was bought off. As nothing else remained for him, he returned to politics.

The 1989 parliamentary election was well prepared by the CD, which again contested the election under the official name of *Lijst Janmaat/Centrumdemocraten*, also because the CD was often confused with the CP. As the party stood candidates in all nineteen voting districts of the country, it won the right to state supported television and radio time. Opponents of the party had tried to contest the legality of the signature lists, which is required of all parties that are not represented in the old Parliament in order to contest elections within a voting district. The 'anti-racists' were not successful, however, as the CD had been able to provide all signatures by genuine party supporters (see DNPP 1990). Although the CD at that time counted a mere 300 members, it was able to distribute thousands of pamphlets and gain a lot of media attention. Eventually the party got what it had worked for, Janmaat's return to the Second Chamber (with 0.9 per cent of the votes).

In the local election of 1990 the CD continued its success, securing eleven seats in eight (big) cities in the Randstad (see Husbands 1992). These were also the strongholds of the provincial election the next year, when the CD gained three seats (in North and South Holland as well as Utrecht). The electoral success also led to a short-lived impulse to develop the organisational side of the party. At the party conference of December 1991, party secretary Wil Schuurman claimed a weekly increase of 100 members in the last months of the year. Even though this will have been an exaggeration, the CD no doubt underwent one of its biggest gains in membership and probably counted some 2,000 (paying) members at the end of 1991. Still, the number of active members remained small, a mere 100 at best, and constituted almost exclusively by party representatives at the various levels. This was also why the party was only 'visible' at the level of representative bodies, although some party delegates were reported to be frequently absent from council debates (see Van Riel and Van Holsteyn 1998).

The super election year of 1994 was approached with much optimism by the CD. Opinion polls had predicted large gains throughout 1993 (see Mudde and Van Holsteyn 1994; Van Holsteyn 1995) and within the party this had led to wild speculations. The first test was the local election in

March, which substantiated the optimism. The CD had put forward candi-dates in only forty-three (of over six hundred) municipalities and gained sev-enty-seven seats (an increase of sixty-six). In almost every city where the CD had participated, it had gained representation. Both within and outside of the party it was expected that the CD would gain more than five seats in the parliamentary election of May. Some people, among them Janmaat, even predicted that the party could get as many as ten seats.

This optimism was harshly tempered by the many scandals in which the CD then became involved. Directly after the local election the party became the victim of its bad organisation and lack of active members. Several local seats were either not filled by the party, as those elected did not take up their seats, or were taken by people who left the party soon afterwards. Some of these joined or founded another party, others kept their seats as independent council members, and yet others left politics altogether (see Van Holsteyn 1995). The party had also been infiltrated by no less than three undercover journalists, who in their publications portrayed the CD as 'a party of fascists, criminals and scum' (Rensen 1994a; also Kooiman 1994; Van Hout 1994). Particular emphasis was put on members that were known for their (former) neo-Nazi links, such as the council member in Purmerend, Richard van der Plas. The biggest impact was caused by the television program *Deadline*, in which a newly elected Amsterdam council member (Yge Graman) was filmed by a hidden camera bragging about having started several fires in centres providing services for foreigners in the early 1980s. The program was broad-cast the weekend before the parliamentary election and led to a public outcry (and later conviction of Graman).

The CD gained only 2.5 per cent of the votes, securing three seats in the Second Chamber. Even though this meant an increase of 1.6 per cent (and two seats), it was well below what was feared by opponents and hoped for by party members, especially given the fact that the election had been one of the most dramatic of the century, with a record number of seats changing hands (Irwin 1995). Moreover, in almost all municipalities where the CD had submitted candidates in March, it received only half the number of votes in May. Nonetheless, even these relatively poor results dismayed some com-mentators and politicians. Wim Kok, leader of the social democratic *Partij van de Arbeid* (Labour Party, PvdA) and premier-to-be, spoke of 'a black day in Dutch history' (Mudde and Van Holsteyn 1994: 132). Most disappointed, however, was Janmaat himself, who blamed the result on the anti-CD cam-paign in the media, which was (as usual) claimed to be part of a larger con-spiracy against the party (directed by the BVD and PvdA).

One day after the parliamentary election, Janmaat, Schuurman and the CD were convicted to a series of fines, ranging from 1,000 to 10,000 Dutch guilders, for incitement to racial hatred (IJA 1994). Although the amount of negative publicity decreased sharply after the election, defections of local council members of the CD remained the order of the day until the European election of June. In that election the CD saw its support fall to a mere 1.0 per cent (against 0.8 per cent in 1989), which was well below the required result to obtain a seat. Because of the record low turnout (35.6 per cent), this meant that only 43,300 people had voted CD, against some 250,000 in May. This time the CD lost in all corners of the country, even in the newly conquered territories of the Southwest.

The rest of the year it remained relatively silent around the party, though reports on scandals with (former) members and on the exodus of local council members kept appearing from time to time. At the end of 1994 the CD acknowledged that 'twenty odd' of its seventy-seven elected council members had left the party.[1] This notwithstanding, the party mentioned that its tenth anniversary had been celebrated in good spirits. The electoral losses were taking their toll on the party though, as members left or looked for cooperation with other extreme right parties (Lucardie 1998). As always, Janmaat remained sceptical towards any initiative outside of his control. In May 1996, for example, he expelled four members of Rotterdam city and district councils for being too closely linked to the local branch of the CP'86 (JPR 1997). Eventually, however, Janmaat gave in and even agreed to coorganise several demonstrations with the CP'86; the most notable were in April 1996 in Zwolle, where some 130 people demonstrated against multiculturalism, and the remembrance of the 'Battle of Kedichem' by some eighty people one month earlier (see JPR 1997). This increased activity led not only to a wave of publicity, but also twice to Janmaat's arrest and later conviction for discrimination and 'inciting racial hatred' (e.g. JPR 1997; DNPP 1998). The cooperation would again not last long, in part because of resistance within the CP'86 (see chapter 6), in part because of distrust by Janmaat. In the approach to the election year 1998 Janmaat distanced himself increasingly from the 'extremist' CP'86, trying to present himself as the 'decent' nationalist alternative.

The 1998 elections became the CD's waterloo. This was not unexpected, as the party had already lost all its seats in the local councils of the province of Brabant in the by-election of November 1996. In the regular local election of March 1998 the party participated in only twenty-two municipalities, against forty-five in 1994, losing all but one of its seventy-seven seats (DNPP 1998: 23). With the one seat in Schiedam the CD was as successful as the NB of arch rival Vreeswijk, which was able to hold on to its seat in Utrecht. Two months later the CD lost all three seats in parliament, gaining just 0.6 per cent of the vote. This meant that after nine consecutive years in

---

[1] The Dutch anti-fascist movement Kafka had come to the same account one month earlier. From its detailed overview one can read that most of the 'twenty odd' have defected to other parties at the extreme right, most notably the *Nederlands Blok* (Dutch Block, NB) – led by the former 'crown prince' of the CD Wim Vreeswijk – and the *Burgerpartij Nederland* (Citizens Party Netherlands, BPN), an initiative of former CD council members in Roosendaal (see *Kafka-nieuwsbrief* 12/94).

parliament, as well as an earlier period of four years, Janmaat was no longer an MP. The dramatric losses were in part caused by new legislation, by and large directed against the extreme right, which had raised the number of required signatures per district from ten to twenty-five. As a consequence, the CD was not able to contest the election in all nineteen districts, despite buying signatures from homeless and addicts with drugs and money, losing valuable percentages. However, the result was also a consequence of a change in political mood as well as the payment for years of internal (and external) bickering and the lack of (positive) political actions.

Janmaat reacted furiously to the electoral results, accusing the state of manipulating the voting computers. He even went as far as to submit a complaint against the Dutch Election Council to the Council of Europe, demanding either new elections or twenty million guilders (his estimate of lost income and subsidies of the party). As so often before, he pointed to a conspiracy by the BVD and PvdA to keep him from power. At the same time, Janmaat grew increasingly worried by the legal pressure, believing the CD would be the next target after the CP'86. To 'outsmart' the state, Janmaat founded the *Conservatieve Democraten* (Conservative Democrats), which was to succeed the (other) CD if it were to be banned. In March 1999 the party lost its two seats in the provincial councils of North- and South-Holland, even though it almost held on to the latter. Three months later, the party contested the European election as the *Lijstverbinding Centrumdemocraten/Conservatieve Democraten*, an 'electoral list' of two names which represented the same one party. The 0.5 per cent the list were able to gather were widely considered to have been the last cramp of a dying party.

For years the CD claimed a membership of some 3,000, despite the fact that it also claimed a rapid increase for years. Journalists and scholars have generally taken this number to be an exaggeration, placing the 'exact' number generally between 1,000 and 1,500 (Buijs and Van Donselaar 1994: 8; Van den Brink 1994: 211–12; Van Donselaar 1997: 9), though some claimed 2,700 (Rensen 1994b: 122, 126). As a consequence of the dramatic 1998 elections, the membership went down rapidly and is now estimated at some 900 (Van den Brink 1998: 237). The group of active members has always been very small (even in the party's heydays counting not more than one hundred) and narrow in terms of composition (mainly party delegates in the various representative bodies). More importantly, Janmaat has built the CD into a family business, being either personally or through his wife (Wil Schuurman) involved in virtually every major and minor party decision (see Lucardie 1998). To Janmaat's big frustration, the CD has never been able to attract many youths or even establish a functioning youth organisation; most extreme right youths were active within the CP'86. The *Jonge Centrumdemocraten* (Young Centre Democrats) were originally founded as a youth wing of the old CP in the early 1980s. Except for some small scandals the group never came into the spotlight. Today, the youth wing, also called *CD-Jongeren* (CD Youth), has only few members who, moreover, come virtually all from the Haarlem area.[2]

Despite the fact that the CD sees itself as being related to other (successful) 'patriotic parties' (*CDi* 7/94), it holds official contacts only with the DVU, FN and VB. Ever since the DVU awarded the Andreas Hofer prize to Schuurman, the CD has been a regular visitor at the annual party meeting in Passau. In 1995 Janmaat was even one of the key speakers, accompanied by a party delegation of some ten members (including Schuurman). The contacts with the FN are basically limited to visiting its annual meeting in Paris, though Janmaat has at times boasted about his good personal contacts with FN-leader Le Pen. The relationship with the VB has always been troublesome, partly because the VB had (better) contacts with rival CP'86 and partly because Janmaat has been frustrated by the fact that he is always contrasted unfavourably to Dewinter in the Dutch press.

Finally, the party has always maintained official contacts with the CP and later CP'86, mainly through its special fusion commission (under the leadership of Schuurman). Relations with other splinter parties at the extreme right fringe have been rare, as most of them had broken away from the CD (such as the NB and BPN). In general, Janmaat pursues a politics of divide and rule towards the different groups, offering favourable conditions for a return (or merger) to some leaders within a group, which, when agreed, he will then make public and retract thereby increasing the already difficult relations within and between these small parties. As far as fusion is genuinely acceptable to Janmaat, it can only be as a take-over of the smaller parties by the CD under his leadership.

## Profiling the literature

### Externally oriented: election programmes

The CD published three election programmes in the period 1984–99. Until 1989 the party had issued neither a party programme nor an election programme, even though it had (unsuccessfully) contested the 1986 parliamentary election.[3] During this period the CD was known by the reputation of its party leader Janmaat and by some scarcely distributed pamphlets, which were almost exact copies of the ten-point pamphlets of the old CP. The picture of the CD changed probably only to a limited extent with the publication of the CD *Partij Programma voor de verkiezingen van 6 september 1989*

---

[2] This information comes from the webpage of the anti-fascist group Kafka. See http://www.antifa.net/kafka.

[3] A summary of (the concept of) the 1986 election programme was published in the party paper *Middenkoers* (1/1/86). The programme was written by Brookman and therefore strongly resembled the old CP ideology.

*van de Tweede Kamer der Staten Generaal* (CD Party Programme for the Election of 6 September 1989 for the Second Chamber of the States General, CD 1989). This election programme is an unkempt document of fifteen A4 pages, which primarily shows the lack of professionalism of the CD. It includes several language and typing errors, with, for instance, two chapters XII. The programme opens with two short general sections: the preamble and the points of departure. Thereafter, the party presents its programme, which is a collection of (122) demands classified in nineteen policy areas.

The second programme was made for the 1994 parliamentary election and had the title *Oost West Thuis Best* (East West, Home Best, CD 1994). It was published under the responsibility of the scientific bureau of the party, the *Thomas Hobbes Stichting*, named after Janmaat's favourite philosopher, and is an elaborated version of the 1989 version containing thirty-two A4 pages. The fact that the programme includes only one new section and an increase of a total of twenty-seven demands, shows that the increase in pages is larger than that of ideology or policy (and is primarily caused by a different lay-out). One of the few interesting new features is the introduction written by Janmaat, which starts with a short history of the development of the programme; the concept was developed by a special programme commission under the leadership of Wim Elshout (council member in Haarlem and party treasurer), which was then amended and approved by the party congress. When the final version of the programme is compared with the 'list of new articles for the 1994 party programme of the Centre Democrats', one can only conclude that the congress was not critical of the concept. From the twenty-seven new articles that were proposed by the commission only three were rejected by the congress.[4]

The third programme was developed for the 1998 parliamentary election and was given the mainstream title *Trouw aan Rood Wit Blauw!* (Loyal to Red White Blue, CD 1998), referring to the colors of the Dutch national flag. It counted thirty pages and was again almost identical in style and content to the earlier programmes. This said, there were some remarkable new points, which were even completely novel to the party literature, as they had not even been touched upon in the party paper.

### Internally oriented: party papers

The party paper of the CD was originally called *Centrumtaal* (Centre Speech) and was first published in January 1986. It was distributed under the auspices of the scientific bureau of the party, at that time called *Stichting*

---

[4] Still, these were not without consequence. For one, whereas the commission proposed to 'change' article 1 of the Dutch constitution, which is the anti-discrimination principle (see Schuijt and Voorhoof 1995: 218), the final version of the party programme argues that the article 'is to go' (see also Rensen 1994b). The fact that the CD wants to abolish this article has been seen by various opponents as proof of its anti-democratic character (e.g. Van den Brink 1994).

*Wetenschappelijke Onderbouwing Centrumdemocratische Ideologie* (Foundation for the Scientific Elaboration of the Centre Democratic Ideology, SWOCI), and counted some thirty A5 pages. *Centrumtaal* was meant to inform the membership every month of the activities of the party, especially of those of Janmaat in the Second Chamber, and to be readable and understandable for all members. For the more intellectual readership, the CD started another paper, *Middenkoers* (Middle Course), also published by SWOCI. *Middenkoers* was published only three times in 1986, generally consisting of under twenty pages. The intellectual level of the paper did not really surpass that of *Centrumtaal* and both were soon to disappear.

Soon afterwards the CD started to publish two new party papers: *CD-actueel* (CD-Up-to-Date, *CDa*) and *CD-info* (CD-Information, *CDi*). *CD-actueel* has been published as a quarterly since February 1987, and seems to be the successor to *Middenkoers*. Originally it was the official paper of the party itself, sent free of charge to all party members (and donors), comprising over thirty A4 pages (since 1991 almost constantly twenty). The articles in the paper were written predominantly by the few better educated members – though primarily by Janmaat, who writes under a wide variety of pseudonyms, and mr. H. Eerlijk (literally mr. H. Honest, a pseudonym for 'party lawyer' L. van Heijningen). Since 1989 *CD-actueel* has been published by the scientific bureau of the party; the SWOCI was renamed Thomas Hobbes Foundation in 1992.

Since 1991 *CD-actueel* is no longer sent free of charge to all party members. Everyone, member or not, has to take out a separate subscription to the journal. However, in January 1988 the party introduced *CD-info*, seemingly as the successor of *Centrumtaal*, although it is unclear whether this latter paper was still published in 1987. Originally the new party paper was also a quarterly but within one year it grew into a monthly; normally it entailed between ten and twelve issues annually. *CD-info* was published by the *Stichting Politieke Kadervorming der Centrumdemocraten* (Foundation for the Political Training of the Centre Democrats) and numbers some ten A4 pages. It was more sketchy and up to date than *CD-actueel*, as well as more sloppy in language and typing errors. The main difference, however, is in goal and substance: only *CD-info* carries information on internal party matters (like appointments to and meetings of national, regional and local party branches). Except for this routine business, *CD-info* contains mainly articles on current political issues and on the discussions of fusion with the CP'86. In the mid 1990s the two party papers were distributed less and less frequently. In 1994 *CD-Info* was published eight times, the next year five, and in 1996 only twice; *CD-Actueel* has not been distributed since 1993. In April 1997 *CD-Info* was renamed *CD-Nieuwsbrief* (CD-Newsletter), which was also the only change made. In terms of counting, lay-out, content, and irregular publishing the paper is identical to its predecessor.

## The Netherlands for the Dutch first!

### State nationalism

The main ideological feature of the party ideology of the CD is nationalism, aptly caught in the (old) party slogan 'The Netherlands (in the first place) for the Dutch'. Above all, the CD wants a Dutch Netherlands, which it sees being threatened by mass immigration and the state policy of multi-culturalism. However, contrary to ethnic nationalist parties the CD does not exclude people on the basis of an ethnic criterion. It hardly ever speaks in terms of the Dutch ethnic community, but almost exclusively in terms of the Dutch *population*. It is a state (or civic) rather than an ethnic nationalist party.

Both forms of nationalism strive for the congruence of state and ethnic community, but the ethnic nationalist works from a closed concept of the ethnic community, using an ethnic criterion, whereas the state nationalist is based on a more open concept, using a civic criterion. According to an ethnic nationalist one is born into an ethnic community for life and is bound to it by life. As each ethnic community should determine its own policies, in essence have its own state, people are bound by birth to one state and can not change their nationality. Within a state nationalist view the state precedes the ethnic community (they generally use the term 'nation'), in the sense that the nation is not a fixed entity. One can either be legally born into it, by being born on the territory of the state or by having two (or one) parents with that nationality, or one can become a member of the nation.

The CD allows foreigners to become part of the Dutch nation, normally referred to as the Dutch citizenship or Dutch population. In fact the party gives them the principal choice between either repatriation or assimilation. In the words of the election programme: 'Foreigners and minorities either adjust to the Dutch ways and customs or leave the country' (CD 1989: II.2). When foreigners assimilate they stop being foreigners and become equal parts of the Dutch population (CD 1989: XII.9).[5] As the party is not ethnic nationalist, it does not exclude any group from this process on a priori grounds.

The CD wants to achieve its nationalist goal of *internal homogenisation* further by reversing state policy. This is clearly stated in the points of departure of the election programmes: 'non-Dutch influences are [to be] pushed back' (CD 1989: 1) and 'stop the anti-Dutch policy' (CD 1989: 2). This would enable a return to the old Dutch society in which there was only one culture, the Dutch one.

> The core of this [centre democratic] ideology contains, on the one hand, the struggle for the preservation and development of the Dutch political and cul-

---

[5] This option is not open to all foreigners: guest workers that are unemployed for a period of more than six months, for example, have to repatriate (CD 1989: XII.2).

tural identity and, on the other hand, the promotion of national solidarity in our country by trying to prevent unwanted discrepancies between distinctive sections of Dutch society, or to come to a harmonious solution to these discrepancies, in which we begin from the complete equality of these social sections. (CD 1989: 1)

One of the few new statements in 1994 was that '(t)he programme of the political party Centre Democrats begins from the indissoluble unity and solidarity of the Dutch ethnic community. It is based on the common history and the culture that originated from that history' (CD 1994: 6). This sounds like a shift towards a more ethnic nationalist position, including an organic view of the ethnic community. There are a few other indications in this direction, for instance the demand that government positions should be open only to people that hold Dutch citizenship in the third generation (CD 1989: I.7). Moreover, in a surprising turn to external exclusiveness, the 1998 programme included the wish for 'the reunification with Flanders and other Dutch speaking territories' (CD 1998: XX.4). However, the same programme introduced the not less surprising point: 'An overarching culture is to be formed through the amalgamation of different cultural features. Precondition for this amalgamation is that the cultural features which are contributed by the minorities are not opposed to characteristic features of the Dutch culture' (CD 1989: III.2b).

This notwithstanding, by and large both the programme and the papers maintain their state nationalist character centred around the choice between assimilation and repatriation. The simple fact that the CD sees assimilation as a possibility suggests that it does not hold a static view on the nation. Moreover, the CD wants Dutch citizenship to be acquired by passing a state exam, testing the applicant's general knowledge, knowledge on constitutional matters, and command of the Dutch language. This is more or less comparable to that of the US, which does not point to a particularly high barrier. What the party does have in common with ethnic nationalists, however, is that it also has a problem with the presence of (large groups of) foreigners and that it considers repatriation as an option (but not the only one) that is to be strongly stimulated (CD 1989: XII.1). As Janmaat formulated this point of view in his 1989 advice for the cabinet formation:

The cabinet will implement a responsible policy on minorities and migration, which is expressed in implementing, among other things, the following measures: a) an end to the policy on family reunion of members of the ethnic minorities that reside here; b) an end to the policy of affirmative action for ethnic minorities; c) the exclusion of economic refugees; d) the forceful adoption of the policy of repatriation of minorities. (CDi 5/89)

The opposition of the CD is therefore primarily directed against the multi-*cultural* society and not against the multi-*ethnic* society. It wants all people that live within the Dutch state to be(come) Dutch citizens, members of the Dutch community. This is to be done, on the one hand, by giving foreigners the choice between assimilation and repatriation, and, on the other hand, by state support of native culture and the cancelation of support for the development of alien cultures (CD 1989: II.2). The only exception to this latter rule is made for education in their own language and culture to foreigners and minorities that have signed a declaration that they will repatriate (CD 1989: IV.1).

In recent years the party's nationalism is increasingly linked to the theme of European integration. The CD has always been sceptic towards the process of European integration. It opposes any limitation of sovereignty of the Dutch state and sees the Maastricht Treaty consequently as one of the many international defeats of the Dutch government. The Treaty was the main inspiration for the new section on territory in the 1994 election programme, in which the CD demanded a constitutional guarantee of the sovereignty of the Dutch state (see also CD 1989: XX.3) and argued that the devolution of national competencies should be made dependent upon the support of both a referendum and of a two-thirds majority of the two chambers of the State General (CD 1989: II.1). The syphoning of national competencies to the European Union is even considered high treason. Mockingly the party states that 'our country is not preserved by our own government, but by other European governments. Because they do not want to follow the Dutch proposals to come to a restriction of their own authority' (*CDi* 6/92).

### Exclusionism

There are some articles in the party literature in which signs of an ethnopluralist reasoning can be detected. The first is a point in regard to multi-cultural marriages:

> The Government is partly responsible for the consequences of multi-cultural marriages. Because of its inconsiderate policy many of the Dutch young people have in their youth been put before irresponsible choices regarding their life partner. The Government should provide all possible facilities to end these marriages, at the will of the Dutch partner, and to send the partner as often as possible back to their country of origin. (CD 1989: II.3)

The second instance is the demand for special attention for the 'interests in the broadest sense' of those Dutch people that live in areas with high concentrations of ethnic minorities, 'because of which' they have come (or threaten to come) to a disadvantaged situation (CD 1989: X.9). This seems to imply that the living together of different cultures leads to a degeneration of the better (off), a rare instance of an ethnopluralist conviction within the CD literature (albeit one that did not return in later programmes). In general, however, the CD's 'ethnopluralist' remarks seem to be mainly inspired by the lack of integration in practice rather than ideology. This can best be seen in the party paper's reaction to a television program on the problems of Moroccan youth in Amsterdam:

This program shows that one cannot be lenient towards the inclusion of people of a different culture into the Dutch society. It causes substantial problems, for both the Dutch and the people from the other cultures, in particular for their children. Culture is an important binding element for a country. Cultural differences can to some extent exist, as long as there are sufficient binding elements, so that the people of the different cultures still feel themselves citizens of one country. (*CDa* 3/90)

In line with its nationalist thinking, the CD strives for a limit in the number of new foreigners admitted to the Netherlands. The programme includes demands that only asylum seekers that face long-term sentences for political reasons should be allowed to enter the country (CD 1989: XII.6). It further wants to limit the possibilities for the adoption of children from the Third World (CD 1989: XII.7). At first sight this seems to indicate a racist or at least Eurocentrist bias, but the CD explicitly includes also people from within the European Union in its demand for stricter norms for the admittance of foreigners (CD 1989: XII.8). However, as this group cannot be refused entry into the country because of European legislation, the party settles for a restriction in their rights. It wants to exclude European foreigners from social services, to discharge the state from any obligations to offer them housing, and even to deport them when they lack means of livelihood (CD 1989: XII.9). As far as the party allows for new guest workers, they are to be placed in a new social system, which is fenced off from the Dutch social system (CD 1989: XII.4 and XII.5).

### Xenophobia

The style in which the party paper in particular addresses the issue of immigration is clearly and openly xenophobic. The multi-cultural society is depicted as a society full of crime and confusion in which the common Dutchman has lost all feeling of belonging and of order. Immigrants are consistently portrayed as a problem at the least and generally as a threat. They do not want to integrate and create their own ghetto's, thereby forcing the native people either out of their own neighbourhood or into isolation within their own area. Although the present situation is already described in a negative way, the CD's portrait of the future in delineated in an even more gloomy manner. A perfect example of this is the 'Open letter to Amsterdammers and other Dutch' (*CDi* 2/89) in which a picture of multi-cultural Amsterdam (as omen for the whole Netherlands) is painted in which Moroccan youth gangs rule the streets, churches are changed into mosques, almost every street contains a coffee house in which foreigners live and terrorise the neighbourhood, illegal aliens get a municipal home before hard working Dutch people, and the police are helpless against the rising crime because of the absurdly low sentences and the soft politics of the left. This apocalyptic vision of a multi-cultural Netherlands is painted in almost every issue of the paper. To prove that it can become reality the party regularly points to the race riots in Los Angeles and the civil war in Yugoslavia; the latter is described as 'a terrific example of a multi-cultural society that explodes. Los Angeles in the large' (*CDi* 7/92).

The topic that brings the CD to its xenophobic peak is Islam. This religion is exclusively described in its fundamentalist version in the party literature: 'veil, headscarf, no pork, the reversal of the emancipation of women and the limitation of freedom of religion' (*CDa* 1/91). This Islamic culture is juxtaposed to the European culture, which means that a Muslim cannot integrate into Dutch society without giving up his or her religion. Islam is always portrayed as an aggressive and expansionist religion. This can be seen, on the one hand, by the Muslims in the West, which expand not only in number of people (as they all have many children) but also of mosques and stores (such as Islamic butchers with their barbaric ritual slaughter). On the other hand, the CD points to the belligerent politics of Islamic countries in the Middle East, for instance in the Gulf war (e.g. *CDa* 1/91). The position of the party *vis-à-vis* the Islam can best be summarised in its own words: 'Wherever there is Islam on earth, there are problems' (*CDa* 3/90).

### Socio-economic policy

The CD devotes a lot of attention to economic and socio-economic issues, both in its internally and its externally oriented literature. This is not to say that the party has a clear and elaborated socio-economic programme, however. The election programmes in particular hold a potpourri of individual demands, and where it is often difficult to see the underlying ideology. If the socio-economic demands – as listed primarily in the sections on economy (III), employment (V), social policy (X) and taxes (XI) – show any coherence, it is in their welfare chauvinism. The rest is an ambiguous mix of social and liberal policies, ranging from rejection of 'forced privatisation' (CD 1989: III.1) and support for raising pension benefits (CD 1989: X.8) to calling for less (complicated) taxes (CD 1989: XI.1 and 3). The only substantive adjustments to the generally supported mixed economic system of the Netherlands (CD 1989: III.1) the CD seems to want is the increase of indirect and direct state support for small businesses (CD 1989: III.3 and 8).

The party papers further contain numerous (small) articles in which the party targets various forms of state interference and the high tax burden (e.g. *CDa* 3/90). A regular theme is that state intervention obstructs the realisation of the 'American dream' of the Dutch businessman. 'Those who work hard, work overtime or are a bit lucky with some small deal, can be squeezed by the state: get packing or otherwise pay' (*CDi* 6/93). Despite some of these neo-liberal hobbyhorses, the CD is not a principal antagonist of state intervention in the economy, as is clear from the many articles against cuts in specific state benefits (mainly for the elderly people) and in support of the welfare state (for the Dutch people). Moreover, various articles call for state support for Dutch small business and agriculture, being the backbone of the Dutch economy.

As with most other issues socio-economic policy is strongly linked to the issue of immigration. The CD stipulates that in the Netherlands there is no basis for the kind of tolerance that a multi-cultural society needs as '(t)he basis [for a peaceful living together] is and remains a healthy economy' (*CDi* 10/93). As a consequence of almost twenty years of bad policies the Netherlands has become 'one of the most heavily taxed countries in the world and one of the poorest in Europe in income' (*CDi* 9/91). This provides the party with the economic proof of the necessity of its welfare chauvinist argument. In short, the CD argues that repatriation of a large number of foreigners and prevention of new foreigners entering the Netherlands are vital conditions to preserve the welfare state for the Dutch population. Jobs are to be given by preference to Dutch unemployed (CD 1989: V.1) and minorities should get jobs only when there are no more Dutch applicants left (CD 1989: V.2).[6]

In the introduction to the 1994 election programme Janmaat defends his plea for 'the Dutch first' with the argument that 'from a historical perspective we Dutch have the oldest rights' (CD 1994: 3). Welfare chauvinism is not only deemed relevant in national politics, but also in international politics. Confused by 'an increasingly diffuse international world' (CD 1994: 3) the programme justifies the emphasis on Dutch national interests. Probably referring to the (implications of the) Maastricht Treaty, Janmaat states that '(e)xactly because of that international entanglement it is more than necessary that our own population is protected by its own government' (CD 1994: 3). The 1994 programme further shows a trend towards more protectionism, especially in the field of economics, as well as some demands for (partial) autarchy of the Dutch defense apparatus (CD 1994: III.3) and agriculture (CD 1994: VIII.3).

### The strong state

Crime is one of the main topics in the party literature, often combined with the (interlinked) issues of drugs and foreigners. According to the CD the Netherlands has become one of the least safe countries in Europe (e.g. *CDa* 2/90). This is the consequence of the failed policies of the established parties, whose reorganisation of the police has led to chaos in organisation and

---

[6] These points are to some extent in conflict with its positive stand on assimilation, as the CD seems to exclude 'minorities' from the group of 'Dutch applicants'. This is at least indicated on some occasions, as for instace: 'The neglect of Dutch employees for the employees of the minorities, whether with the Dutch nationality or not, has to be made illegal' (CD 1989: V.1). However, it might also be the result of the general sloppiness of the party programme and the confusing terminology that is used in the Netherlands concerning *foreigners* (people that do not have the Dutch nationality) and *minorities* (people that are of non-Dutch descent but might have the Dutch nationality).

competencies. Moreover, the policy of affirmative action within the police has introduced an irrelevant criterion into the selection process and thereby decreased the standards of the force (e.g. *CDa* 1/92). And even when the police capture criminals, despite the lack of resources and the opposition by the political elite, these criminals are given ridiculously low sentences which often do not even have to be served because of the lack of prison space. This all has created a reverse situation in the Netherlands, in which the criminals can walk the streets freely whereas the ordinary citizens increasingly lock themselves in their houses and no longer dare to come out.

The only way to overcome this chaos is by introducing tough law and order policies. The 1989 programme calls for higher sentences, which are to be served under severe conditions (CD 1989: XIII.1 and 2), an expansion of both the competencies and the capacity of the police (CD 1989: XIII.4 and 7), and the extradition of foreign criminals (CD 1989: XIII.2). In 1994 the party expanded the section on justice with four new demands, of which the introduction of the death penalty was the most extreme (CD 1994: IV.1b). Further law and order measures that appear in the party literature are the preservation of border patrols (also after the Schengen Treaty) and the building of more prison cells, so that all criminals have to serve their (full) time. If the Dutch state fails to take these measures, the CD claims that it will lose its right of existence as it can no longer protect its citizens against rising crime (e.g. *CDa* 1/92; *CDi* 9/93).

Compared to its law and order policies, the party's views on the military are not that far-reaching. The CD wants the Dutch defense apparatus to have at its disposal the best material, though it does not demand a substantial increase in its capacity or competencies. The only new role the party desires is training for combating terrorism and city guerrillas which might be a problem in the future. In the 1994 programme the section on defense is extended and toughened, including the demand that the defense budget should not be lowered. However, the fact that the CD wants to introduce a compulsory waiting period of two years between secondary school and higher education in which people have to make themselves useful to society through either compulsory military or national service (CD 1989: IV.9), does indicate some support for a strong state, but at the same time shows at best a weak militaristic outlook.

### Populist anti-party sentiment

Every issue of the party papers holds at least one populist anti-party sentiment. The established parties and politicians are accused of having squandered the interests of the Dutch people and of misleading the voters with their sloganising during the election campaign. Consequently, the party regularly states that it first and foremost holds the government, and not the foreigners, responsible for the disruption of society (that is, the multi-cultural society).

The various populist anti-party sentiments of the CD come together when discussing the fight against their own party. It claims that the established parties attack the CD so hard because it is the only genuine opposition party. Moreover, it is the only party that puts the finger on the sore spot, the multicultural society (e.g. *CDa* 4/93). To cover up their own failure in this area the established parties use every trick in the book. For one, they ignore every opposition to multi-culturalism, from the man in the street as well as from a parliamentary party such as the CD. If ignoring the opposition does not help the established parties demonise the opposition by accusing them of racism, and linking them to fascism and so on.

In this battle for political life and death, the established parties are helped by lackeys such as the media, which are dependent on the subsidies they receive. The established parties even created a whole infrastructure of so-called 'anti-racist' and 'anti-fascist' organisations which, with the help of legal collectives, are full-time fighters against the CD and any other opponents of the multi-cultural society. As all these organisations have to justify their large subsidies, they 'exaggerate with all their will for the subsidy mill' (*CDi* 3/93). According to the party the fight against the CD has already cost the state a total of more than one quarter of a billion Dutch guilders (*CDi* 6/94).

The struggle is not only fought on the level of the media or politics. More and more the established parties have sought salvation in legal measures. To try and achieve the multi-cultural society even against the will of the people, they have introduced a multitude of anti-discrimination laws, which in practice favour the minorities and discriminate against the indigenous people. Most of these laws are primarily directed against the CD. According to the CD this holds true also for almost every other change that might have a negative effect on the party, ranging from changes in the electoral law to the subsidising of political parties.

At the same time the party papers are filled with articles in which the major influence of the party on governmental policy and the public debate is described (e.g. *CDa* 4/88). Almost every measure the government takes regarding asylum seekers or minorities which (slightly) resemble policies proposed by the CD, is seen as a triumph for the party (e.g. *CDa* 4/91). With great regularity it proclaims a turn in the tide of public opinion or politics favouring the party (e.g. *CDa* 2/92). Typical are also the articles, often written by Janmaat, in which it is claimed that Janmaat had won a debate in parliament (if the ministers and MPs were courageous enough to debate with him), or that the government is on the brink of falling (as a consequence of the opposition by the CD). In similar vein the party always predicts an enormous victory in coming elections. The fact that the expected results are far above those in the opinion polls proves the fact that these latter are manipulated to keep down the CD. When the party finally polled far fewer votes than expected, it would blame the entire anti-CD conspiracy again.

### Democracy

The CD devotes regular attention to the issue of democracy. The bulk of these articles address the alleged breaches of democracy in the Netherlands. According to the CD the present Dutch state is not a democracy, as it does not allow true opposition. The party even stated that 'in its methods of oppression our government seems to surpass the brutal methods of Stalin' (*CDi* 8/91). This is not to say that the CD considers the political system itself undemocratic or to be rejected. The party is an open and consistent supporter of parliamentary democracy. It even sees itself exclusively as an election party, believing that 'victory in elections is the only way to go and to exercise influence' (*CDa* 4/91). However, it accuses the established parties of having perverted the good system of parliamentary democracy to protect (and prolong) their own power and jobs (e.g. *CDa* 1/89). They have even fixed elections, which is why the CD claims to have asked the UN to send observers for the 1989 parliamentary election (*CDa* 2/89). To make the system function democratically once more the politicians of the established parties have to be voted out of power and replaced (primarily) by CD members.

In recent years the CD has found a new threat to Dutch democracy: the European Union. The party had always considered international organisations, and the outside world in general, to be hostile towards the Netherlands. That is also why it argues for a modest foreign policy in which the Netherlands do not interfere in the politics of other countries and vice versa. Dutch membership in the main international organisations was accepted with great reservation. Generally, the party speaks scornfully of such organisations as the UN, describing them as superfluous, inefficient and profligate bureaucracies. An exception to this was NATO, which had the goal of keeping the West safe from communism and which was also deemed necessary after 1989, as the Russians remained dangerous and a new enemy was also easily found, international Islam.

### Ethical Values

Originally the CD did not put much emphasis on ethical values. Topics like abortion and euthanasia were virtually not discussed by the party. At times there would be articles in the party papers in defense of traditional values, mainly citing the family as the cornerstone of society. As part of this quest the party opposed various 'progressive' organisations that would undermine the family, such as the relief centres for runaway children (e.g. *CDa* 1/89). One of the few shifts that could be detected in the 1994 programme was towards a more conservative outlook, stressing law and order as well as traditional morals and values. The section on culture was elaborated by conservative pleas for the banning of hardcore pornography and a limitation on the screening of violence on Dutch television (V.5) as well as limitations on the possibility to divorce (V.6 and 7). This shift to a protection of traditional morals might also explain why the party dropped its plea for the inclusion of condoms in the national health program. This development was continued in the 1998 programme, which put increasing emphasis on the protection of the family, including making divorce (particularly in case of families with children) more difficult (e.g. CD 1998: III.6c and 7).

A topic in which the party's concerns on values comes to the fore most clearly is that of AIDS. Throughout the years AIDS has been a regular topic within the party literature. The (large) section of the programme on public health for instance, contains no less than three (of the nine) points that concern this disease (CD 1989: XVI.4, 7 and 8). Moreover, one of the few brochures ever published by the scientific bureau of the CD also addressed the issue (Johnstone and Knappert 1994). The report *AIDS: Ghost or Threat*, written by two members of the Unification Church of Sun Myung Moon (Van den Brink 1995),[7] paints a picture of a dangerous disease which is the consequence of the present moral crisis. As AIDS is mainly caused by 'specific behaviour' (i.e. sexual promiscuity, homosexuality and drug addiction), the disease can be stopped only through prevention. However, pressured by 'the dictatorship of a minority' (Johnstone and Knappert 1994: 16), by which they mean the homosexual lobby, the medical issue has become a political issue:

> In fact, under the pretext of fighting against homophobia and turning zeropositives into scape-goats, we are coming to the point of making the society feel guilty and to make the zeropositive less responsible in regard to the risks that they make others run, especially their sexual partners. (Johnstone and Knappert 1994: 17)

According to the CD, if we want to save ourselves from an AIDS explosion in the West we will have to overcome the present moral crisis and moral relativism and return to traditional morality. In extremis, we should return to no sex until marriage and to the family as 'the school of love' (Johnstone and Knappert 1994: 31). Though the brochure is atypical for CD literature (in that it is relatively well written, argued and researched), it fits well within the party's thinking. The main point is that a problem is not solved as a result of a conspiracy of the political elite.

## Conclusion

The CD does not possess a very elaborated ideological programme. The party literature contains at best a shallow ideology, focusing on only a lim-

---

[7] For years, Willem A. Koetsier, a prominent member of the 'Moonies' in the Netherlands, worked at the party office of the CD. He also wrote in the party papers. This notwithstanding, the Unification Church was never mentioned in the party papers and it seems that it also never had a real say within the party.

ited number of themes. This holds true especially for the party paper *CD-Info*, which by and large deals with four main (linked) themes: opposition to the multi-cultural society, populist anti-party sentiment, the undemocratic struggle against the own party, and (fighting) crime. And, although the election programmes address a fairly wide variety of policy areas, the ideological content again remains limited. It contains the idea that people should live in a mono-cultural state which is not crowded by too many inhabitants. Immigrants are given the choice between assimilation and repatriation. The role of the state should not be too big, neither in national nor in international politics, and the state should first and foremost take care of its own population, ensuring a relatively generous welfare system without, however, hindering private initiative (for instance, by high taxes) or overspending (for instance, on subsidies). The state should play a strong and dominant role only in strictly ensuring law and order. Within the world view of the party this can be realised within the current political system, but only when the CD is accepted within that system and when several current actors are ousted of power (mainly the PvdA and BVD).

# 6

# Centrumpartij'86

### Reservoir of the fringe

After the expulsion of the Janmaat group at the end of 1984 the troubles of the *Centrumpartij* were far from over. Party leader Konst was put under increasing pressure by his employer to resign as party chairman or lose his job as teacher at a state school; vice-chairman De Wijer had already been temporarily suspended as teacher at another state school (DNPP 1987; Schikhof 1998). Only a few months after the split Konst resigned and was succeeded by former party treasurer Albrecht Lier, (in)famous in the Netherlands for his claim to be an illegitimate son of prince Hendrik.[1] In the 1985 by-election the CP gained one seat in the new province of Flevoland and one in the new municipality of Leerdam. Despite the decreasing trend, the party contested the local election of March 1986 with moderate success (winning six seats). The last surge of optimism for the parliamentary election of two months later was shattered by the defection of party leader Lier to the CD (Lucardie and Voerman 1990). The eventual blow in winning just 0.4 per cent of the votes was softened only slightly by the 0.1 per cent won by its main rival the CD.

Lier's successor, former party treasurer Danny Segers, was unable to turn the tables for the rapidly disintegrating party. Since the split the membership of the CP had fallen back to merely 100. Moreover, almost the whole top echelons of the party had either left politics altogether or moved to the CD. The situation became even more devastating as the CP had become involved in a series of court cases as a consequence of its preparation for the local election. A group of people who had signed the CP electoral list in Heerlen later claimed to have been misled by the party, as they had been told that they signed for something else. The court acknowledged their complaint and fined the CP 50,000 Dutch guilders. As the party could not pay the fine, it

---

[1] German-born Hendrik Wladimir Albrecht Ernst (1876–1934) became prince of the Netherlands after marrying Queen Wilhelmina in 1909. Hendrik's only official child, Juliana, succeeded Wilhelmina as queen in 1948.

was declared bankrupt on 13 May 1986 (DNPP 1988). The successor was founded exactly one week later, conveniently named *Centrumpartij'86* (Centre Party'86, CP'86).

Though its legal successor, the new CP'86 was no more than a weak copy of the old CP. From the approximately 3,500 members the CP had claimed in its heyday, only a mere fifty were willing to begin with the CP'86. Yet even within this small group the internal disputes continued. In 1987 chairman Segers withdrew from his position and was succeeded by Ema Bouman, a relatively unknown member until she was elected as a council member in Amsterdam in 1986. At the end of 1988 she also suddenly left the CP'86, in protest against the radicalisation of the party (Schikhof 1997), and was replaced by Wim Beaux, then council member in both the municipality of Almere and the province of Flevoland and a long-time leading member of the CP. He was superseded shortly afterwards by another major driving force of the new party, Wim Wijngaarden, also a long-time activist within the CP. This time the succession was not the result of an internal dispute, and Beaux remained part of the party executive.

Except for internal disputes, the CP'86 had several other problems to deal with. For instance, election material of the party was confiscated at its German printer (the same printer as was used by the North Rhine-Westphalian branch of the NPD). Moreover, it was involved in a legal battle with the CD over the legacy of the CP. The CP'86 won the case in the first instance and was appointed the sole legal heir to the CP. This meant it could profit from several publicity and electoral advantages, as the CP was relatively well-known and represented in several municipal and provincial councils. However, the CP'86 could not make much use of it at the time, as internal difficulties and a general decline prevented it from contesting the 1989 parliamentary election.

In the 1990 local election the CP'86 gained four seats, a disappointing result compared to the eleven seats of the CD. There was good news for the party as well, since it won its legal case over the heritage of the CP in the second instance too, despite the fact that the CD had claimed before the Council of State that it should also be considered and treated as a successor to the CP (DNPP 1992). More important was the remarkable growth in membership which the CP'86 experienced, with an influx of between 50 and 100 youths. They originated predominantly from the *Jongerenfront Nederland* (Youth Front Netherlands, JFN), at that time the largest right-wing extremist youth movement in the Netherlands with some 200 members. After a Breda court had labelled the JFN a criminal organisation (in a case against two of its members in May 1990), leader Stewart Mordaunt called upon his supporters to follow him into the CP'86, for which party he had been elected to the municipal council of The Hague earlier that year (FOK 1992).

This expansion brought the total membership of the CP'86 to approximately 300 at the end of 1991. In addition, the youth and activism of the new members gave the party a new impulse. In particular, following an almost hidden existence for five years the young activists brought the CP'86 back into the spotlight by distributing pamphlets. Favourite targets for the young militants were young people and inhabitants of areas with a high concentration of foreigners and ethnic minorities or of areas where ethnic tensions had recently erupted. In addition to the people that were directly approached, the CP'86 also made its actions as provocative as possible in order to spread its message to other people through the consequent (large) media attention – a strategy that had already been the trade mark of the JFN.

The revitalisation of the CP'86 did not bring an end to the internal disputes, however. After party secretary Egbert Perée had been ousted from the party leadership in August 1990, his successor Wim Geurts experienced the same fate in the beginning of 1991. The same year the party contested the provincial election in four provinces, all without success. Shortly thereafter, Wim Kock, who had been heading the election list in the province of South Holland and had been the assistant of Mordaunt in the council of The Hague, was expelled from the party. In most cases the veterans were replaced by members of the former JFN. In early 1992 the party executive included five people of which (the first) three came from the old CP and (the last) two from the JFN: Wijngaarden (chairman), Theo Termijn (council member in Rotterdam), Beaux (vice-chairman), Mordaunt and Tibor Mudde (secretary).

The next three years were characterised by a remarkable unity and growth. Through its large number of local actions the CP'86 was able to steadily increase its membership to some 500 at the end of 1994. Among the new members were former members of the CP (such as Segers), as well as small groups of (former) neo-Nazis. This latter group was partly attracted by the large autonomy the local branches of the party enjoyed. Especially in the area of Rotterdam the (former) neo-Nazis were able to put their imprint on the local party.

The election year 1994 was approached with much optimism by the CP'86. Henk Ruitenberg, a relative newcomer to the extreme right and to the CP'86, had succeeded the ill Wijngaarden as party leader in early 1994. The party campaigned actively throughout the whole country, distributing thousands of pamphlets, mostly in so-called disadvantaged areas. Despite the fact that the CP'86 was overshadowed by the CD in the March local election it more than doubled its number of seats, from four in 1990 to nine in 1994 (see Mudde and Van Holsteyn 1994; Van Holsteyn 1995). Though the successes outside of the big cities were exclusively in municipalities in which the CD had not contested the election, the leadership saw the result as proof of the viability of their party (next to the CD) and anticipated its (re)entry into the Second Chamber. This optimistic view was supported by some opinion polls, which showed that the party was receiving sufficient support to win a parliamentary seat (Van Holsteyn 1995).

The final result in the parliamentary election, when it won just 0.4 per cent, therefore signified a rude awakening. The party remained below the score needed for one seat (0.67 per cent) and well behind its main rival the CD, which increased its number of seats from one to three. After some soul searching the party concluded that one of the main reasons for its poor results was that it was too often mistaken for the CD by the voters. It had tried to avoid this problem by stamping its election material with the text 'Centre Party'86 absolutely not to be confused with Janmaat's CD'. On 19 November 1994 the party decided on a more drastic measure, renaming itself as *Nationale Volkspartij/CP'86* (National People's Party/CP'86, NVP).

There had also been another reason for this change of name, however: legal pressure. The CP'86 had always been the target of anti-racist organisations and on several occasions attempts had been made to get the state to start legal proceedings against the party to either convict or ban it for incitement to racial hatred. In 1994 vice-chairman Beaux was convicted on two occasions, once, together with five other members, for possessing and distributing racist pamphlets (IJA 1995). But most importantly, after years of discussions and under mounting pressure from anti-racists organisations and various political parties (most notably PvdA and D66), the state finally started legal actions against the party itself. In 1995 an Amsterdam court ruled that the CP'86 constituted a criminal organisation, as it consistently spread racial hatred; in addition, five of its leaders were convicted of heading a criminal organisation (e.g. JPR 1997).

The conviction hit the party hard, most notably the 'moderate' leader Ruitenberg, who had tried to bring the party into a more acceptable position. Feeling pressured by both the legal repression and the increasing internal opposition from the 'radical' wing, he sought a rapproachement with the CD, offering something close to a full merger of the two parties on Janmaat's terms. In addition, the two parties cooperated in some high profile demonstrations (e.g. Zwolle), where leaders of CP'86 and Janmaat marched and spoke side by side. In May the cooperation came to a sudden end, when the CP'86 membership by large majority rejected Ruitenberg's fusion proposal. In reaction, Ruitenberg resigned as party chairman, defecting to the CD shortly afterwards, and was succeeded by party veteran Beaux. However, the bitter struggle between the 'moderate' nationalist wing and the 'radical' neo-Nazi wing continued to divide the party.

Officially, it was the open neo-Nazi behaviour and contacts of the group around Rotterdam council member Martijn Freling[2] which caused the 'mod-

---

[2] Freling had returned to the Netherlands in the beginning of the 1990s after having lived in Germany for several years. He originated, like Mordaunt, in the youth-wing of the NVU, the *Nationaal Jeugdfront* (National Youth Front), but left after a dispute with Glimmerveen. In 1983 he co-founded the *Onafhankelijk Verbond van Nationaal Socialisten* (Independent Alliance of National Socialists), which became the Rotterdam branch of the JFN, infamous for

erate' leadership headaches. However, several party leaders were at least as worried about Freling's party ambitions, as well as irritated by his defiance of the official party line, which proclaimed that open neo-Nazism was not allowed. At the same time the leadership was hesitant to split the tiny movement even further. After much lingering Freling was finally expelled from the party in October 1996; however, not by an unanimous party leadership decision. To some surprise a disgruntled Mordaunt choose Freling's side, which led to his expulsion a few weeks later. In November Freling countered by organising a meeting of loyal party members, in which they claimed the party, elected Mordaunt as chairman and Freling as secretary, and expelled the 'moderate' leadership (e.g. Kafka 1998; Lucardie 1998). After months of confusing bickering, the Freling-Mordaunt group obtained the legal right to the party, and changed the name back to CP'86. The 'moderates', on their part, dismantled the NVP in February 1997 and founded the *Volksnational-isten Nederland* (Ethnic Nationalists Netherlands, VNN).[3]

Both groups are just weak shadows of the old party; in 1998 their memberships were estimated at some forty members per party (Van den Brink 1998). Various influential and active members, among them Mudde and Marcel Rüter, had left party politics altogether, devoting all their energy to the Dutch branch of Voorpost (see Kafka 1998; Van den Brink 1998). The two successor parties were unable to make any impression in elections. In the local election of March 1998 they lost all their seats and neither of the parties has contested any elections since. However, the parties did make the headlines on various occasions, particularly the CP'86 of Freling and Mordaunt. Freling has always held close contacts with journalists, who repaid this privilege by (over)reporting his every move (see Van Donselaar *et al.* 1998). In 1996 the group organised various meetings which were also attended by prominent neo-Nazis from outside of the party, most notably NVU-leader Glimmerveen. At some of these meetings speakers threatened prominent Dutch persons, including the Surinamese-born MP of *Groen-Links* (Green Left), Singh Varma, an outspoken anti-racist. Ironically, it was particularly the remarks of Glimmerveen, not a party member, which provided the final push in the legal battle against the party. In reaction mainly

its neo-Nazism. Though he also joined the JFN, Freling devoted most of his time to the *Aktiefront Nationale Socialisten* (Action Front of National Socialists), which he co-founded in 1984 as the Dutch branch of the German organisation with the same name led by Michael Kühnen (see Ten Haaf 1992; Kafka 1998).

   [3] On 3 July 1998 the party became the *Nieuwe Partij Nederland* (New Party Netherlands), allegedly a new party uniting the Dutch extreme right, but in reality not more than the former VNN and some veterans of the 'centre movement'. Already in October it was disbanded and the 'new' *Nieuwe Nationale Partij* (New National Party) was founded, which today constitutes a mere sect of some forty people, virtually all veterans (of the 'moderate' wing) of the old CP'86.

to his remarks, the whole parliament (with the exception of the CD) urged the Goverment to start criminal investigations into the CP'86, with the (unspoken) aim of a party ban (see JPR 1997).

In October 1997 the High Court confirmed the ruling of the Amsterdam court of two years earlier, which had found both the CP'86 and five of its leaders guilty of inciting racial hatred (Van den Brink 1998). Though the actual sentences were marginal, one month suspended sentences and fines of a few thousand guilders, the ruling was generally considered as the first step to the banning of the party, which was now for the first time officially labelled a 'criminal organisation'. At the same time, various people questioned the usefulness of a ban, given the deplorable state of the party as well as the bizarre situation that only one of the five convicted 'leaders' was still a member of the party. This notwithstanding, Minister of Justice Sorgdrager announced her intention to ban the party and started the preparations for the 'ghost trial' a few days after the ruling. It would take until 18 November 1998 before the party was officially banned and disbanded by the Amsterdam court. By that time, the CP'86 was not more than an empty vessel, probably containing only the inactive 'party leader' Freling, who had lost all his former comrades as well as the party's funds, allegedly as a consequence of his drug addiction.

Throughout its existence the CP'86 has constantly been involved in some form of negotiations about a possible fusion with the CD, and at times also with other parties at the extreme right fringe. In 1992 the Belgian VB tried to bring a wide variety of these parties together – among them the CP'86, CD, and NB – with the idea of creating one big Dutch nationalist party. The negotiations failed completely and even the agreement to constitute one electoral list in the 1994 European election lasted only for a few days. As in earlier years the main obstacle had been Janmaat, who had demanded that all other parties and persons would grant him and his party the leading role. At the CP'86 party conference of 1992 the membership almost unanimously rejected the possibility of a merger with the CD if it would include the elimination of their own party (which it would do again in 1996). Though contacts concerning possible cooperation were never terminated for long, it would take until 1996 before serious talks between CP'86 and CD were held again. It was these talks that led to the demise of the CP'86, putting the already tense relations between the 'moderates' (i.e. Ruitenberg, Mudde, De Boer and Hoogstra) and the 'radicals' (i.e. Freling and Mordaunt) under even more strain.

Although the CP'86 never maintained a large membership, many of those within the party (leadership) have been highly active in the extreme right scene, both inside and outside of the Netherlands. The party held official contacts with the Flemish VB (and VBJ) and Voorpost, the German NPD (and JN), the British National Party, and the South African *Boerestaatparty*

(Boer State Party). High-ranking party members had personal contacts with organisations like the American National Alliance and (sections of) the Ku Klux Klan, the French *Nouvelle Resistance* (New Resistance) and the Austrian *Aktionsgemeinschaft für Politik* (Action Community for Politics). The CP'86 was also for years officially represented at the annual *Ijzerbedevaart* in the Flemish town of Diksmuide, where it had a prominent stand in the hall of Voorpost.

## Profiling the literature

### Externally oriented: programmes

In the period 1986–99 the CP'86 published three election programmes and two party programme (or programmes of principle). The first election programme was the undated (probably 1987) 'party programme' *Voor een veilig en leefbaar Nederland!* (For a Safe and Livable Netherlands!, CP 1987), which was an almost exact copy of the programme *Naar een veilig en leefbaar Nederland* (Towards a Safe and Livable Netherlands) with which the CP had contested the 1986 parliamentary election. The main difference was that the CP had used the logo of a traffic sign in which an arrow to both the left and right was crossed (illustrating the slogan 'not right, not left'), whereas the CP'86 used a (Dutch) lion with a sword. The programme contained thirty chapters (policy areas) on a total of twenty-seven unpaged A5 pages. It was never used in elections; neither was the revised 1990 programme with the same title, including a short new introduction, some new demands and the eradication of several old demands (CP 1990). In 1993 the party published a new version titled *Partijprogramma* (Party Programme), with which the party contested the 1994 local and parliamentary elections (CP 1993). Except for the fact that the CP'86 had changed the title of the programme and the supplement to the party name (from 'The national democratic movement in the Netherlands' in 1989 to 'Own people first!' in 1993), the revisions in the programme were almost unnoticeable.

In 1989 the CP'86 presented its first party programme, under the title *Nationaaldemocratische gedachten voor een menswaardige toekomst* (National Democratic Thoughts for a Human Future, CP 1989). The first version included fifteen unmarked A4 pages, some of which featured advertisements for the party. The second version was published as a 'programme of principle' in 1990, containing an identical title and content. It included thirteen unmarked A5 pages, had a more professional lay-out, and was distributed more broadly. The programme was an almost literal translation of the 1987 NPD programme, entitled *Nationaldemokratische Gedanken für eine lebenswerte Zukunft*, although passages that were placed in a typically German context in the original were – using similar phrasing – placed in a typically Dutch context in this new version (see Mudde 1995: 220). In May 1996 the then NVP adopted a new party programme with the title *Wie wij zijn & wat wij willen* (Who we are & what we want, CP 1996), written by Rüter and Mudde. The so-called 'Yellow Booklet', referring both to the color of the programme and to the 'Green Booklet' by Libyan leader Moamar Quadaffi, counted thirty-two pages and included five sections: the history of the NVP/CP'86, the ideology, the aims, the statutes and the former national anthem *Wien Neerlands Bloed* (Whose Dutch Blood).

### Internally oriented: party paper

In 1987 the CP'86 started publishing a quarterly national party paper with the title *Centrumnieuws* (Centre News, CN) and the sub-title *Blad voor de Centrumpartij'86* (Paper for the CP'86). The final supervision of the paper rested with the 'scientific bureau', which only existed on paper at that time. In December 1987 the paper was restyled for the first time, introducing the logo of the Dutch lion and the Latin slogan 'Vincit Amor Patriae' (Patriotism Conquers) on the front page, as well as a slightly revised sub-title *Partijorgaan van de Centrumpartij'86* (Party Paper of the CP'86). Though the number of (unnumbered) pages was extended to fifteen, the paper maintained its poor quality in language and lay-out. Most of the articles were short and vague, printed in a broad variety of different letter types and containing many typing errors. The last 1988 issue introduced a new extension to the sub-title: 'the national democratic movement in the Netherlands'. In the following years the style remained basically the same, but the size of the paper increased to some thirty pages.

After the influx of the young JFN members a new editorial board was created under the leadership of its former chancellor and then CP'86 secretary Tibor Mudde. As of the third issue of 1991 the party paper was drastically restyled. For the first time in its existence it was paginated, and the number of language and typing errors decreased rapidly. Moreover, the paper became more conveniently arranged. It was (re)structured into several columns, of which most contained exclusively articles on a single theme (mainly foreigners). The paper also featured more drawings, cartoons and quotations from like-minded journals abroad, portraying Viking and Celtic warriors as the true European heroes of the past. Under the new guidance the party paper expanded its size considerably, numbering between thirty-nine and sixty-four pages in the later years. In late 1993 it changed its cover and lay-out again. The extension 'the national democratic movement in the Netherlands' was deleted and the paper was named plainly *Centrumnieuws* – with, in the middle of the name, a Celtic cross and two hands that break free from handcuffs, one of which features a dollar sign, the other a hammer and sickle. The style was not changed until the beginning of 1995, when the now *Nationale Volkspartij/CP'86* introduced the radically improved party paper *De Revolutionair Nationalist* (The Revolutionary Nationalist, RN). It had a lay-out quite similar to *Revolte*, the journal of the Great-Netherlands action group Voorpost. In addition to the drastic restyling, the new party paper also used a new slogan: *Voor Volk en Vaderland* (For Ethnic Community and Fatherland). With the split of the party, the paper disappeared; the VNN tried for a while to publish a somewhat similar paper as the *RN*, while the CP'86 seeked inspiration in its predecessor *CN*.

## In search of an identity

### Ethnic nationalism

The CP'86 has always identified itself as a nationalist party, mostly using the term *volksnationalist* (ethnic nationalist). This is also the main theme in the party literature. What ethnic nationalism precisely means to the party, however, is often simply assumed to be clear to the reader. Sporadically one can find a clear-cut description such as the following: 'Country and ethnic community should be one!' (*CN* 1/89). The party holds this to be a universal truth. It acknowledges the right to self-determination of all ethnic communities and strives for a world of independent and genuine nation-states. Consequently, it sees its main enemy in imperialism, i.e. the expansion of a certain state beyond its 'natural' territorial borders.

Despite the frequent reference to its own ethnic community and the use of terms like 'true Dutchmen' and 'paper Dutchmen', the CP'86 has problems in defining the own ethnic community. In the pamphlet 'national democratic guidelines regarding our national consciousness', based on a similar pamphlet of the NPD, it states: 'The race is the determining factor for the identity of every ethnic community' (*CN* 1/89). In another instance the party depicts a somewhat organic view of the notion of an ethnic community, declaring that '(y)our soil, your own ethnic community, culture and traditions form the unmistakable recognition of the roots of your own existence' (*CN* 1/89). Despite the confusing usage of the terms race and ethnic community, the broader idea of the party is relatively clear: only those people are members of the Dutch ethnic community 'whose preceding generations originated from Dutch parents, and among whom the language, culture and way of life is acknowledged and practised as the only way' (*CN* 3/90). Accordingly, children born in the Netherlands with foreign (grand)parents (so-called *allochtonen*) are not considered to be truly Dutch. Though never stated openly, it is clear from the party literature that truly Dutch people are part of the 'white race'. Interestingly, though the party portrays the Dutch ethnic community always as a homogeneous group in contrast to 'the' foreigners, at the same time it believes that the Dutch ethnic community includes several sub groups (such as the Frisians), who live harmoniously together in one state (*CN* 1/89).

Part of its ethnic nationalist ideology is the feature of *external exclusiveness*, the claim that the Dutch state should encompass all members of the Dutch ethnic community. The 1990 programme, for example, states: 'The highest goal for us national democrats is a sovereign, non-aligned Dutch speaking nation-state in which the whole Dutch speaking part of the nation in Europe is united.' In line with this vision the separation of the Netherlands and Flanders, referred to as the Northern and Southern Netherlands, is labelled a *volkstegenstrijdige scheiding* (a partition which is hostile to the ethnic community).

> We, national democrats, envisage a Dutch ethnic state, which is congruent geographically with the Northern and Southern Netherlands together, and is inherent to a territory in which the Dutch language, Dutch culture and truly Dutch traditions are commonplace. It is the character and will of the ethnic community that determines the ethnic state and its borders. (CP 1990: 29.8)

This Great-Netherlands state would stretch geographically 'from Dollart through Southern Flanders' (*CN* 3/89), i.e. the current Netherlands, plus Belgian Flanders and French Flanders (an area in the Northwest of France). Remarkably, the rather extreme demand of external exclusiveness features prominently in the externally oriented literature, both in the election programmes (after 1987) and in the programme of principle, yet hardly figures in the internally oriented party papers.

A topic that is prominent in the whole party literature is *internal homogenisation*, i.e. the demand that only Dutchmen can live in the Dutch state. The CP'86 wants to repatriate all foreigners, starting with those who are illegal and those who are or were criminal (and have lived in the Netherlands for less than five years). The few foreigners that will be needed for economic reasons can stay in the Netherlands, but only on a temporary basis. These people should not be allowed to bring their families nor should they (be forced to) integrate into Dutch society. Foreigners who have been naturalised in the last decades, condescendingly referred to as 'paper Dutchmen', are also to be repatriated to their countries of origin. Finally, the 1990 programme includes the new demand that all unemployed foreigners, who have not yet reached retirement, as well as all 'social refugees', will be obliged to repatriate (CP 1990: 7.9–10).

All election programmes stress the need to bring Dutch policy on immigration into accord with European policy. The European argument is used solely when other European countries have a policy more favourable to the CP'86.

> At least what has to be avoided is that the Netherlands will take an exceptional position in Western Europe, by a too negligent adoption of generally accepted rules of conduct with regard to the policy on foreigners. The Netherlands can not become a haven for foreigners that are rejected everywhere else. (CP 1993: 7.3)

The CP'86 further demands that acquiring Dutch citizenship should be made far more difficult. According to the party, it is not meant to provide foreigners with social and financial security or the (established) political parties with 'improper electoral gains' (CP 1990: 5.19). Should foreigners wish to acquire Dutch citizenship, they have to make it clear that they indeed want to become Dutch, will speak Dutch, and will freely and fully 'harmonise into the Dutch cultural pattern' (CP 1999: 5.20).

Until the *volksstaat* (ethnic state) is realised the party wishes to pursue a policy of 'our own people first' which, for the most part, means 'our own money for our own people'. It would also mean the introduction of legal pluralism, as the CP'86 wishes to bring conditions regarding admission, employment, housing and expulsion of foreign nationals into accord with the respective policies of the countries of origin of these foreigners. Consequently, the few foreigners that are allowed to live in the country are accepted only under clear conditions (to work for a specific period of time) and under very strict rules.

### Exclusionism

Given the lack of an elaborated ideology more complex features like ethnopluralism can be traced only by combining different statements within the party literature. In the early years the party limited itself mainly to fighting the payment of subsidies for forced integration of ethnic customs and cultures into existing cultural patterns. In the 1990s this opposition was not only radicalised, but was also (slightly) more substantiated.

> The requisition of shelters for asylum seeking aliens, in particular in small communities, is polluting the environment and discriminating against our own ethnic community. Moreover, it is an unbearable burden for the whole Dutch society and is rejected by us as inhuman. (CP 1990: 22.12)

According to the party the flood of foreigners has led to the loss of identity in the Dutch ethnic community, as ghettos of foreigners have made them into a minority in their own land. But the foreigners have also lost their identity, since they have been the victims of a 'foreigner-hostile integration policy (a forced Dutchifying)' (CP 1989). As 'the struggle for homogeneity and the living together with similar people is anchored in human nature' (*CN* 3/92), the policy of multi-culturalism and integration is perceived as inhuman. Moreover, integration uproots the foreigners, which leads to confusion and consequent criminal and amoral behaviour, particularly among the youth. Therefore, the CP'86 equates a multi-cultural society with a 'multi-criminal society'. This whole line of argument is applied exclusively to non-white foreigners, however. Within the 'white race', often simply equated with the European culture, integration seems to be possible, according to the party literature. Hence, it considers European foreigners as posing far less of a threat than non-Europeans.

Probably the most outspoken example of ethnopluralist reasoning is found in the party's support for a Europe of Ethnic Communities. The first programme had contained a very positive European chapter, proclaiming the process of European integration as 'vital for our political, economic and societal system' (CP 1987: 28.1) and stating that the Netherlands has to be an 'inspiring but particularly loyal ally' (CP 1987: 28.2). Though it acknowledged some problems with(in) the European Community – such as the wasting of money, the alienation from the people and the lack of democratic control – the institution as such was viewed as extremely positive. The CP'86 even wanted to increase the autonomy of the European Commission, arguing that it should be able to decide by simple majority. This is therefore a world apart from the 1990 programme, which called the European Community imperialist and described it as a perilous threat to Dutch identity (CP 1987: 28.1). EU-phoria had given way to an ethnopluralist EU rejection:

> National democrats support the European co-operation of independent ethnic communities, including the East European countries, but resist any form of European integration in which our national identity could be endangered. (CP 1987: 28.3).

The CP'86 maintains that the different ethnic communities in (East and West) Europe share enough common history and culture to work closely together, yet are at the same time too different to give up their separate identities and autonomy. Thus, each different ethnic community should have its own independent nation-state (including, among others, the Bretons and Basques), which should work together on specific matters, mainly economic and military.

The frequent usage of the term race, at times used interchangeably with the term ethnic community, could point to a racist argumentation, hidden behind the more open ethnopluralist argumentation. The party does consider race to be the determining factor for the identity of every ethnic community and argues that '(o)nly the recognition and the acceptance of the substantial differences between the races guarantees respect between ethnic communities' (CN 3/88). Even in its typically ethnopluralist defense of the South African apartheid regime it uses racial categories: 'There is no racism in South Africa, but a healthy racial consciousness, which is the positive thinking that grants every race or ethnic community the right to self-determination, self-development and its own identity' (CN 1/90). However, the belief in the existence (and importance) of races is not (openly) combined with statements that any race is superior or inferior – even though members of non-white races are always portrayed negatively in the party literature.

### Xenophobia

The entire party literature of the CP'86 has always been drenched with xenophobia. The party paper in particular has a special interest in the negative sides of immigration. Favourite topics are crimes by foreigners of all kinds (guest workers, asylum seekers, illegal aliens), preferably rapes and murders. Originally the party paper would print copies of newspaper articles about crimes (allegedly) by foreigners. Following its restructuring special columns like 'adaptation problems', based on a similar column in the German extreme right journal *Nation [und] Europa*, printed lists of excerpts from these newspaper articles. In addition to these more or less neutral presentations of facts, all issues of the paper include at least some xenophobic comments on the multi-cultural society, from either readers or the editors. The main argument that a multi-cultural society can only be a multi-criminal society is 'proven' by pointing to examples such as former Yugoslavia (the civil war) and Los Angeles (the race riots of 1994). According to the party the mass influx of foreigners and the consequent policy of multi-culturalism can lead only to civil war:

> After all, the ongoing stream of aliens from ever different countries, next to the millions of non-Europeans who have already penetrated Europe, are a direct attack on our economy, on our sense of justice, on our social consciousness, on our national values and on our personal freedom! (*CN* 5/87)

Nor are the party programmes free from xenophobia, which is clearly visible, for instance, in the section of the 1989 party programme with the title 'the inner peace and security is being seriously endangered by the massive influx of aliens into our country'. Since 1990, the introduction of the election programme declares 'our resistance against the uncontrolled influx of hundreds of thousands of criminal and parasitic aliens in our overpopulated country' (CP 1993) to be one of the main pillars of the political thinking and actions of the party.

### Ethical values

The preservation of traditional ethical values has always been a regular feature in the party literature. The election programme originally included a moderately conservative view, stating that abortion for social reasons should remain illegal, but not demanding any new (stricter) measures (CP 1987: 5.11). In the 1990 version the position had toughened: abortion was referred to as 'the mass murder of the unborn child' (CP 1990: 12.9) and the creation of a living climate in which pregnant women would not have to consider abortion for social reasons was demanded. This toughening was also visible in the party position on the related issue of euthanasia. The 1987 programme had not yet formulated a standpoint on euthanasia, stating that a policy paper would be published (it never appeared). In 1990, the programme also contained the demand that euthanasia should remain illegal (CP 1990: 5.10).

The CP'86 considers the traditional family as the cornerstone of society, within which the most ideal and non-replaceable environment for the upbringing of children is provided. A special role in the revival of (ethnic) community spirit is ascribed to the family. The new election programmes even include a demand for a specific constitutional guarantee for the protection of the family. Moreover, the party also demands that everything should be done to restore positive future expectations for the family and a general joy of life, as only then will the family be able to maintain its indispensable place in the (ethnic) community. The position on the family has consequences for other beliefs. For instance, the party does not look favourably upon homosexuality. In an Amsterdam council meeting Beaux described it as 'an interpersonal practice that goes against nature' (CN 1/93). In general, however, homosexuality is ignored rather than attacked in the party literature. This also goes for feminism, which is not regarded positively, though seldom addressed (if mentioned at all, feminists are portrayed as men-hating lesbians). The CP'86 sees man and woman as equal in rights, but with different tasks in life. It wants a society that is friendly towards children and that recognises and enables 'the sublime role of housewife and mother' (CP 1989).

The CP'86 wants the state to become more involved in upholding morals and values, though it concedes that only a change in mentality can bring back the desired values of 'order, discipline, tolerance, refined speech, courtesy, honesty and being well-groomed' (CN 3/87). These values seem a world apart from the current state of affairs, described as:

> Self-enrichment, criminal materialism, devaluation of our basic values, secularisation, corruption and deceit are features of our modern society with the resulting excesses: unbridled abortion and euthanasia practices, pornography, incest, drug addiction, unlimited mental suffering of the many, destruction of marriage and family morals, uncontrollable crime as a consequence of the lack of a just and adequate penal system, a criminal foreigners policy and finally exploitation and humiliation of those that have landed at the bottom of the social ladder, such as the elderly, handicapped, disabled, unemployed and minimum wage earners. (CN 2/89)

The CP'86 believes that the two 'materialist' and 'hedonist' systems of capitalism and socialism (normally referred to as communism) are at the core of the current moral decay in the (Western) world; after the fall of the Berlin Wall 'liberal capitalism' was declared its main enemy. At the elite level these systems have led to a situation in which the economically powerful are no longer bound by a country (or ethnic community), which is in itself juxtaposed to the nationalist spirit. At the mass level the systems made people into 'consumer slaves who are devoid of culture', so that they are easier to control and thus stimulate the profit of big capital (CN 2/92). Only if these materialist and hedonist systems (and cultures) are overcome, is it possible to achieve a return to traditional ethical values.

### Socio-economic policy

Originally the CP'86 professed a rather liberal economic view which featured primarily in the election programme. It stressed the importance of decentralisation and privatisation of state tasks, the reduction of collective spending and tax and premium reductions where and whenever possible (CP 1987: 9.7; also chapter XIII). It further pledged support for reducing the financial deficit, for a policy of wage restraint, for government support for the Dutch small business community, and for specially subsidised (research on) technological innovation and education.

The later programmes were less liberal and more welfare chauvinist in outlook. They proclaim the full economic and financial dependency of the Netherlands on international (read US) capitalism (CP 1990: 9.1). According to the new party line, the economic actions of the Dutch government should make sure that 'our own ethnic community and not the multinational companies profits optimally from the benefits of the market' (CP 1993: 9.3). The party increased the number of demands to protect the Dutch economy and business community from negative effects of international capitalism. The programmes are also less friendly towards employers (e.g. CP 1990: 11.13). This transformation had already been visible in the party paper. Increasingly the party was acting in defense of people in a weak socio-economic position. In contrast to the popular picture of right-wing extremist parties in which there is normally very little sympathy for poor people that 'live off the state', the CP'86 hardly ever attacks the welfare system or those who are dependent upon it. On the contrary, there are regular features in which outrage is expressed over the poor conditions under which elderly people in particular have to live. The party rejects any further cuts in several social benefits, often even calling for increases. The support for the socially weak falls within a broader pro-worker discourse, also particularly visible in the paper, in which the party identifies with the common working man who is threatened by various forces (among others, foreigners, big business and the government).

The CP'86 claims to aspire to an 'economic third way', i.e. a system that is neither capitalist nor socialist, both of which are perceived as purely materialist economic systems, operated by the two imperialist powers (the US and the USSR) to alienate Eastern and Western Europe. They should be replaced by a common pan-European new economic order. According to the 'national democratic guidelines regarding economic and social policy', the crunch of this new order is that '(a)ll citizens that are dependent upon wages should, by participating in the productive capacity of the economy, become jointly responsible and jointly influential as well as sharing in the profit' (CN 1/89). This new order, the so-called *volkseconomie* (ethnic economy), is further built on the basis of private initiative (which is considered an essential feature of human nature) and the strengthening of small business.

According to the 1989 programme '(t)he future lies in a socioeconomic order that serves our own ethnic community, bears responsibility for country and culture, and engenders community spirit'. The 'national revolution', which will create the ethnic economy, will have to bring an end to the 'scandalous exploitation, humiliation and uprooting of our ethnic community by these so-called necessary cuts, reductions and abolitions that have as their sole target the abolishment of our social system' (CN 1/88). As far as concrete measures are concerned, they remain limited to the repatriation of foreigners. In sharp contrast to 'our own people', foreigners that profit from the Dutch welfare state are depicted as 'parasites' who do not want to work and who do their utmost to get as much as possible on the backs of the hard-working Dutch population. At the same time those that work thereby steal scarce jobs from 'our own people'. If the foreigners are repatriated, the party believes that the Dutch welfare state can be brought back to its old (higher) levels of the 1970s and 1980s.

### The strong state

A theme that has always featured prominently in the party literature, both externally and internally oriented, is law and order. The 1987 programme mentioned 'safe' as one of two pivotal terms in the title, and the introduction contained the statement: 'As a guarantee for the individual freedom of all citizens, we deem an effective police force as well as a merciless combating of all forms of crime to be absolutely vital.' The programme also included demands for 'the absolute necessity that sentences are served fully and under simple and sober conditions' as well as for the (re-)introduction of the death penalty (CP 1987: 6.7). The 1993 programme holds the same tough law and order policies plus the demand for obligatory detoxification for drugs addicts (CP 1993: 6.9).

In the party paper the omnipresent issue of crime is usually linked to either foreigners or to the left (both defined in the broadest sense). According to the CP'86 a so-called 'gang of 50' terrorises the Netherlands under such names as anti-fascists, anti-racists, anti-materialists, squatters, etc. Though officially the enemy of the Dutch state, the gang is tolerated by large parts of the state apparatus because it has proven valuable in the fight against the CP'86. Crime by foreigners is another dominant topic in the party paper (not only in the special columns). The party normally confines itself to simply presenting the facts and a simple solution: deport all criminal foreigners to their countries of origin! In the brochure 'national democratic guidelines regarding crime' it demands the following additional law and order policies: introduction of working camps and of the death penalty, stern discipline in prisons, higher sentences, putting the victim at the centre, less administrative disturbance for the police, and more local policemen (CN 1/89).

A topic that is linked to a variety of themes, mainly traditional values and crime, is drugs. The CP'86 regards both soft and hard drugs as 'enemy number one of the ethnic community'. The poisonous ideas of the (extreme) left and the general moral decay they have caused especially among Dutch youth are perceived as the primary causes of the broad circulation of drugs in the Netherlands. Although the party proposes a more general change in moral values, it mainly wants to fight the drugs menace with law and order solutions: 'death penalty for drug dealers; impounding of all possessions of drug dealers; mandatory detoxication for junkies; and immediate expulsion of foreign junkies' (CN 3/92).

Defense receives little attention in the party literature of the CP'86. The party paper addressed the matter only once or twice, whereas the election programmes always included a separate chapter on defense policy. It originally numbered no less than sixteen demands, of which the main message was full support to NATO and all the obligations that stem from the membership. There was no sign of a militarist outlook, however, and it explicitly stressed the exclusively defensive tasks of the Dutch army, with no mention of any calls for the enlargement of personnel or competencies. The later programmes saw a substantive reduction in the number of points (to six), mainly as a consequence of the changed position towards NATO. The 1993 programme, for example, declared the deployment in peacetime of (parts of) the Dutch army under foreign leadership to be 'in violation of the tasks of our army' (CP 1993: 30.6). The emphasis on the exclusively defensive tasks of the Dutch army has also been sharpened. Whereas the 1990 programme had spoken of this as the 'first and most important task', the 1993 programme stated that the protection of the freedom and independence of the country and its citizens was 'the only task of our army' (CP 1993: 30.2). Moreover, in line with the public debate in the Netherlands, though contrary to the generally militaristic ideal, the party supported the abolition of compulsory military service and the introduction of a professional army (CP 1993: 30.1).

### Ecologism

The environment and its protection are major concerns of the party programmes as well as making for frequent topics in the party papers. The second pivotal term of the 1987 programme, 'livable', referred to a combination of social (protection of certain weaker groups such as disabled and elderly people), nationalist (rejection of the multi-racial society) and ecological views (protection of the environment), of which only the latter one was really prominent in the programme. The chapter on the environment calls for a radical change of mentality towards 'an environmentally conscious acting and thinking' (CP 1987: 21.3). It also includes demands for more policy at all governmental levels to protect the environment as well as for more knowledge and research on environmental problems and environmentally friendly production techniques.

The CP'86 holds an ecological view on the relation between economy and environment. Man should return to his harmonious relation with nature, the ethnic community and the family. Only when man is consciously part of these larger entities can he experience his identity to the full. As man is part of nature, he should take good care of it. According to the pamphlet 'national democratic guidelines regarding protection of our life and our environment', '(e)conomic growth is acceptable only when neither the natural landscape, our environment or the health of the people are destroyed because of it, nor when the natural resources are plundered in an unbridled manner' (CN 1/89). To accomplish this the party presents some concrete measures, such as an increase in the taxation on cars and free public transport. In accordance with its law and order approach the party calls for a tougher policy on pollution, in which the polluter pays. However, real progress can be made only by 'a revolution in human thinking', which would replace materialism and consumerism by 'experiencing nature, the care for irreplaceable cultural values as well as for the social security in the family, in our own area, and in our own country' as constituting the meaning of life and the condition of human happiness (CN 1/89).

The topic of the (protection of the) environment has also increasingly featured in articles about foreigners, especially in the party paper. In the beginning the link between foreigners and the environment was made indirectly, through the issue of overpopulation. The first election programme, for instance, stated that overpopulation forced the Netherlands to a restrictive policy on foreigners as well as stringent rules in the areas of environmental protection and planning (CP 1987: 20.1). The later programmes added a direct linkage to this, declaring that '(o)ur dear fatherland is made unlivable as a consequence of the absolute failures of the government and in part because of the policy on foreigners, which is destructive of the environment' (CP 1993: 21.20).

### Populist anti-party sentiment

One of the dominant features in the party papers is anti-party sentiment which is linked to virtually all other themes, most notably the multi-cultural society. In line with its ethnopluralist vision the party argues that the foreigners are victims too, victims of the multi-cultural society and the integration policies of (national and international) politicians. It is the foreigner policy and the people behind it that are seen as the prime enemies of the ethnic community. Consequently, the party states: 'Our actual goal is not "the removal of the foreigners" but of the clique that has brought them here, keeps them here and that will immediately bring them here again in the case that they will be again "needed"' (CN 2/91). Though the CP'86 mainly targets the established political parties, the 'clique' it speaks of is far bigger.

> At a safe distance from the day-to-day problems and worries of the ordinary man, party bosses, trade unionists, priests, journalists, church officials, radio and tv dictators and more of that riffraff shack up in their remote and, above all, safe villas, wondering about the hostility against foreigners and blathering on about integration, or even worse, deciding that our country is an immigration country. (CN 2/88)

The party considers the fact that the established parties present themselves as different alternatives, by using labels like liberal or socialist, as mere window-dressing. In the eyes of the CP'86 all (major) political parties are responsible for the current misery, which is primarily caused by their 'away-with-our-own-people' politics (a term copied from the VB). There is only one way out of the emerging catastrophe: 'Change the politicians, before they change the ethnic community' (CN 2/93). This change cannot be realised by supporting Janmaat and his CD, however, since that party presents no real alternative to the anti-Dutch clique. Various articles in the party paper accuse them of misusing the issue of nationalism out of political opportunism. The only goal of these 'pseudo-nationalists' is acceptance by the Establishment, not the realisation of genuine nationalist ideals.

There is only one force that can, will and does fight against this evil clique: the ethnic nationalists of the CP'86. This is also acknowledged by the established parties themselves as 'they' consider it ('us') their main enemy. Moreover, this is proven by the fact that the party is attacked so vigorously. Many articles in the paper describe the violations of the democratic rights of the party and its members, ranging from 'state terror' (e.g. arrests, court cases and house searches), attacks by the state's 'subsidised thugs' (e.g. anti-fascists and other left-wing organisations), to elections ('the biggest deception of the public'). The CP'86 is convinced that it is not given an honest chance to compete for the voters' support and consequently considers the Netherlands to be an undemocratic state. That is, for a large part, why the party strives to change 'the political system of the parliamentary dictatorship into that of an ethnic democracy' (CN 3/94).

### Conspiracies

Until 1990 the election programme of the CP'86 had been free from any reference to international conspiracies. The 1987 programme had shown a moderately sceptical world view, being very positive with regard to relations with international organisations like the EC and NATO, but wary of the United Nations. In general the programme was reserved concerning relations with former colonies (except Indonesia) and interference with the internal affairs of sovereign states. The party argued that the Netherlands is a small country and should thus be moderate in its foreign political dealings. By the time of the 1990 programme, however, this moderate scepticism had become more or less open paranoia. The now national democrats took their lead from the International Third Position (ITP) philosophy, which aspires to a nationalist third way between the two imperialist roads of international capitalism/liberalism and international communism/socialism (CP 1990: 29.1). The ITP philosophy introduced a host of dark forces into the programme:

> We consider multinational and international organisations as accomplices of either international capitalism or international communism. With these we have

in mind, for instance, the UN, the EC, the IMF, the World Bank, the World Council of Churches, etc. These organisations are manipulated also by the American CFR (Council for Foreign Relations) which wants to bring about a one-world government. The CFR is hard at work to realise what Brezhnev already predicted in 1975, i.e. the superpower that controls both the Gulf and South Africa controls the whole world, since that superpower controls 75% of the oil supplies and ca. 70% of all strategic minerals on earth. (CP 1990: 29.2)

What had already figured in the party paper now also made its entrance in the election programmes. The CP'86 firmly believes that evil forces are at work behind the scenes. They control all major governments (American, Russian, West European), important international organisations (IMF, World Bank, UN and World Council of Churches) as well as the media (especially the American). The main goal of these sinister forces is to form a one-world government. To achieve this they have to break the spirit of the different ethnic communities, which they do by 'mixing' them and undermining them both mentally and morally (by materialism and consumerism).

In the 1980s the conspiracies had been mainly linked to world communism. Large parts of the party paper were filled with virulent anti-communist articles, dealing for the most part with the atrocities of the USSR and with accusations against the West European (extreme) left for supporting them. The fervent anti-communist stand did not lead to a pro-NATO standpoint, however. The party treated the US as an enemy, which worked secretly together with the USSR. Some articles spoke of the 'Finlandisation of Western Europe', claiming that the US and USSR together kept Europe, Germany in particular, divided so that they could rule the world (a typical NPD argument). Other articles, mainly published before the fall of the Berlin Wall, claimed that the US (especially president Roosevelt) was in reality pro-communist and had given parts of Europe to Stalin. On a higher level these conspiracies were always part of the overriding conspiracy of a one-world government.

### Anti-semitism

Although the party is careful not to state who precisely lies behind the one-world conspiracy it does at times give indications. At the top of the conspiracy are the 'trilateral commissions' and the Bilderberg Group. These organisations are primarily (if not exclusively) formed by Jews, as is 'hinted' by names such as Rothschild, Kissinger and Oppenheimer. At one time the party paper explicitly referred to the *Protocols of the Meetings of the Learned Elders of Zion* (an anti-Semitic forgery of the Czarist secret service) as proof of Jewish involvement (*CN* 1/90). This issue was never distributed for fear of legal punishment, however. In the next issue the matter was phrased with a more veiled wording: 'We know who controls the global media including the international press agencies' (*CN* 2/90).

The occasional anti-Israel articles also fit well into the anti-Semitic conspiracy. Israel, often referred to as 'the Jewish state', is believed to control all Western governments and media, enabling it to build a 'Great Israeli Reich' (*CN* 1/93) without being called to order by the international community. Several European and virtually all American politicians are 'outed' as helpers of Israel in the party paper. Even Janmaat is depicted as a helper of Israel, as he supported the deployment of Dutch Patriot missiles to defend Israel during the Gulf war (in which the CP'86 supported Iraq against the 'imperialist Zionist aggression'). In other articles the party pays disproportionate attention to violence by the Israeli state or citizens against the Palestinians. The CP'86 fully supports the Intifada, the Palestinian uprising in the occupied territories, which it describes as 'a reaction to the genocide policy of the Jewish government' (*CN* 1/92). It demands a boycott of all products from and relationships with Israel and, moreover, advocates immediate military action in the occupied territories as well as the destruction of all nuclear weapons by means of a short-term occupation of Israel (*CN* 2/93).

Another example of anti-Semitic conspiracy thinking was apparent in the many articles on the trial of Ivan Demjanjuk, a Ukrainian-American who was accused of committing war crimes as a Treblinka camp guard during the Second World War. The Israeli court case against Demjanjuk received a lot of attention in the world media as well as in the party paper of the CP'86. From the outset Demjanjuk was depicted in the paper as an innocent man, who was 'extradited by the US to a Jewish blood council' (*CN* 1/89). According to the party the whole purpose of the show trial was to 'keep the memory to the 'continuous story of the six million' alive' (*CN* 1/92). Though this statement hints at a denial of the Holocaust or at least at the accusation that Israel (or 'international Jewry') uses it to further its own goals, revisionism was never openly expressed in the party literature.

### Democracy

All party programmes include positive standpoints on the constitutional state and on parliamentary democracy. The party stresses the need for the different state organs to control and be controlled by each other and by independent outsiders. And from the beginning the CP'86 has pushed for an increase in the influence of the people and for a considerable improvement of the involvement of the citizen with the local and regional councils (CP 1990: 4.4). Remarkably, given its vast critique of politicians, it has also called for an increase in the number of members of both the Senate (from 75 to 100) and the Second Chamber (from 150 to 200). Moreover, the party uses the (unpatriotic) argument that this would bring the Netherlands more in accord with the ratios in other EC countries (CP 1990: 3.7). Notwithstanding its support for the system itself, the CP'86 repeatedly points to the flaws of the current political practice, which according to the party are falsely referred to as the pluralist community. The main thorns concern the lack of freedom of speech (especially for 'nationalists'), the corruption of the Estab-

lishment, and the political control of the judiciary. It wants to (re)create a
real democracy, in which the will of the people can freely develop.

> One condition to accomplish that goal is the full sovereignty of the entire Dutch
> speaking community as a democratic state, which joins all sub-interests as
> guardian of the whole, protects the rights of the own minorities, respects the
> constitution, and is supported as the sovereign by the people. (CP 1989)

In this *volksdemocratie* (ethnic democracy) there will be no place for the
'personal and group egoism [which] have led to an excessive deterioration
of responsible thinking and acting' (CP 1989). What it actually will contain
remains rather vague. 'Power to the people at all governmental levels' (*CN*
3/94), is the only elaboration given to the term. And the only concrete
demand the party has voiced in this regard is the introduction of the so-
called *volksreferendum* (ethnic referendum), an optional plebiscite which is
open exclusively to members of the Dutch ethnic community. Throughout
its existence the CP'86 has supported the introduction of a referendum to
break the power of the corrupt elite and return it to the Dutch people. The
party has also used a more opportunist reasoning: 'Every ethnic referendum
will support us, so we demand the introduction of an ethnic referendum'
(*CN* 1/88). Except for the introduction of a referendum the CP'86 does not
give any details about the creation of the proposed 'three V's', which stand
for *Verandering, Vernieuwing en Verbetering* (change, renewal and improvement).

## Conclusion

The CP'86 does not have a particularly well-developed ideology. Its election
programmes hold scanty introductions, which precede long lists of unsub-
stantiated demands. The only party programme it ever presented was copied
literally from another party. Its paper mainly contains articles on current
affairs. Substantial articles dealing with questions of the present or future are
absent. This notwithstanding, the literature of the CP'86 is larded with
terms that seem to be part of an elaborated ideology, such as 'third way' or
'national revolution'. The elaboration of these terms (and the ideology
behind them) remains vague if not totally absent and, in addition, terms
come in and out of vogue quickly. Originally, the CP'86 remained loyal to
its predecessor by calling itself a 'right-wing political people's party' (CP
1987). At the end of 1988 this was replaced by the label 'the national democratic movement in the Netherlands', and since 1994 the party refers to itself
as a 'national revolutionary party'.

The CP'86 began as a relatively moderate nationalist party in the tradition
of its predecessor the CP. Within a few years it had radicalised into an ethnic
nationalist party, striving for both external exclusiveness and internal
homogenisation. The new goal is an ethnically homogeneous Great-Nether-

lands in which political power is put in the hands of the Dutch people (mainly through the introduction of an ethnic referendum). The main change has to come through policies, most notably ensuring stricter law and order, a return to traditional ethical values and ecological consciousness. The socio-economic policy will support a strong national welfare state. The Great-Netherlands will take its place in a 'Europe of Nations', based on the cooperation of independent and genuine nation-states. This Europe will have to defend itself against the many national and international helpers of the conspiracy to establish a (Jewish) one-world government.

# 7

# Comparative perspectives

Following the detailed analysis at the level of the individual parties, this chapter will now focus on the comparative dimension. At the core of this study is the idea of the party family, a distinct group of parties with a shared core ideology. In the following comparison the similarities of the ideologies of the five parties will therefore be at the fore, albeit in a manner which remains conscious of key differences.

## Comparing the literature

On average the five parties distribute a moderate amount of literature, but there are also large differences within the group. Regarding the externally oriented literature, which is directed at the potential voters, all parties publish some kind of election programme. In almost all cases the first programme was more or less copied from another party or organisation: the CP'86 copied the programme of its predecessor the CP in full, while the CD copied substantial parts of that same programme. The first election programme of the REP was heavily inspired by that of the CSU, from which party its leaders had originally split. The DVU programme is a selection of twelve points from the DV programme, itself a collection of the programmes of its various action groups. The VB published its first election programme only in 1991, but its first programme (of principle) was very similar to that of the Flemish nationalist organisation Were Di.

Most of the parties did not change their election programmes extensively in content or style. The programmes of the DVU and the CD are particularly stable, while the CP'86 changed the outlook rather than the look of its programme. The VB was late in developing a distinct election programme and has since proved rather consistent. The only party that effected substantial changes in both the structure and content of its programme is the REP, which replaced its original CSU-like programme within two years with a far shorter and more radical manifesto. This latter would function as the ideological

core of the later programmes, which maintained the radical tone of the manifesto but combined it with the structure of the first programme.

There are big differences between the parties in terms of the size of the
programmes. At the two extremes are the DVU, with its programme of five
(short) pages, and the REP, with its 1993 programme of one hundred (large)
pages. The election programmes of the other parties average some twenty-
five pages. There are also substantial differences in the variety of party literature distributed by the parties. All parties publish some kind of election
programme, but in the case of the German parties this is the only externally
oriented literature that they distribute. The CP'86 published an additional
programme of principle, while the CD published a thematic brochure. In
both cases, however, the items were more or less copied: the CP'86 literally
translated its first programme of principle of the German NPD, while the
CD distributed a brochure on AIDS which was developed by and for the Unification Church. The only party that issued a wide variety of (original) externally oriented literature is the VB, which began with a programme of
principle and later added election programmes and a range of thematic and
general brochures in the 1990s.

Of all the parties, the DVU is the only one that does not officially publish
internally oriented literature in the form of a party paper. It compensates for
this with the vast amount of literature distributed by the empire of its party
leader, Gerhard Frey, which includes two (previously three) weekly newspapers. The Dutch parties CD and CP'86 issue official party papers although
of a very poor quality (containing various letter types or many language and
typing errors). Moreover, the party papers of the CD appear rather irregu-
larly, the CD-actueel in particular, while the CP'86 paper until recently fluctuated heavily in both structure and volume. The papers of the VB and the
REP make a professional impression, especially since the late 1980s, and are
published regularly (every month) and consistently.

One of the most remarkable differences between the parties is in the
breadth of the literature. At one extreme is the CD, which is virtually a
single-issue party, opposing the creation of a multi-cultural society in the
Netherlands. Few attempts are made in the literature to substantiate this
opposition through ideological arguments. This is not much different from
the DVU, although this party's dominant theme is the rehabilitation of Germany. Both parties address a very limited number of issues and seem to
accept the main socio-political and socio-economic characteristics of the
present society. At the other extreme is the VB which offers a comprehensive ideological programme. Throughout the years, and mainly in the 1990s,
the party consistently extended its programme to cover an increasing range
of topics through thematic conferences and brochures. The other two parties are in between these extremes, but differ substantially from each other.
The REP has never claimed to be an ideological party and started out more
or less pragmatically, copying most of its programme from the CSU but with-

out the Christian outlook. Soon afterwards it radicalised and became overtly nationalist, but the party never reputed its claim or put much effort into the development of its own ideology. The CP'86, on the other hand, has always claimed to be an ideological party, and although it uses a discourse that suggests an elaborated ideological programme, it has never developed an ideology (of its own) and has proven very inconsistent in its terminology.

## Evaluating the analysis

Most studies of party ideology use only election programmes as the source of analysis. These programmes have the advantage of being officially endorsed by the party membership or leadership and consequently 'represent and express the policy collectively adopted by the party' (Borg 1966: 97). However, this is also the main problem with election programmes: that is, they deal with *policy* rather than *ideology*. If this analysis had been based exclusively on the election programmes of the five parties, for example, the picture of the core 'ideology' of the different parties would certainly have appeared different, first and foremost because the ideological arguments behind policies are at best often vague, and at worst absent. In addition, similar policy demands can be based on different arguments (in different countries). For example, the call for unification by the German parties is based on legal arguments such as upholding the German constitution and international law, while the same call by the VB and the CP'86 is based on nationalist arguments of external exclusiveness.

In addition, most (extreme right) political parties follow more or less the same structure in their election programmes. Hence, ideologically different parties address often similar issues. A good example is the environment, an issue which has been absent from few election programmes since the rise of Green parties in the 1980s. Another example is socio-economic policy, which features prominently in many programmes and which might explain why some authors choose to emphasise this particular aspect of the ideology of extreme right parties (e.g. Betz 1994; Kitschelt 1995). In both cases the number of demands appears to indicate the importance of the issue, and the content of the demands appears to point to a certain ideological outlook. These indications remain vague, however, and sometimes contrast with the attention they receive and with the positions that are adopted elsewhere in the party literature.

Given the often shallow character of election programmes it is difficult if not impossible to determine the importance of the different features within the (core) ideology of the party. To apply the *causal chain approach* one not only needs the arguments that lie behind the individual policy demands, but also a substantiated description of a more holistic nature, such as, for instance, those which address the desired model of human cooperation or state organisation. The addition of party programmes or so-called programmes of principle proved to be very fruitful in this respect, as they provide a more elaborated and thorough description of the party's (fundamental) values and goals. Unfortunately, however, not all parties publish such programmes, and hence party papers were seen to provide effective substitutes. Party papers are usually less elaborated in argument than party programmes, but are clearly more elaborated than election programmes. Moreover, party papers provide a clear indication of the importance of the various ideological traits, especially in terms of how *often* and how *centrally* they feature within the broader ideological argument.

The key question that remains, of course, is whether these sources reveal all that there is. Some authors, for example, claim that extreme right parties in particular do not show their true face 'front-stage', i.e. to the general public, but reserve it for the 'back-stage', i.e. the real supporters (see Van Donselaar 1991: 16; also Eatwell 1992: 174). However, this thesis is difficult to validate or even to test since, in contrast to the front-stage, the back-stage is not that easy to define and analyse. Who are the 'real supporters'? Moreover, can the back-stage be researched at all? To avoid the thesis from becoming a conspiracy theory in which the back-stage is always the one behind that which is being researched (cf. Dahl's (1989: 272) argument regarding the testing of theories of minority domination), this study has sought to distinguish the two 'stages' of the parties on the basis of the primary orientation of the party literature. Externally oriented literature such as election and party programmes, as well as brochures, were taken as indicators of the front-stage, whereas internally oriented literature such as party papers were seen as indicators of the back-stage.

In one of the few similar studies of party ideology, both in sources and in method, Spruyt (1995: 263–76) comes to the conclusion that the VB deceives its voters by presenting different themes in its propaganda (front-stage) to those in its programme (back-stage). There are two reasons why this conclusion is too harsh. First, the selection of propaganda material is too confined, since it includes exclusively literature that is distributed on the initiative of the party itself and therefore excludes, for example, election and party programmes. Second, the difference that Spruyt depicts is mainly in the elaboration of the themes rather than in the ideological position that is taken in the different sources. The VB does not present a different *ideological* position in its propaganda; it simply does not present the ideological *argument* in its entirety. To a large extent this is the result of the strict selection of the propaganda items, since election pamphlets generally include only a few (catchy) slogans and (short) demands rather than the ideological elaboration of these slogans and demands.

What is most important to emphasise, however, is that when the front-stage and back-stage are defined on the basis of the primary orientation of the party literature, the differences between the externally and internally oriented literature of the individual parties can be seen to be generally limited to secondary features and themes. In fact, and this must be underlined, the core ideology of the parties is (prominently) present in the entire literature. If there is one exception in this regard, then it is the DVU, which does not publish its own official party paper. Even in this case, however, both the externally and the internally oriented literature do reflect the core ideology of the party. Moreover, when we apply the same distinction to the VB, we can see a remarkable similarity in ideological content, with even the more sensitive features such as ethnopluralism and revisionism featuring in both sources. Indeed, the only small proof of the thesis that certain particularly sensitive features are hidden from the front-stage is found in the fact that anti-Semitism is exclusively expressed back-stage, i.e. through the internally oriented literature. However, although the ideology of the 'extreme right' might include more of such sensitive features than other parties, they are certainly not the only parties that keep these features from the general public. More to the point, they express (most of) their core ideology quite openly in their literature.

## Comparing the ideology

### Nationalism

All of these parties are nationalist parties (see table 7.1, which offers a summary of the relevance to each party of the various features discussed in this section), striving for the congruence of state (the political unit) and nation (the cultural unit). In the case of the VB, nationalism is primarily expressed through the demand for Flemish independence: the party wants to divide Belgium and create a sovereign Flemish state. The two German parties DVU and REP voice their nationalism chiefly through the demand for complete German independence, claiming that Germany is still limited in its sovereignty by the (former) Allies. This demand has become somewhat less prominent since the four-by-two agreement in 1990, which was seen as the basis for not only the German unification but also the 'normalisation' of the international position of Germany.

In the case of the two Dutch parties, CD and CP'86, nationalism is predominantly expressed though the demand for *internal homogenisation*, i.e. the claim that only members of the Dutch nation are permitted to live in the Dutch state. For the CP'86 this primarily means that all non-European foreigners have to repatriate while European foreigners can assimilate, whereas the CD wants all foreigners to either assimilate or repatriate. The nationalist sub-feature of internal homogenisation is also prominent in the party literature of the other three parties. The VB, for example, makes a similar distinction as the CP'86 between Europeans and non-Europeans – the German parties do not address this issue in detail. What all five parties have in common is the idea that their country should be (at least) mono-cultural and that this should be realised by an active state policy of (at least) repatriation.

The second nationalist sub-feature, *external exclusiveness*, constitutes part of the ideologies of only the VB and the CP'86. Both parties strive for the inclusion of *all* members of the Dutch ethnic community within the Dutch state, which means the unification of the Netherlands and Flanders into a Great-Netherlands state. The VB explicitly states that this should be a federalist state, whereas the CP'86 does not address this issue. Surprisingly, both parties mention this relatively radical ideal of a Great-Netherlands principally in their externally oriented literature, most notably in their programmes of principle. In the case of the VB this might be the result of the fact that the party considers unification undesirable in the short term, given that the party believes that the (Northern) Netherlands is currently undergoing a process of left-wing decay.

*Table 7.1*   Summary table of ideological features per party[a]

| Feature | REP | DVU | VB | CD | CP'86 |
|---|---|---|---|---|---|
| Nationalism | C | C | C | C | C |
|   Internal homogenisation | C | C | C | C | C |
|   External exclusiveness | i | i | C | | C |
|   Ethnic nationalism | i | i | C | | C |
|   State nationalism | | | | C | |
| Exclusionism | | | | | |
|   Ethnopluralism | | i | C | | C |
|   Anti-Semitism | p | C | | | C |
| Xenophobia | C | C | C | C | C |
| Strong state | | | | | |
|   Law and order | C | C | C | C | C |
|   Militarism | | i | | | |
| Welfare chauvinism | C | C | C | C | C |
| Traditional ethics | C | p | C | p | p |
| Revisionism | C | C | C | | i |

[a] I have left out ideosyncratic (core) features, such as in the case of the DVU chauvinism or ecologism for the CP'86.
(C = core; p = present, not core; i = indication, not explicit).

Despite the fact that the literature of both German parties is drenched with expressions of open support of German unification, which is perceived as most important and urgent, the DVU and REP adopt legal rather than nationalist arguments in support of their case. Both claim that the German constitution as well as international law still recognises the 'German Reich of 1937' and consequently demand the reinstatement of these borders through negotiations. The unification of 1990 was regarded as just a first step in the process of full 'reunification', as it included only West Germany (the FRG) and 'Central Germany' (as they call the former GDR), and not the genuine East Germany (the so-called *Ostgebiete* behind the Oder-Neiße border). Moreover, and in contrast with the assumptions of external exclusiveness, the parties also accept the fact that certain parts of the German nation live outside of the German state. For example, although they both consider the Austrians to be part of the German nation, they accept the fact that they live in an independent Austrian state.

These variations are the result of a more fundamental distinction, namely that between *ethnic* and *state nationalism*. The VB and the CP'86 are ethnic nationalist parties and consider the ethnic community as the prime basis for human organisation and social solidarity. The ethnic community is defined on the basis of ethnic criteria, mainly through blood ties. Members of the Dutch ethnic community are (only) those who are born to Dutch parents, and ethnic nationalists consider the state as nothing more than the political arm of the ethnic community. The state should therefore have the same borders as the ethnic community, a goal which can be realised by separation and unification. In the case of the VB the two are even combined, since the party first wants to separate Flanders from Belgium and then to unify Flanders with the Netherlands into a federal Dutch state.

State nationalists, on the other hand, consider the state as the prime basis of human organisation and solidarity. The nation is constituted from the people that are born within the state borders or that live within the state and want to naturalise. The nation has to be culturally homogeneous but not necessarily ethnically homogeneous. This is why state nationalist parties emphasise *both* repatriation *and* assimilation as policies to make the state internally homogeneous. Of the five parties, the CD is, in fact, the only state nationalist party. The two German parties are clearly nationalist, and use ethnic nationalist rhetoric (with terms such as *Volksgemeinschaft*). However, the literature of the parties specifies neither the criterion for defining the 'own group' nor the specific relationship between state and nation, and it thereby clouds their categorisation within the different subgroups.

## Exclusionism

In line with the difference in nationalism the parties also vary in the arguments they use to include and exclude people from the 'own group'. The two ethnic nationalist parties VB and CP'86 are openly *ethnopluralist*, believing that people are inextricably linked to a specific ethnic community and that both the people and their ethnic communities are unequal but equivalent. Hence, they demand the repatriation of foreigners on the grounds that all people should live 'according to their own nature'. However, as they believe that Europeans are linked by a sort of European meta-culture, these parties also accept the possibility of assimilation in the case of European foreigners. The ideologies of the two German parties are too nebulous to include such elaborated world views as ethnopluralism, although vague indications are present in the literature of the DVU. The state nationalism of the CD, on the other hand, does not allow for ethnopluralism, and with the exception of an occasional hint, this kind of argument is absent from the literature of that party.

*Racism* is not an evident part of the party ideology of any of the five parties. The majority of the parties do not even formally speak of 'races' and the two parties that use this terminology (the VB and the CP'86) express a belief in the existence of different races without proclaiming the superiority of any one of these. For the CP'86 in particular the distinction of humans into races precedes that into ethnic communities and seems to be of even greater importance. It primarily demands the separation of races and is far less strict with regard to the separation of different ethnic communities within one race (the VB has a similar argument but within the European meta-culture). Whether the absence of an openly expressed belief in hierarchy of races is caused by legal pressure, especially in Germany and the Netherlands (see Van Donselaar 1995), is impossible to ascertain on the basis of this study.

What speaks against a moderating effect of legal pressure is the fact that *anti-Semitism* is clearly visible in the case of both German parties (mainly the DVU) and the CP'86. While the CD and the VB do not consider Jews to be an issue and neither attack nor address them, the three other parties persistently portray Jews in a negative manner in their literature. The REP mainly addresses Jews in reaction to allegations of racism and anti-Semitism by Jewish persons and organisations, while the DVU shows an interest in Jews (and Israel) that borders on an obsession. The three parties generally address Jews as part of a classic conspiracy theory in which they are portrayed as a closed group of internationally powerful people that conspire either against Germany (in the case of the DVU and, to a lesser extent, the REP) or are trying to create a one-world government (in the case of the CP'86).[1]

### Xenophobia

As is evident from the whole party literature, and most notably the party papers, all parties are xenophobic. Everything what is considered 'alien', or deviating from their own nation and conventions, is portrayed as negative and is perceived as threatening. This applies not only to the cultural values of other ethnic communities, but also to the values of particular minorities within their own ethnic community, such as homosexuals and the left. Moreover, xenophobia has an international dimension in that all of the parties perceive the world as hostile towards their own group. In this respect the German parties point mainly to the actions of the former Allies, while the CP'86 sees a conspiracy to establish a one-world government. All parties perceive the process of European integration in general, and the abolition of

---

[1] As the parties never describe Jews in strictly racial terms and primarily address the threat of Jewish power, their anti-Semitism is closer to xenophobia than to racism.

internal borders in particular, as a threat to the character of their own group. Except for the CD, the parties all also point to the threat of the growing influence of American culture ('Cocacolonisation') in Europe.

Most attention in the xenophobic party literature is paid to the threat of (mass) immigration and the creation of a multi-cultural society. All parties portray an image of a 'flood' of immigrants which is out of control and which is kept hidden by 'the Establishment'. Immigrants are seen as competitors, since they take away jobs, money and houses from the 'own people'. They are also linked to every other threat or problem in the country (and even in Western Europe more generally), such as rising crime, moral decay, or in the case of the Dutch parties (most notably the CD), overpopulation. The multi-cultural society is portrayed as a 'multi-criminal society'; indeed, according to the ethnic nationalists (VB and CP'86), this is inevitable since the people that live outside their own ethnic community become uprooted and consequently morally degenerate, whereas the other parties claim simply that the immigrants do not want to integrate.

Though the xenophobic propaganda of all five parties is rather similar in argumentation, there are differences in the groups that function as the main targets in the respective literature. Originally the VB had targeted mainly European immigrants, but it shifted in the 1980s to the group that is also the main target of the two Dutch parties, Muslim immigrants from Turkey and Morocco in particular. In addition to the usual allegations about foreigners (lazy, criminal, backward), the Muslims are depicted as the fifth column of a fundamentalist and backward religion. Asylum seekers generally featured less prominently in the literature of the Dutch speaking parties, though this changed when this issue gained salience in the public debate in these countries during the 1990s. In the case of the German parties asylum seekers have always been the most targeted group of foreigners, even though their importance increased even more during the asylum debate in the early 1990s. For these parties the Muslim immigrants seem to constitute a major new target in their xenophobic propaganda.

### The strong state

A general belief in the importance of *law and order* is present in the ideology of all five parties, though only the VB expresses this in an open manner, stating that human life is only possible in a well-ordered community. In the case of the other parties the belief is mainly addressed by means of a rejection of permissiveness and the call for a strong state. This strong state should provide for a police force that is extensive in terms of personnel, equipment and competencies. Moreover, the judiciary system should be purged of left-wing elements and should deliver harsher sentences which would then be executed to the full, under strict conditions and covering a wider variety of crimes. Except for the VB and the REP, all parties call for the introduction of the death penalty. The issue of crime is also generally linked to that of immigration and increasingly to that of 'the left' in general, and to 'anti-fascists' in particular.

In contrast to their strict and prominent law and order position, the parties are relatively modest in their attention to and position on defense issues, showing no signs of *militarism*. All election programmes include a section on defense in which the institution of a national army is supported, albeit without calling for significant expansions in personnel or competencies. Moreover, the parties stress the purely defensive tasks of the army and are wary of international deployment. Most parties accepted NATO as a lesser of two evils during the Cold War, for example, and since then they have found in international Islam a new reason for continuing that support. The CP'86, however, changed to an openly anti-NATO position at the end of the 1980s, following its 'conversion' to national democracy.

A special position is taken by the DVU, which is the only party that shows signs of a militaristic outlook, and it supports a strong army in which civilians are not expected to play a leading role. More importantly, it argues that the German army should be strictly independent, and consequently it has always opposed NATO membership. The foundation of its militaristic position is to be found in the legacy of the past rather than in present day politics, however. Indeed, one of the most prominent features of Frey's newspapers in particular has been the rehabilitation of the German soldiers who fought during the Second World War and time and again the militaristic virtues of these soldiers are applauded as part of this rehabilitation.

### Welfare chauvinism

Socio-economic policy features prominently in the externally oriented literature of all five parties, yet is far less visible in their internally oriented literature. Only the party papers of the REP and the CD devote regular attention to this theme, albeit without presenting a clear socio-economic programme. As with all other parties, they support the core aspects of the current system of a mixed economy in their respective countries, and only the VB tries to present a more or less alternative system based on a sense of solidarism. For the VB, the solidarist 'people's economy' is achievement-oriented and builds on the duty to work and on the central role of the family. This solidarist system does not differ very much from the systems of the mixed economy favoured by the other parties, however, which are also (more or less) achievement-oriented and family-friendly. Despite the fact that all parties support some form of welfare state, most regularly cite neo-liberal rhetoric and return regularly to various neo-liberal hobby horses, such as the limitation of public subsidies and an emphasis on the 'squandermania' of the state and its bureaucracy.

The main distinctive feature of the socio-economic policy of all parties is *welfare chauvinism*: that is, they believe that the fruits of the national economy should first and foremost (if not exclusively) come to the benefit of their 'own people'. This means not only that jobs and money should be used for their own people rather than for immigrants, but also that the state should protect certain sectors of the 'native economy' against foreign competition. All parties stress the importance of national agricultural production, for example, although this point is most prominently emphasised in the (early) literature of the REP. Even in the beginning, when the party programme still included a pro-EC position as part of the legacy of its CSU origins, the REP paper called for the protection of German farmers to the point of leaving the EC. In addition, a call for support for their 'own' small businesses and for the protection of this 'backbone of the national economy' against multi-nationals is present in the whole literature of all five parties. These points became more prominent with the increasing level of European integration, and most notably the signing of the Maastricht Treaty, which all parties consider a serious threat to the viability of the national economy.

### Traditional ethics

Though all parties hold a traditional view on ethical values, not all devote much attention to the issue in their literature. Moreover, some parties worry mainly about and warn against the alleged ongoing process of moral decay (the REP), which is part of an international conspiracy (the CP'86), while others present an elaborated alternative programme (the VB). All parties, however, stress the importance of the traditional nuclear family (including one man, one woman and many children) and reject any possible threat against it (such as abortion, homosexuality or divorce). Moreover, with regard to gender relations most parties also (try to) present themselves as more progressive than they actually are. Despite efforts to accept the working woman, most parties see women first and foremost as mothers, although this is less the case for the Dutch parties. In general the values that are defended are presented as part of a European culture which is based on both Christian and humanist traditions. Christianity itself is not an issue for the parties and they are generally hostile towards 'organised Christianity' (Church authorities), which is portrayed as degenerated, left-wing and anti-national (especially in the case of the German parties).

### Revisionism

One of the aspects in which the two Dutch parties deviate most clearly from the other three parties is in the fact that they devote almost no attention to the Second World War. In sharp contrast, the party papers of the DVU deal more with this issue than with current affairs. Most of the articles that address the role of the Germans during the war, and its legacy on post-war Germany, contain a clearly revisionist view. Either they call for the rehabilitation of German soldiers and their actions or they stress the war crimes of the Allies during and after the war (so-called *Aufrechnung*). The party never goes so far as to condone (major aspects of) Nazi-Germany, however. The

REP shares this feature of revisionism with the DVU, although it is more moderate in its arguments and in the attention it devotes to the topic. For the REP in general, and for Schönhuber in particular, revisionism is mainly part of the attack against alleged anti-national politicians (among their favourite targets was former German President Richard von Weiszäcker).

The VB also devotes a lot of attention to the legacy of the Second World War, most notably through the issue of amnesty. As in the case of the two German parties, it identifies with those who lost the war, the radical wing of the Flemish movement, but without fully condoning their ideology. However, whereas the German parties mainly try to defend the actions of the German soldiers by pointing to their lack of choice ('they had to do their duty') or by pointing to similar actions by soldiers of other countries (mainly from the former Allies), the VB openly condones the actions of the Flemish collaborators. According to the party they acted 'for the good of Flanders' and that is the only criterion for deciding between good and evil. Moreover, while the German parties keep some distance from 'contaminated' people (this applies less to the DVU) the VB openly applauds former leading collaborators and accepts them in leading positions within the party.

## The extreme right party family: fact or fiction?

In the first chapter I discussed the (comparative) literature on extreme right parties of the third wave (1980–99). As could be seen, different scholars grouped different parties together and did this under different labels. Some consensus could nevertheless be uncovered. First, the term extreme right (or right-wing extremist) is still broadly accepted as the most satisfying collective noun. Second, this term is generally used to describe an ideology containing a combination of several distinct features. Third, and despite several borderline cases, there is a large number of political parties whose extreme right status is not debated. On the basis of this consensus, the following propositions were constructed:

1   The extreme right party family consists of a distinct group of parties that shares a common ideological core.
2   This common ideological core includes (at least) that combination of features generally defined as right-wing extremist.
3   Within the broader extreme right party family at least two subgroups can be distinguished on the basis of ideological extremity.

Having compared the literature and ideology of the parties in detail, I will now turn my attention to the consequences of these findings for the 'extreme right party family'. In the following discussion, I will assess in what way the findings support or reject each of the three propositions.

### The common ideological core

The foregoing analysis has clearly demonstrated that all five parties share an ideological core which is built around the nucleus of *nationalism*. All parties are first and foremost nationalist parties, aspiring for the congruence of state (the political unit) and nation (the cultural unit). The state should implement a policy of *internal homogenisation* to create a mono-cultural society which at least includes the repatriation of (some) foreigners. In addition, *xenophobia* determines the world view of the parties in which everything 'abnormal' (or better: that which is perceived as deviating from their own nation and conventions) is seen as negative and threatening. This includes both 'internal enemies' (e.g. immigrants, homosexuals) and 'external enemies' (e.g. supranational organisations). The combination of nationalism and xenophobia determines the preferred socio-economic policies of the parties, which can best be described as *welfare chauvinist*; that is, the state should ensure that employment and welfare policies work to the (exclusive) benefit of 'the own people'. Consequently, foreign policy should be directed at protecting the sovereignty of the own state and at the welfare of the own people. A fourth core ideological feature is a belief in *law and order*, in which the state should maintain a strict legal system and should enforce these rules actively and rigorously. Again, the underlying arguments are based on nationalism and xenophobia, i.e. protecting the nation from evil outside forces. For all parties this belief in law and order includes a moral dimension, though this is not always a core feature of the party ideology.

Before testing whether the core ideology is also indeed extreme right, as is generally assumed, the matter of distinctiveness may be taken a step further, by questioning the extent to which this core might also be shared by two other groups of parties that are sometimes believed to overlap considerably with the (alleged) extreme right family: left-wing extremist parties and (neo-)conservative parties. For example, one of the theoretical schools within the study of right-wing extremism (see Mudde 1996), the extremism-theoretical school, emphasises the similarities between right-wing and left-wing extremist parties, pitting both against (left-wing and right-wing) democratic parties. Moreover, the shared core feature of all these 'extremist' parties is generally defined as the rejection of (core aspects of) democracy (e.g. Backes 1989; Pfahl-Traughber 1992). In this case, however, as we have seen, rejection of democracy is not in fact part of the core ideology of the five parties with which this study is concerned; indeed, despite much criticism, all five accept (parliamentary) democracy. Moreover, while some authors have argued that pluralism is a core feature of democracy, and that extremist parties are essentially anti-pluralist or better monist in that they treat cleavages and ambivalences as illegitimate (e.g. Lipset and Raab 1970), this is also not that helpful for an understanding of this group of parties. For although the core ideology of the five parties includes some form of monism, most notably in the struggle for a *mono*-cultural state, on other aspects the parties do accept a plurality of ideas and organisations.

A more problematic border seems to exist between extreme right and (neo)conservative parties. According to some authors these two groups are part of the same 'silent counter-revolution' (Ignazi 1992). Neo-conservatism has been primarily associated with a political philosophy within Anglo-Saxon countries (with thinkers like Daniel Bell, Nathan Glazer and Peter Viereck), with the most significant party political representatives being probably the Conservative Party under Margaret Thatcher and the Republican Party under Ronald Reagan. What characterised these parties was first and foremost 'a revival of classical liberalism' (Green 1987: 2), with the core of the neo-conservative ideology being summarised as a combination of economic liberalism and socio-cultural conservatism (cf. Dubiel 1987; Girvin 1988; Ignazi 1992). It is particularly in the feature of socio-cultural conservatism that a similarity between the extreme right and neo-conservatism can be seen. For, although this is not part of the core ideology of the 'family', all five parties certainly do share a (secular) traditional ethical view, and in the case of some parties (most notably the VB), it is even a core feature of the party ideology. Various authors (e.g. Ignazi 1992; Betz 1994; Kitschelt 1995) have also stressed the salience of economic liberalism for extreme right parties. Indeed, some definitions of radical right (populist) parties come very close to the definition of neo-conservatism. As noted, however, these five parties do not in fact advocate 'rightist free market economics', as Kitschelt (1995: 2) argues, but rather support some form of welfare system, if only for their 'own people'. Moreover, the two groups of parties differ even more fundamentally in that the extreme right parties in general, and the ethnic nationalists in particular, put their emphasis on the collective, whereas neo-conservatives put an emphasis on the individual. In addition, while neo-conservative parties appear to accept the primacy of economics, 'extreme right' parties are intent on restoring the primacy of (national) politics.

### An extreme right core

Having established that the core ideology of the five parties is distinctive, both in general and in relation to the core of left-wing extremism and neo-conservatism, I now turn to the question whether this core ideology does indeed fit the label 'extreme right', as is generally assumed to be the case. As we have seen (on pp. 10–11), the concept of right-wing extremism is usually defined as a political ideology composed of a number of different features. Five such features are mentioned in particular, in one form or another, by a majority of the authors involved: nationalism, racism (including ethnopluralism), xenophobia, anti-democracy and the strong state (Mudde 1995: 206). To speak of right-wing extremism in this sense does not require that all five features need be present, but rather that there should be *a* combination of some of the features. Three different approaches to the problem of defining the necessary combination of features can be distinguished: a quantitative, a qualitative and a mixed approach (Mudde 1995: 218–19).

In a quantitative approach all five features are considered of equal importance and the only criterion used to define the necessary combination of features is the actual *number* of features. So, for example, one can argue that at least half of the features should be present, which means three or more. In this study, we have indeed found that half of the five features that are part of the definition of right-wing extremism are also part of the common ideological core of the five parties, namely nationalism, xenophobia and law and order (the latter as part of the strong state). Consequently, if the quantitative criterion is set at (at least) half of the number of features, the combination of nationalism, xenophobia and law and order is sufficient to constitute right-wing extremism, and the party family identified in this study can be said to hold an extreme right core ideology.

In the qualitative approach, on the other hand, one or more features are considered to be 'more equal' than others: for instance, in the extremism-theoretical tradition there can be no (right-wing) extremism without the feature of anti-democracy. So even if all four of the other features are present, they would not constitute extremism. As we have already seen above, the core ideology of the five parties does not include the feature of anti-democracy and therefore the party family is not (right-wing) extremist according to the extremist-theoretical school. However, if the prime feature were to be nationalism or xenophobia, the parties would certainly be labelled extreme right.

The third approach combines the quantitative and qualitative approaches: for example, it requires at least two features, and of these two at least one has to be 'exclusionist' (i.e. nationalism, racism or xenophobia) and at least one has to be 'hierarchic' (i.e. anti-democracy or strong state). Utilising this combination of one exclusionist and one hierarchic feature, a combination which is also revealed in studies of right-wing extremism at the individual level (Meijerink et al. 1998), the core of the party family can again be classified as extreme right. Two features of the core ideology can be categorised as exclusionist (nationalism and xenophobia), while law and order is a hierarchic feature.

In conclusion, the core of the party family ideology identified in this analysis, which entails a combination of nationalism, welfare chauvinism, xenophobia and law and order, can be labelled extreme right according to all three approaches, though it seems to constitute a borderline case. Moreover, a problem that any scholar of the extreme right is confronted with, is that semantically the terms 'extreme right' and 'right-wing extremist' point to the wrong direction. After all, the extreme right ideology is neither an extreme form of right-wing thinking, as the communist theory postulates (e.g. Kühnl 1992), nor a right-wing form of extremist thinking, as the extremism-theoretical school argues (e.g. Backes 1989).

This might be the reason that a growing group of scholars work with alternative labels, often explicitly denouncing the term extreme right. However, as has been argued above (in chapter 1, pp. 11–14), these 'new' labels are generally defined in rather similar terms and therefore hardly constitute real alternatives. This is most notably the case with the term 'radical right', which is also most often used interchangeably with the term 'extreme right'. But even most definitions of the various forms of 'populism' do not differ much from those of 'right-wing extremism'. The main advantage that these definitions offer is that they generally do not (explicitly) include the feature of anti-democracy (see Backes 1991; Taggart 1995), nor its semantic meaning. This said, they put the emphasis on the feature of populism, which is predominantly defined as a particular political style rather than a specific ideological feature (e.g. Betz 1994; Pfahl-Traughber 1994). As the concept of party family is defined in (exclusively) ideological terms, this would mean stretching the concept.

A final option would be to use either more or less demanding concepts, i.e. to travel up or down Sartori's famous ladder of abstraction (Sartori 1970). At the bottom of that ladder one would find the most demanding concepts like fascism and National Socialism, which generally include the five features of right-wing extremism *as well as* some additional features. Though some of these additional features are of an ideological nature, such as 'palingenesis' (Griffin 1995) or a 'Third Way' (Eatwell 1995), most refer to forms of political organisation or style (e.g. Payne 1995). In either case, the term fascism offers no way out, introducing either even more demanding or non-ideological features. In contrast, concepts at a higher ladder of abstraction, most notably nationalism, are too general and provide too little discriminating power. Though the identified ideological core is clearly nationalist, not all nationalisms include also the features of xenophobia and law and order (e.g. Kohn 1945; Tamir 1993).

It seems therefore most useful to stick with the term 'extreme right'. Though the ideological core falls only just within the definition of right-wing extremism, and the term provides some semantical confusion, alternative labels do not overcome these problems. Therefore, they do not justify the rejection of what is still the most generally used term to describe this particular party family.

### A moderate and a radical subgroup

The third proposition holds that all extreme right parties can be grouped together on the basis of a certain shared core of ideological features, while at the same time certain parties can also be grouped together in subgroups based on a more specific core. What is essential in this approach to classification is that these subgroups also share all features of the whole group (cf. Sartori 1970), such that while the extreme right party family as a whole shares the core ideology of the four features listed above, the subgroups will have to share these four features *and* one or more additional features.

The most commonly identified basis for distinction between subgroups of extreme right parties is the presence/absence of a 'fascist legacy', which in essence is seen to emerge in the party's (negative) position on democracy. This has been elaborated most explicitly by Ignazi (1992), who defines the whole extreme right party family on the basis of two criteria and adds a third criterion to distinguish between two subgroups. So while all extreme right parties are placed at the far right of the national political spectrum (the spatial criterion) and have a negative attitude toward the political system (the attitudinal-systemic criterion), one subgroup includes features of a 'fascist corpus' in its party ideology (the old/traditional subgroup) and one does not (the new/post-industrial subgroup). The subgroup of the new/post-industrial extreme right parties is considered to be more 'moderate', while the old/traditional subgroup is depicted as more 'radical'. Indeed, rejection versus acceptance of the democratic system is usually also seen as the main distinction between right-wing extremist and right-wing populist parties, although most authors use this criterion to distinguish between two groups rather than two *sub*groups (e.g. Backes 1991; Betz 1994; Taggart 1995).

In contrast to the views of these authors the analysis of the ideology of these five parties does not support a distinction within the group on the basis of their stand on democracy. All five parties accept democracy, including the CP'86 and the DVU which are generally classified as old/traditional extreme right (see Ignazi 1992: 10). The criterion of 'a fascist legacy', though creating more problems in its application, leads to the same conclusion. According to Ignazi, the criterion is to be interpreted simply as 'a reference to myths, symbols, slogans of the inter-war fascist experience' (1992: 10). If applied somewhat loosely, this would mean that all parties except for the CD would qualify as being old/traditional extreme right parties. If applied rigidly, only the VB (if any) would qualify, since this party is at least the most open and positive in its references to (Flemish) inter-war fascist movements. In both instances, however, the two subgroups would include totally different parties than those identified in the general classifications (Ignazi 1992; see also Kitschelt 1995).

Even more important is the fact that the distinction between subgroups on the basis of a fascist legacy or (anti-)democratic character does not address the core of the ideologies of these parties. As noted, all extreme right parties share an ideological core of nationalism, welfare chauvinism, law and order and xenophobia. The main ideological distinction within this extreme right family is therefore between the *ethnic* and *state nationalist* parties. Thus, the ethnic nationalist subgroup combines the extreme right core with an ethnic nationalist and ethnopluralist outlook. Within this view their own group, their own ethnic community, is defined on the basis of a (rigid) ethnic criterion and should live according to its own nature. This means that the congruence of state and ethnic community is accomplished by both internal homogenisation (repatriation) *and* external exclusiveness (unification or separation). The second subgroup holds a state nationalist outlook in which their own group is defined on the basis of a civic (and more flexible) criterion. Generally, all people who are born within a certain state or who want to naturalise are considered as part of their own group. The congruence of state and nation is to be accomplished exclusively by internal homogenisation, and more concretely by the choice between assimilation or repatriation.

Two of the five parties belong to the subgroup of the *ethnic extreme right parties*, namely the VB and the CP'86. To some extent this subgroup most closely resembles the generally accepted image of the extreme right party, since it is generally ethnic nationalism that is described as 'extreme', or 'ultra' nationalism and ethnopluralism that is generally depicted as racism in the many definitions of right-wing extremism (see Herz 1975; Mudde 1995). Given the fact that it uses a more rigid criterion for defining its own group, it can also be labelled the (more) 'radical' subgroup. The 'moderate' subgroup of the *state extreme right parties* includes only one of the five parties, namely the CD. This leaves us with the two German parties DVU and REP, which are clearly part of the extreme right family, but which cannot be categorised in one of these two subgroups. This results for the most part from the vagueness of their ideological programmes, as neither party clearly identifies the basis of its definition of its 'own group'.

Finally, it is also worth noting that various authors have linked the extremity of the ideology of extreme right parties with the levels of their electoral success. Indeed, most authors believe that ideologically 'moderate' extreme right parties are electorally more successful than the ideologically 'radical' parties (e.g. Ignazi 1992; Greß 1994; Kitschelt 1995; Jackman and Volpert 1996). Following the distinction of this study, between a radical subgroup of ethnic nationalist and a moderate subgroup of state nationalist extreme right parties, the VB and CP'86 belong to the radical subgroup while the CD constitutes the moderate 'subgroup'. And although the number of parties is rather small, not least because of the fact that the two German parties cannot be categorised into either of the two subgroups, the proposition that moderate extreme right parties are electorally most successful is not sustained. The radical subgroup contains both the most and the least successful parties (the VB and CP'86 respectively) and the 'moderate' CD falls in between these two. Consequently, the difference in the electoral performance of parties within the group(s) is not only larger than that between the groups, but it is also confounded by the case of the VB, which is by far the most successful in electoral terms, and at the same time the most radical in ideological terms.

## Final thoughts

As of yet, the research on political parties in general and party families in particular that has been conducted on the basis of an ideological approach has been very limited in both range and quantity. This lack of research is particularly apparent in comparative studies (Lawson 1976; Dierickx 1994), and seriously constrains the capacity of cross-national research to build on a notion of the party family as a means of determining which parties may be usefully compared to one another. And although this study has focused only on extreme right parties, and moreover within only a limited number of countries, it hopes to have provided a more general model for such research which could be applicable to all sorts of parties (extreme right or otherwise) and in all types of countries (also beyond Western Europe).

This study also reveals the limitations of the ideological approach. In-depth studies of party ideologies are clearly very time consuming and are therefore limited in the extent to which they can be usefully employed. Moreover, every researcher is not only limited by time but also by language, and given that these studies must include the analysis of primary literature, which is usually available only in the original language, the number of parties that can be studied by any single researcher is unquestionably limited (no matter how much time is available). There are, however, some ways in which to overcome most of these practical problems. For one, it is not necessary that one particular scholar should analyse the party ideology of all parties of a particular family to find the core of that ideology; indeed, it is the sort of research work which is ideally suited to the collaboration of teams of scholars from different countries working to a common cross-national framework. Moreover, studies of a single party can also provide important and useful data for cross-national studies on party families. What is essential, however, is that studies on party ideologies employ concepts that are clearly defined, that are used more generally in the field, and that can 'travel' (Sartori 1970; Rose 1991).

The categorisation of political parties according to broader families has by now become a more or less standard procedure in the numerous cross-national studies of political parties, and distinctions between party families have thereby become fundamental elements in studies in such diverse sub-fields as coalition formation (Budge and Keman 1990; Laver and Schofield 1990) and policy analysis (Esping-Andersen 1985; Van Kersbergen 1995). At the same time, one of the main problems with these varied applications has often been the shallowness and ambiguity of the categorisations, both in terms of the character of the individual families and of the differences and borders between them, and therefore of the whole enterprise itself.

The matter of these borders and classifications is far from merely academic, for they determine which parties are part of which group, and therefore which parties may be compared in cross-national research as being 'alike'.

The proof of various theses that involve political parties is therefore highly dependent on the accuracy with which the initial classification of the parties is conducted. To classify the Scandinavian Progress Parties as (neo-)conservative rather than extreme right, for example, as seems to be more appropriate, will have serious consequences for our understanding of both the beginning and the breadth of the current third wave of extreme right parties. At the same time, however, there is no reason to believe that the problems of defining borders and reclassifying parties apply solely to the extreme right party family. In fact, doubts on the ideological homogeneity may be, and have been voiced for all party families. In this sense, it is hoped that further studies of political parties in general, and of party families in particular, that apply the ideological approach can provide a clarification of the ideological core of the various families and of the borders between them, so providing a more robust basis for the classification of individual parties, and for the testing of many of the more important theses in comparative politics.

## Appendix A

# List of extreme right parties in Western Europe

The following list includes political parties which are generally considered to be members of the extreme right party family of Western Europe and which contested nation-wide elections (i.e. parliamentary or European) at least once in the period between 1980 and 1999.

| Country | Extreme right parties |
| --- | --- |
| Austria | Freiheitliche Partei Österreichs |
| Belgium | Agir |
| | Front National |
| | Front National Belge |
| | Parti des Forces Nouvelles |
| | Vlaams Blok |
| Denmark | Dansk Folkeparti |
| | Fremskridtspartiet |
| France | Alliance Populaire |
| | Front National |
| | Front National – Mouvement National |
| | Mouvement pour la France |
| | Parti des Forces Nouvelles |
| Germany | Deutsche Volksunion (-Liste D) |
| | Nationaldemokratische Partei Deutschlands |
| | Die Republikaner |
| Greece | Chryssi Avghi |
| | Ethniki Politiki Enosis |
| | Enomeno Ethniko Kinema |
| Italy | Alleanza Nazionale |
| | Lega Lombarda |
| | Lega Nord |
| | Lega Veneto |
| | Movimento Sociale Italiano (-Destra Nazionale) |
| | Movimento Sociale Italiano – Fiamma Tricolore |

| | |
|---|---|
| Luxembourg | Nationalbewegong |
| Netherlands | Centrumpartij |
| | Centrumdemocraten |
| | Centrumpartij'86 (/Nationale Volkspartij) |
| | Nederlandse Volks-Unie |
| Norway | Fedrelandspartiet |
| | Fremskrittspartiet |
| Portugal | Força Nacional-Nova Monarquia |
| | Partido da Democracia Crista |
| | Partido de Solidariadade Nacional |
| Spain | Allianza por la Unidad Nacional |
| | Alternativa Democratica Nacional |
| | Falange Española Autentica de las JONS |
| | Falange Española de las JONS |
| | Falange Española Independiente |
| | Fuerza Nueva/Frente Nacional |
| | Union Nacional |
| Sweden | Ny Demokrati |
| | Sverigedemokraterna |
| Switzerland | Freiheitspartei der Schweiz |
| | Lega dei Ticinesi |
| | Nationale Aktion für Volk und Heimat |
| | Schweizer Autopartei/Parti Suisse des Automobilistes |
| | Schweizer Demokraten/Démocrates suisses |
| | Schweizerische Republikaner Bewegung/ Mouvement Républicaine Suisse |
| | Vigilance |
| United Kingdom | British National Party |
| | National Front |

# Appendix B

# Ideological features and themes

**Nationalism**: The belief that the political unit (the state) and the cultural unit (the nation or ethnic community) should be congruent.

*State nationalism*: The state is the primary unit of organisation, while the nation consists essentially of the people living within the borders of the state. Membership of the nation is based on civic criteria like the *ius soli* and citizenship requirements.

*Ethnic nationalism*: The ethnic community is considered the primary unit, while the state is seen as essentially the political expression of the ethnic community. Membership of the ethnic community is based on ethnic criteria such as the *ius sanguinis* and ethnicity.

*Internal homogenisation*: Only people belonging to the X-nation have the right to live within the borders of the X-state. Foreigners are accepted only as (temporary) guests with limited rights; most notably, non-nationals are not allowed to have political rights.

*External exclusiveness*: State X needs to have all people belonging to the X-nation within its borders. The state is linked to an ethnic community, which again is linked to a certain territory.

**Exclusionism**: The distinction between groups whereby one group (they) is excluded from certain aspects of the life of the other group (we).

*Racism*: The belief in natural (hereditary) and permanent differences between groups of people with the centrality of a hierarchy of races.

*Ethnopluralism*: The belief in permanent (natural or hereditary) differences between groups of people (races and/or ethnic communities) with the centrality that all groups are equivalent but different; people should live within their own group and the groups should live separated; people have both the right and the duty to live according to their own 'natural way'.

*Ethnocentrism*: The belief in cultural and (in principle) temporal differences between groups of peoples, with the centrality that the own group is superior to the others.

*Anti-semitism*: The belief that the Jewish race or ethnic community is in its entirety bad; variants of a Jewish-led world conspiracy (in the tradition of the Protocols) with the conclusion that the Jews ('they') are essentially against the 'own group' ('us').

**Xenophobia**: Fear, hate or hostility with regard to groups that are perceived as 'alien' or 'strange', such as foreigners, immigrants, asylum-seeker, etc. The idea that anything 'alien' is threatening.

**Anti-democratic features**: Criticism of 'democracy' as a political system; views that are opposed to (various) core features of democracy (like pluralism, parliamentarism, political equality, etc.).

*Elitism*: The belief that people are divided by birth into leaders and followers; a small elite should lead the masses without their interference; the common man is not able to decide on difficult matters (such as politics).

*Führerprinzip*: One person is gifted by nature with the qualities that good leadership requires. This leader is the heart of the (ethnic) community and has absolute power. His leadership is above discussion, as only he is able to decide what is good and bad for the (ethnic) community.

*Monism*: The tendency to treat cleavage and ambivalence as illegitimate; rejection of contradistinctions within the (ethnic) community and the state are not accepted; the part (individual) is nothing without the whole (state) and they thus have the same interests.

*Organic vision of the state*: The state is regarded as an organism. This means that one is born into it, and that one has a fixed role to play in the state; it further implies a hierarchic order; *Fremdkörper*, i.e. people who do not perform their correct role or who do not have a role to play in the state, make the state ill and have to be taken out of the process.

*Technocracy*: Technocrats, i.e. people who are not elected but are qualified on the basis of their skills, should have a leading role in political and economic matters.

**Populism**: The belief in the soundness of the common man; anti-elitism; support for direct democratic measures on the basis of letting the people decide; call for referendums at various levels and to go back to the grass-roots.

**Anti-party sentiments**: Systematic criticism of political parties, directed either at the institution itself or at the policies and behaviour of 'the' political parties.

*Extremist anti-party sentiments*: The political party as an institution is rejected, often on the grounds of its divisive nature or on the basis of the fact that it forms a barrier between the rulers and the ruled.

*Populist anti-party sentiments*: Certain political parties (usually the major or established parties) are rejected, often because of their bad functioning or because of the group they (do not) represent.

### The strong state

*Law-and-order*: The belief in order and authority, accompanied by the demand for strong punishment of breach of the rules (e.g. high sentence, sober prison conditions, capital punishment); to maintain order the state should have a strong police force in terms of personnel, equipment and competencies.

*Militarism*: The call for a strong army to protect the national interests; serving in the army as the highest honour; war is considered the natural condition; peace is considered an artificial period between wars; war is considered to be more than a means to pursue the 'national will' as it is the ultimate goal. Positive and unique attributes are ascribed to war and the soldier functions as a role model.

## Environmental position

*Ecologism*: The vision that nature should be carefully exploited by men; the search for a balance between economic growth and environmental protection; warning for the exhaustion of natural resources; criticism of economic growth at all costs; the belief in technology and human inventions to reach this goal.

*Environmentalism*: The vision that nature is equal to man and should be treated with the same respect; no attack on nature on the basis of materialist arguments; the belief that this can only be realised by a new way of thinking (i.e. the rejection of the belief in progress through expansion) and not solely by technological improvements.

## Ethical outlook

*Traditional ethics*: Concern with the breakdown of the nucleus family, community, religion, and traditional morality from a non-religious viewpoint; values are grown as historical basis of society and their decline means the breakdown of society. For a strict ban on non-ethical behaviour (pornography, abortion, homosexuality); a plea for duties, honour, order, dignity etc. over materialist and hedonist motives.

*Religious ethics*: Concern with the breakdown of religious values as the backbone of society; emphasis on a combination of values like the nucleus family, community and religious morality; opposition to modernisation of the Church.

*Libertarianism*: Putting the autonomous individual and his rights and duties at the centre; support for freedom of choice (abortion, euthanasia, drugs); opposition to state regulation state of ethical questions.

## Socio-economic policy

*Corporatism/solidarism*: Support for trilateral governing, which involves the state as well as the workers and the employers; economy should come to the good of the whole nation and not to specific groups; national solidarity instead of class struggle.

*(Neo-)Liberalism*: Strong belief in the natural working of the market; a minimum of state intervention in the economy; deregulation of economy; support of private enterprise; strong emphasis on freedom and individualism.

*Socialism*: Support of strong state control over sectors of the economy; support of strict and detailed planning of the economy; nationalisation of vital sectors of the national economy.

*Welfare chauvinism*: Socio-economic policy should be directed first and foremost to the 'own group'. Priority in jobs and social benefits for the own people. State protection of certain areas of the national economy against foreign competition.

# Bibliography

**Primary literature**

*Centrumdemocraten (CD)*

**Election programmes**
CD 1989. CD *Partij Programma voor de verkiezingen van 6 september 1989 van de Tweede Kamer der Staten Generaal*
CD 1994. *Oost West Thuis Best*
CD 1998. *Trouw aan Rood Wit Blauw!*

**Brochures**
Johnstone, R. and J. Knappert
 1994. *AIDS. Ghost or Threat*

**Party papers**
*Centrumtaal*
*Middenkoers*
*CD-Actueel (CDa)*
*CD-Info (CDi)*
*CD-Nieuwsbrief*

*Centrumpartij'86 (CP'86)*

**Election programmes**
CP 1987. *Voor een veilig en leefbaar Nederland!*
CP 1990. *Voor een veilig en leefbaar Nederland!*
CP 1993. *Partijprogramma*

**Party programmes**
CP 1989. *Nationaaldemocratische gedachten voor een menswaardige toekomst*
CP 1996. *Wie wij zijn & wat wij willen*

## Party papers
*Centrumnieuws* (CN)
*De Revolutionaire Nationalist* (RN)

### Deutsche Volksunion (DVU)

## Programmes
DVU 1987. *Programm der DVU-Liste D*
DVU 1989. *Schwerpunkt-Programm der DVU zur Europa-Wahl am 18. Juni 1989*
DVU 1993. *Partei-Programm*

## Party papers
*Deutsche Anzeiger* (DA)
*Deutsche National-Zeitung* (DNZ)
*Deutsche Wochen-Zeitung/Deutsche Anzeiger* (DWZ)

### Die Republikaner

## Party programmes
REP 1983. *Grundsatzprogramm*
REP 1985. *Das Siegburger Manifest*
REP 1987. *Programm der Republikaner*
REP 1990. *Parteiprogramm*
REP 1993. *Wir machen uns stark … für deutsche Interessen*
REP 1998. *Partei-programm (Kurzform)*
REP 1999. *Deutschland und Europa*

## Books
Schönhuber, Franz 1989. *Ich war dabei*, Munich, Non Stop, 5th edition.

## Party papers
*Republikanische Anzeiger* (RA)
*Der Republikaner* (Rep)
*Der neue Republikaner*

### Vlaams Blok

## Election programmes
VB 1991. *Uit zelfverdediging*
VB 1995. *Nu afrekenen!*
VB 1997. *Een Programma voor de Toekomst van Vlaanderen*
VB 1999a. *Het Toekomstplan*
VB 1999b. *Het Veiligheidsplan*

## Party programmes
VB 1980. *Grondbeginselen*
VB 1990. *Grondbeginselen. Manifest van het rechtse Vlaams-nationalisme*

## Brochures

Annemans, Gerolf
  1988. *Dit leven is in gevaar: Een Vlaams Blok-brochure over Abortus*
  1991. 'De grondslagen van een gezinspolitiek', in *De Gezinspartij*, 9–25.
  1992. *Abortus en 24 november*
Annemans, Gerolf and Filip Dewinter
  1989. *Dossier Gastarbeid*
  1991. *Dossier vreemdelingen. Deel 1: Gastarbeid*
Annemans, Gerolf and Willy Smout
  1990. *Onafhankelijkheid moet en kan. Deel I*
  1993. *De kostprijs van België. Noord-Zuid-transferten in België anno 1992*
Annemans, Gerolf et al.
  1991. *De Gezinspartij*
  1998. *Projekt Vlaamse staat*
Ceder, Jurgen and Luk Dieudonné
  1994. *De Hetze van 24/11/91 tot 24/11/93*
De Man, Filip
  1991. 'De demografische tijdbom', in *De Gezinspartij*, 27–39
  1993. *Aids: geen paniek? Het actieplan van het Vlaams Blok tegen de aids-epidemie*
De Man, Filip and Filip Dewinter
  1991. *Dossier vreemdelingen. Deel 2: Politieke vluchtelingen*
Dewinter, Filip
  1989. *Zwartboek 'progressieve leraars'*
  1990. *Eigen volk eerst. Antwoord op het vreemdelingenprobleem*, Brecht, De Roerdomp
  1991. *Weg met ons? Antwoord aan Paula D'Hondt*, Antwerpen, Tyr
  1992. *Immigratie: De oplossingen. 70 voorstellen ter oplossing van het vreemdelingenprobleem*
  1996. *Immigratie: de tijdbom tikt*, Antwerp, Tyr
Dewinter, Filip, Pieter Huybrechts and Jan Penris
  1992. *Immigratie: De kostprijs. Sociaal-economische aspecten van het vreemdelingenprobleem*
**Dewinter, Filip and Jan Penris**
  1993. *Zwartboek Werkloosheid. Het aandeel van de vreemdelingen in de werkloosheid*
Dillen, Karel
  1992, *Vlaams Blok, partij van en voor de toekomst*
Van Hauthem, Joris and Wim Verreycken
  1991. *Onafhankelijkheid moet en kan. Deel II*
Verreycken, Wim
  1991. 'Staatsvorm' in *Onafhankelijkheid moet en kan. Deel II*, 63–132.
  1992. *Voeren is geen pasmunt*
  1993. *Amnestie*
  1994. *Europa barst?*, Antwerpen, Tyr
Vlaams Blok
  1992. *'Zeggen wat u denkt'*
  1992. *10 vooroordelen tegen het Vlaams Blok*
  undated. *100 Vragen. Vragen aan en antwoorden van Vlaams-Blokpropagandisten*

## Party papers

*De Vlaams Nationalist* (VLN)
*Vlaams Blok* (VLB)

*Vlaams Blok Magazine* (VBM)
*Kaderblad*
*VVBM-Nieuwsbrief*

## Secondary literature

Abramowicz, M. and W. Haelsterman (1998), 'Belgium', in J. Y. Camus (ed.), *Extremism in Europe*, Paris, éditions de l'aube/CERA, 59–85.

Alexander, R. J. (1973), *Latin American Political Parties*, New York, Praeger.

Anckar, D. and V. Ramstedt-Silén (1981), 'Relating preferences to policy: three problem areas', in K. E. Rosengren (ed.), *Advances in Content Analysis*, Beverley Hills, Sage, 89–108.

Arndt, I. and A. Schardt (1989), 'Zur Chronologie des Rechtsextremismus. Daten und Zahlen 1946–1989', in W. Benz (ed.), *Rechtsextremismus in der Bundesrepublik. Voraussetzungen, Zusammenhänge, Wirkungen*, Frankfurt am Main, Fischer, 273–324.

Assheuer, T. and H. Sarkowicz (1990), *Rechtsradikale in Deutschland. Die alte und die neue Rechte*, Munich, Beck.

Backes, U. (1989), *Politischer Extremismus in demokratischen Verfassungsstaaten. Elemente einer normativen Rahmentheorie*, Opladen, Westdeutscher.

Backes, U. (1990a), 'Nationalpopulismus und Rechtsextremismus im westlichen Deutschland. Kritische Betrachtung zum neuerlichen "Hoch" in Politik und Literatur', *Neue Politische Literatur*, 35:3, 443–71.

Backes, U. (1990b), 'The West German Republikaner: profile of a nationalist, populist party of protest', *Patterns of Prejudice*, 24:1, 3–18.

Backes, U. (1991), 'Nationalpopulistische Protestparteien in Europa. Vergleichende Betrachtung zur phänomologischen und demokratietheoretischen Einordnung', *Österreichische Zeitschrift für Politikwissenschaft*, 20:1, 7–17.

Backes, U. (1996), 'Organisationen 1995', in U. Backes and E. Jesse (eds), *Jahrbuch Extremismus und Demokratie*, Vol VIII, Baden-Baden, Nomos, 117–29.

Backes, U. (1997), 'Organisationen 1996', in U. Backes and E. Jesse (eds), *Jahrbuch Extremismus und Demokratie*, Vol IX, Baden-Baden, Nomos, 133–42.

Backes, U. and G. Hertel (1996), 'Dokumentation 1995', in U. Backes and E. Jesse (eds), *Jahrbuch Extremismus und Demokratie*, Vol VIII, Baden-Baden, Nomos, 130–49.

Backes, U. and E. Jesse (1989), *Politischer Extremismus in der Bundesrepublik Deutschland. Band II: Analyse*, Cologne, Wissenschaft und Politik.

Backes, U. and E. Jesse (1993), *Politischer Extremismus in der Bundesrepublik Deutschland*, Berlin, Propyläen.

Backes, U. and P. Moreau (1994), *Die extreme Rechte in Deutschland: Geschichte – gegenwärtige Gefahren – Ursachen – Gegenmaßnahmen*, Munich, Akademischer Verlag München, 2nd edition.

Bank, J. (1998), 'Post-war politics and the legacy of Nazism in the Netherlands', in S. U. Larsen (ed.), *Modern Europe after Fascism 1943–1980s*, Boulder, Social Science Monographs, 1389–422.

Bardi, L. (1994), 'Transnational party federations, European parliamentary party groups, and the building of Europarties', in R. S. Katz and P. Mair (eds), *How Parties Organize: Change and Adaptation in Party Organizations in Western Democracies*, London, Sage, 357–72.

Bartsch, G. (1975), *Revolution von rechts? Ideologie und Organisation der Neuen Rechten*, Freiburg, Herderbücherei.

Bell, D. (ed.) (1960), *The End of Ideology: On the Exhaustion of Political Ideas in the Fifties*, Glencoe, The Free Press.

Benz, W. (1989), 'Die Opfer und die Täter. Rechtsextremismus in der Bundesrepublik', in W. Benz (ed.), *Rechtsextremismus in der Bundesrepublik. Voraussetzungen, Zusammenhänge, Wirkungen*, Frankfurt am Main, Fischer, 9–37.

Betz, H. G. (1990), 'Politics of resentment: right-wing radicalism in West-Germany', *Comparative Politics*, 23:1, 45–60.

Betz, H. G. (1993), 'The two faces of radical right-wing populism in Western Europe', *Review of Politics*, 55:4, 663–85.

Betz, H. G. (1994), *Radical Right-Wing Populism in Western Europe*, Basingstoke, Macmillan.

Borg, O. (1966), 'Basic dimensions of Finnish party ideologies: a factor analytical study', *Scandinavian Political Studies*, 1, 94–117.

Bouw, C., J. Van Donselaar and C. Nelissen (1981), *De Nederlandse Volks-Unie. Portret van een racistische splinterpartij*, Bussum, Het Wereldvenster.

Braasch, S. (1996), '25 Jahre "Deutsche Volksunion"', *Blick nach Rechts*, 13:2, 3–5.

Braasch, S. (1998), 'Schlierer-Partei vor Zerreißprobe', *Blick nach Rechts*, 15:10, 3.

Brants, K. and W. Hogendoorn (1983), *Van vreemde smetten vrij. Opkomst van de Centrumpartij*, Bussum, De Haan/Unieboek.

Budge, I. and H. Keman (1990), *Parties and Democracy: Coalition Formation and Government Functioning in Twenty States*, Oxford, Oxford University Press.

Budge, I., D. Robertson and D. Hearl (eds) (1987), *Ideology, Strategy and Party Change: Spatial Analyses of Post-War Election Programmes in 19 Democracies*, Cambridge, Cambridge University Press.

Buijs, F. J. and J. Van Donselaar (1994), *Extreem-rechts: aanhang, geweld en onderzoek*, Leiden, LISWO.

Butterwege, C. *et al.* (1997), *Rechtsextremisten in Parlamenten. Forschungsstand – Fallstudien – Gegenstrategien*, Opladen, Leske & Budrich.

Canovan, M. (1981), *Populism*, New York, Harcourt Brace Jovanovich.

Childers, T. (1983), *The Nazi Voter: The Social Foundations of Fascism in Germany, 1919–1933*, Chapel Hill, University of North Carolina Press.

Christian, W. and C. Campbell (1974), *Political Parties and Ideologies in Canada: Liberals, Conservatives, Socialists, Nationalists*, Toronto, McGraw-Hill Reyerson.

Coffey, A. and P. Atkinson (1996), *Making Sense of Qualitative Data: Complementary Research Strategies*, Thousand Oaks, Sage.

Cohn-Bendit, D. and T. Schmid (1993), *Heimat Babylon. Das Wagnis der multikulturellen Demokratie*, Hamburg, Hoffmann und Campe.

Conradt, D. P. (1989), *The German Polity*, New York, Longman, 4th edition.

Crotty, W. (1991), 'Political parties: issues and trends', in W. Crotty (ed.), *Political Science: Looking to the Future. Vol IV: American Institutions*, Evanston, Northwestern University Press, 137–201.

Dahl, R. A. (1989), *Democracy and its Critics*, New Haven, Yale University Press.

Dalton, R. J. (1991), 'Comparative politics of the industrial democracies: from the Golden Age to island hopping', in W. Crotty (ed.), *Political Science: Looking to the Future. Volume Two: Comparative Politics, Policy, and International Relations*, Evanston, Northwestern University Press, 15–43.

Damen, S. (1998), 'Strategiën tegen extreem-rechts: het cordon-sanitaire rond het Vlaams Blok', M.A. thesis, University of Antwerp.

Dammann, C. (1999), 'Franz Schönhuber – ein rechtsextremer Saubermann', in J. Mecklenburg (ed.), *Braune Gefahr. DVU, NPD, REP Geschichte und Zukunft*, Berlin, Elefanten, 70–90.

Day, A. J. (ed.) (1988), *Political Parties of the World*, Harlow, Longman, 3rd edition.

De Schampheleire, H. (1991), 'Extreem rechtse populistische partijen in West-Europa: problematiek', in H. De Schampheleire and Y. Thanassekos (eds),

*Extreem rechts in West-Europa. L'extrême droite en Europe de l'ouest*, Brussels, VUB-Press, 31–7.

Deschouwer, K. (1991), 'Small parties in a small country: the Belgian case', in F. Müller-Rommel and G. Pridham (eds), *Small Parties in Western Europe: Comparative and National Perspectives*, London, Sage, 135–51.

De Wever, B. (1992), 'Het Vlaams-nationalisme tussen democratie en fascisme', in R. Van Doorslaer (ed.), *Herfsttij van de 20ste eeuw. Extreem-rechts in Vlaanderen 1920–1990*, Leuven, Kritak, 47–63.

Dewinter, F. and K. Van Overmeire (1993), *Eén tegen Allen. Opkomst van het Vlaams Blok*, Antwerp, Tyr.

Dierickx, G. (1994), 'Christian democracy and its ideological rivals: an empirical comparison in the Low Countries', in D. Hanley (ed.), *Christian Democracy in Europe: A Comparative Perspective*, London, Pinter, 15–30.

Dierickx, G. (1996), 'Ideology: the theoretical construct and its empirical consequences', paper presented at the ECPR Joint Sessions of Workshops, Oslo, March–April.

Dittrich, K., R. Kleykers and P. W. Tops (1986), 'De overheid gereinigd? Een analyse van de PvdA-verkiezingsprogramma's 1981, 1982 en 1986', *Socialisme en Democratie*, 43:2, 51–6.

DNPP (19XX), *Jaarboek Documentatiecentrum Nederlandse Politieke Partijen 19XX*, Groningen, DNPP.

Dubiel, H. (1987), 'Neokonservatismus', in I. Fetscher and H. Münkler (eds), *Piper's Handbuch der politischen Ideen. Band 5. Neuzeit: Vom Zeitalter des Imperialismus bis zu den neuen sozialen Bewegungen*, Munich, Piper, 475–79.

Dudek, P. and H. G. Jaschke (1984), *Entstehung und Entwicklung des Rechtsextremismus in der Bundesrepublik Deutschland. Zur Tradition einer besonderen politischen Kultur. Band 1*, Opladen, Westdeutscher.

Duverger, M. (1951/64), *Political Parties*, London, Methuen.

Dvoraková, V. (2000), 'The politics of antipolitics? The radical right in the Czech Republic', in L. Sorenson (ed.), *Liberalism, Fascism and Social Democracy in Central Europe. Past and Present*, Aarhus, Aarhus University Press.

Eatwell, R. (1992), 'Towards a new model of generic fascism', *Journal of Theoretical Politics*, 4:2, 161–94.

Eatwell, R. (1995), *Fascism. A History*, London, Chatto & Windus.

Epstein, S. (1996), 'Extreme right electoral upsurges in Western Europe: the 1984–1995 wave as compared with the previous ones', *Analysis of Current Trends in Antisemitism*, 8.

Esping-Andersen, G. (1985), *Politics against Markets: The Social Democratic Road*, Princeton, Princeton University Press.

Falter, J. W. (1991), *Hitler's Wähler*, Munich, Beck.

Falter, J. W. and S. Schumann (1988), 'Affinity towards right-wing extremism in Western Europe', *West European Politics*, 11:2, 96–110.

Fennema, M. (1996), *Some Theoretical Problems and Issues in Comparison of Anti-Immigrant Parties in Western Europe*, Barcelona, Institut de Ciències Polítiques i Socials.

Fennema, M. and C. Pollmann (1998), 'Ideology of anti-immigrant parties in the European Parliament', *Acta Politica*, 33:2, 111–38.

Ferraresi, F. (1996), *Threat to Democracy: The Radical Right in Italy after the War*, Princeton: Princeton University Press.

Fischer, S. L. (1980), 'The "decline of parties" thesis and the role of minor parties', in P. H. Merkl (ed.), *Western European Party Systems*, New York, The Free Press, 609–13.

Fitzmaurice, J. (1983), *The Politics of Belgium: Crisis and Compromise in a Plural Society*, London, C. Hurst & Company.

Flechtheim, O. K. (1974), 'Parteiprogramme', in K. Lenk and F. Neumann (eds), *Theorie und Soziologie der politischen Parteien. Band 2*, Darmstadt und Neuwied, Luchterhand, 179–86.

Fleck, C. and A. Müller (1998), 'Front-stage and back-stage: the problem of measuring post-Nazi antisemitism in Austria', in S. U. Larsen (ed.), *Modern Europe after Fascism 1943–1980s*, Boulder, Social Science Monographs, 436–54.

Flohr, H. (1968), *Parteiprogramme in der Demokratie. Ein Beitrag zur Theorie der rationalen Politik*, Göttingen, Otto Schwarz & Co.

FOK (1992), *Jaaroverzicht 1991: Extreem-rechts in Nederland*, Amsterdam, FOK.

Frisch, P. (1990), 'Die Herausforderung unseres demokratischen Rechtsstaats durch Extremismus und Terrorismus', in *Rechtsextremismus in der Bundesrepublik Deutschland*, Bonn, Der Bundesminister des Innern, 7–26.

Gallagher, M., M. Laver and P. Mair (1995), *Representative Government in Modern Europe*, New York, McGraw Hill, 2nd edition.

Gardberg, A. (1993), *Against the Stranger, the Gangster and the Establishment: A Comparative Study of the Ideologies of the Swedish Ny Demokrati, the German Republikaner, the French Front National and the Belgian Vlaams Blok*, Helsinki, Universitetstryckeriet.

Gerring, J. (1998), *Party Ideologies in America 1828–1996*, Cambridge, Cambridge University Press.

Gijsels, H. (1992), *Het Vlaams Blok*, Leuven, Kritak.

Gijsels, H. (1994), *Open je ogen voor het Vlaams Blok ze sluit*, Leuven, Kritak.

Girvin, B. (1988), 'Introduction: varieties of conservatism', in B. Girvin (ed.), *The Transformation of Contemporary Conservatism*, Beverley Hills, Sage, 1–12.

Goedbloed, F. (1991), 'De dilemma's van de georganiseerde Vlaamse oud-Oostfrontstrijders', *Belgisch Tijdschrift voor Nieuwste Geschiedenis*, 22:3–4, 395–450.

Gooskens, M. P. J. (1994), 'The budget approach: political distance measured in Kroner', *Acta Politica*, 29:4, 377–407.

Gossweiler, K. (1995), 'Faschismus aus der "Mitte der Gesellschaft"?', *Marxistische Blätter*, 33:1, 35–44.

Green, D. G. (1987), *The New Conservatism. The Counter-Revolution in Political, Economic and Social Thought*, New York, St. Martin's.

Greß, F. (1994), 'Rechtsextremismus in Europa. Generelle Aspekte und das italienische und das französische Beispiel', in W. Kowalsky and W. Schroeder (eds), *Rechtsextremismus. Einführung und Forschungsbilanz*, Opladen, Westdeutscher, 185–211.

Griffin, R. (1995), 'Post-war fascisms: introduction', in R. Griffin (ed.), *Fascism*, Oxford, Oxford University Press, 311–16.

Haller, M. and G. C. Deiters (1989), 'Alte Parolen, neue Parteien. Die Republikaner und die Deutsche Volksunion-Liste D', in W. Benz (ed.), *Rechtsextremismus in der Bundesrepublik. Voraussetzungen, Zusammenhänge, Wirkungen*, Frankfurt am Main, Fischer, 248–72.

Hartel, V. (1989), 'Zur Einstimmung: Spiel mir das Lied vom Tod', in C. Leggewie, *Die Republikaner. Phantombild der neuen Rechten*, Berlin, Rotbuch, 11–16.

Hartmann, U., H. P. Steffen and S. Steffen (1985), *Rechtsextremismus bei Jugendlichen. Anregungen, der wachsender Gefahr entgegenzuwirken*, Munich, Kösel.

Helenius, R. (1969), 'The Profile of Party Ideologies', Ph.D. dissertation, University of Helsinki.

Herz, T. A. (1975), *Soziale Bedingungen für Rechtsextremismus in der Bundesrepub-*

*lik Deutschland und in den Vereinigten Staaten. Eine vergleichende Analyse der Anhänger der Nationaldemokratischen Partei Deutschlands und der Anhänger von George C. Wallace*, Meisenheim am Glan, Haim.

Hirl, L. (1987), 'Der organisierte Rechtsextremismus in den Niederlanden nach 1945 unter besonderer Berücksichtigung seiner Tradition', Ph.D. dissertation, University of Vienna.

Hirsch, K. and H. Sarkowicz (1989), *Schönhuber: Der Politiker und seine Kreise*, Frankfurt am Main, Eichborn.

Hoffmann, J. and N. Lepszy (1998), *Die DVU in den Landesparlamenten: inkompetent, zerstritten, politikunfähig. Eine Bilanz rechtsextremer Politik nach zehn Jahren*, Sankt Augustin, Konrad-Adenauer-Stiftung.

Holzer, W. I. (1981), 'Zur wissenschaftlichen Propädeutik des politischen Begriffs Rechtsextremismus', in Dokumentationsarchiv des österreichischen Widerstandes (ed.), *Rechtsextremismus in Österreich nach 1945*, Vienna, Österreichischer Bundesverlag, 13–50.

Hoogerwerf, A. (1971), 'The Netherlands: from politics to administration', in M. Rejai (ed.), *Decline of Ideology?*, Chicago, Aldine, Atherton, 140–59.

Husbands, C. T. (1981), 'Contemporary right-wing extremism in Western European democracies: a review article', *European Journal of Political Research*, 9:1, 75–99.

Husbands, C. T. (1992), 'The Netherlands: irritants on the body politic', in P. Hainsworth (ed.), *The Extreme Right in Europe and the USA*, London, Pinter, 95–125.

Husbands, C. T. (1996), 'Die Anhängerschaft der Rechtsextremismus in Westeuropa: eine Überprüfung der Wellenhypothese anhand von Umfragen-Zeitreihen in fünf Ländern', *Politische Vierteljahresschrift – Sonderheft Rechtsextremismus: Ergebnisse und Perspektiven der Forschung*, 27, 313–28

Huyse, L. (1986), *De gewapende vrede. Politiek in België na 1945*, Leuven, Kritak.

Iddekinge, P. R. A., and A. H. Paape (1970), *Ze zijn er nog ...* Amsterdam, De Bezige Bij.

Ignazi, P. (1989), *Il polo escluso. Profilo del Movimento Sociale Italiano*, Bologna, Il Mulino.

Ignazi, P. (1992), 'The silent counter-revolution. Hypotheses on the emergence of extreme right-wing parties in Europe', *European Journal of Political Research*, 22:1–2, 3–34.

Ignazi, P. (1994a), *L'estrema destra in Europa*, Bologna, Il Molino.

Ignazi, P. (1994b), 'Antidemocratic antipolitics: the re-emergence of the extreme right', paper presented at the colloquium 'Vienna Dialogue on Democracy', Vienna, July.

Ignazi, P. (1994c), *Postfascisti? Dal Movimento Sociale ad Alleanza Nazionale*, Bologna, Il Mulino.

Ignazi, P. (1996), 'The crisis of parties and the rise of new political parties', *Party Politics*, 2:4, 549–66.

IJA (1994), *Antisemitism World Report 1994*, London, Institute of Jewish Affairs.

IJA (1995), *Antisemitism World Report 1995*, London, Institute of Jewish Affairs.

Ionescu, G. and E. Gellner (eds) (1969), *Populism. Its Meanings and National Characteristics*, London, Weidenfeld & Nicholson.

Irwin, G. A. (1995), 'The Dutch parliamentary election of 1994', *Electoral Studies*, 14:1, 72–6.

Jackman, R. W. and K. Volpert (1996), 'Conditions favouring parties of the extreme right in Western Europe', *British Journal of Political Science*, 26:4, 501–21.

Jäger, S. (1991), 'Wezenlijke kenmerken van het actuele modernistische extreem rechts in de Duitse Bondsrepubliek', in H. De Schampheleire and Y. Thanassekos (eds), *Extreem rechts in West-Europa. L'extrême droite en Europe de l'ouest*, Brussels, VUB-Press, 31–37.

Janda, K. (1980), *Political Parties: A Cross-National Survey*, New York, The Free Press.

Janda, K. (1993), 'Comparative political parties: research and theory', in A. W. Finifter (ed.), *Political Science: The State of the Discipline*, Washington, APSA, 2nd edition, 163–92.

Jaschke, H. G. (1994), *Die "Republikaner". Profile einer Rechtsaußen-Partei*, Bonn, Dietz, 3rd edition.

Jesse, E. (1990), 'Biographisches Porträt: Adolf von Thadden', in U. Backes and E. Jesse (eds), *Jahrbuch Extremismus und Demokratie*, Vol. II, Bonn, Bouvier, 228–38.

Jesse, E. (1997), 'Wahlen 1996', in U. Backes and E. Jesse (eds), *Jahrbuch Extremismus und Demokratie*, Vol. IX, Baden-Baden, Nomos, 119–32.

JPR (1997), *Antisemitism World Report 1997*, London, Institute for Jewish Policy Research.

Kafka (1998), *CP'86 met name genoemd*, Breda, Papieren Tijger.

Katz, R. S. and P. Mair (1992), 'Introduction: the cross-national study of party organizations', in R. S. Katz and P. Mair (eds), *Party Organizations: A Data Handbook on Party Organizations in Western Democracies, 1960–1990*, London, Sage, 1–20.

Kepplinger, H. M. (1989), 'Content analysis and reception analysis', *American Behavioral Scientist*, 33:2, 175–82.

Kitschelt, H. (in collaboration with A. J. McGann) (1995), *The Radical Right in Western Europe. A Comparative Analysis*, Ann Arbor, The University of Michigan Press.

Klingemann, H. D., R. I. Hofferbert and I. Budge (1994), *Parties, Policies, and Democracy*, Boulder, Westview.

Klußmann, U. (1998), 'Wie ein Windhund', *Der Spiegel*, 13 July.

Knütter, H. H. (1991), *Hat der Rechtsextremismus in Deutschland eine Chance?*, Bonn, Der Bundesminister des Innern.

Kohn, H. (1945), *Idea of Nationalism: A Study in Its Origins and Background*, New York, Macmillan.

Kooiman, K. (1994), 'Undercover in de CD', *De Groene Amsterdammer*, 118:12, 6–11.

Kopecky, P. (1999), 'Political Competition and Institutionalization of Parliaments: The Czech and Slovak Republics', Ph.D. dissertation, University of Leiden.

Kowalsky, W. and W. Schroeder (1994), 'Rechtsextremismus – Begriff, Methode, Analyse', in W. Kowalsky and W. Schroeder (eds), *Rechtsextremismus. Einführung und Forschungsbilanz*, Opladen, Westdeutscher, 7–20.

Kühnl, R. (1992), 'Der Aufstieg der extremen Rechten in Europa', *Blätter für deutsche und internationale Politik*, 37:6, 730–41.

Kühnl, R., R. Rilling and C. Sager (1969), *Die NPD. Struktur, Ideologie und Funktion einer neofaschistischen Partei*, Frankfurt am Main, Suhrkamp, 2nd edition.

Lange, A. (1993), *Was die Rechte lesen: fünfzig rechtsextreme Zeitschriften. Ziele, Inhalte, Taktik*, Munich, Beck.

LaPalombara, J. (1966), 'Decline of ideology: a dissent and an interpretation', *American Political Science Review*, 60:1, 5–16.

LaPalombara, J. and M. Weiner (1966), 'The origin and development of political parties', in J. LaPalombara and M. Weiner (eds), *Political Parties and Political Development*, Princeton, Princeton University Press, 3–42.

Laver, M. and N. Schofield (1990), *Multiparty Government. The Politics of Coalition in Europe*, Oxford, Oxford University Press.

Lawson, K. (1976), *The Comparative Study of Political Parties*, New York, St. Martin's Press.

Lazarsfeld, P. F. and A. H. Barton (1951), 'Qualitative measurement in the social sciences: classification, typologies, and indices', in D. Lerner and H. D. Lasswell (eds), *The Policy Sciences*, Stanford, Stanford University Press, 155–92.

Leggewie, C. (1989), *Die Republikaner. Phantombild der neuen Rechten*, Berlin, Rotbuch.

Lepszy, N. (1989), 'Die Republikaner. Ideologie – Programm – Organisation', *Aus Politik und Zeitgeschichte*, B 41–2, 3–9.

Linke, A. (1994), *Der Multimillionär Frey und die DVU. Daten, Fakten, Hintergründe*, Essen, Klartext.

Linz, J. (1967), 'Some notes toward a comparative study of fascism in sociological historical perspective', in W. Laqueur (ed.), *Fascism: A Reader's Guide*, Berkeley, University of California Press, 3–121.

Lipset, S. M. (1960), *Political Man*, London, Heinemann.

Lipset, S. M. and E. Raab (1970), *The Politics of Unreason. Right-Wing Extremism in America, 1790–1970*, New York, Harper & Row.

Lipset, S. M. and S. Rokkan (1967), 'Cleavage structures, party systems, and voter alignments', in S. M. Lipset and S. Rokkan (eds), *Party Systems and Voter Alignments: Cross-National Perspectives*, New York, The Free Press, 1–64.

Livingstone, S. M. (1989), 'Audience reception and the analysis of program meaning', *American Behavioral Scientist*, 33:2, 187–90.

Löblich, E. (1998), 'Polit-Zombies', *Blick nach Rechts*, 15:9, 2–3.

Löblich, E. (1999), 'Hintertür für die NPD', *Blick nach Rechts*, 16:5, 2–3.

Lucardie, P. (1996), 'Prophets, prolocutors and pyromaniacs: new parties in the Netherlands', paper presented at the ECPR Joint Sessions of Workshops, Oslo, March–April.

Lucardie, P. (1998), 'Een geschiedenis van vijftien jaar Centrumstroming', in J. Van Holsteyn and C. Mudde (eds), *Extreem-rechts in Nederland*, The Hague, Sdu, 9–30.

Lucardie, P. and G. Voerman (1990), 'Extreem-rechts in Nederland. De Centrumdemocraten en hun radicale rivalen I', *Namens*, 5:5–6, 22–7.

Macridis, R. C. (1989), *Contemporary Political Ideologies: Movements and Regimes*, Glennview, Scott, Foresman and Company, 4th edition.

Mair, P. (ed.) (1990), *The West European Party System*, Oxford, Oxford University Press.

Mair, P. (1994), 'Party organizations: from civil society to the state', in R. S. Katz and P. Mair (eds), *How Parties Organize: Change and Adaptation in Party Organizations in Western Democracies*, London, Sage, 1–22.

Mair, P. and C. Mudde (1998), 'The party family and its study', *Annual Review of Political Science*, 1, 211–29.

Mayer, S. (1998), 'Zehn Jahre Deutsche Volksunion als politische Partei', in U. Backes and E. Jesse (eds), *Jahrbuch Extremismus und Demokratie*, Vol. X, Baden-Baden, Nomos, 184–98.

Mecklenburg, J. (1999a), 'Die Deutsche Volksunion (DVU)', in J. Mecklenburg (ed.), *Braune Gefahr. DVU, NPD, REP Geschichte und Zukunft*, Berlin, Elefanten, 12–22.

Mecklenburg, J. (1999b), 'Gerhard Frey – Multimillionär und rechtsextremer Medienmogul', in J. Mecklenburg (ed.), *Braune Gefahr. DVU, NPD, REP Geschichte und Zukunft*, Berlin, Elefanten, 23–7.

Meijerink, F., C. Mudde and J. Van Holsteyn (1998), 'Right-wing extremism', *Acta Politica*, 33:2, 165–78.

Merkl, P. H. (1993), 'Conclusion: a new lease on life for the radical right?', in P. H. Merkl and L. Weinberg (eds), *Encounters with the Contemporary Radical Right*, Boulder, Westview, 204–27.

Michels, R. (1911/78), *Political Parties. A Sociological Study of the Oligarchical Tendencies of Modern Democracy*, Gloucester, Peter Smith.

Mitra, S. (1988), 'The National Front in France – a single issue movement?', *West European Politics*, 11:2, 47–64.

More, G. (1994), 'Undercover surveillance of the Republikaner party: protecting a militant democracy or discrediting a political rival?', *German Politics*, 3:2, 284–92.

Moreau, P. (1994), *Les héritiers du IIIe Reich. L'extrême droite allemande de 1945 à nos jours*, Paris, Éditions du Seuil.

Moreau, P. and U. Backes (1998), 'Federal Republic of Germany', in J.Y. Camus (ed.), *Extremism in Europe*, Paris, éditions de l'aube/CERA, 150–77.

Mudde, C. (1995), 'Right-wing extremism analyzed. A comparative analysis of the ideologies of three alleged right-wing extremist parties (NPD, NDP, CP'86)', *European Journal of Political Research*, 27:2, 203–24.

Mudde, C. (1996), 'The war of words: defining the extreme right party family', *West European Politics*, 19:2, 225–48.

Mudde, C. (1998), 'Het programma van de Centrumstroming', in J. Van Holsteyn and C. Mudde (eds), *Extreem-rechts in Nederland*, The Hague, Sdu, 31–46.

Mudde, C. (1999), 'The single-issue party thesis: extreme right parties and the immigration issue', *West European Politics*, 22:3, 182–97

Mudde, C. E. and J. J. M. Van Holsteyn (1994), 'Over the top: Dutch right-wing extremist parties in the elections of 1994', *Politics*, 14:3, 127–34.

Müller, L. A. (1989), *Republikaner, NPD, DVU, Liste D ...* Göttingen, Lamuv.

Müller-Rommel, F. (1991), 'Small parties in comparative perspective: the state of the art', in F. Müller-Rommel and G. Pridham (eds), *Small Parties in Western Europe. Comparative and National Perspectives*, London, Sage, 1–22.

Naess, A. (1980), 'Ideology and rationality', in M. Cranston and P. Mair (eds), *Ideology and Politics – Ideologie et Politique*, Alphen aan den Rijn, Sijthoff, 133–42.

Nandlinger, G. (1996), '"Heute die demokratische Rechte"', *Blick nach Rechts*, 13:21, 2–3.

Nandlinger, G. (1998), 'Nach rechts rudern', *Blick nach Rechts*, 15:24, 2–3.

Neugebauer, W. (1981), 'Die FPÖ: vom Rechtsextremismus zum Liberalismus?', in Dokumentationsarchiv des österreichischen Widerstandes (ed.), *Rechtsextremismus in Österreich nach 1945*, Vienna, Österreichischer Bundesverlag, 308–28.

Niethammer, L. (1967), 'Die NPD. Führer, Anhänger, Wähler', *Der Monat*, 19:223, 21–35.

Nooij, A. T. J. (1969), *De Boerenpartij. Desoriëntatie en radikalisme onder de boeren*, Meppel, J. A. Boom en Zoon.

Ohne, B. (1999), 'Freys Rechnung', *Blick nach Rechts*, 16:12, 3.

Osterhoff, A. (1997), *Die Euro-Rechte. Zur Bedeutung des Europäischen Parlaments bei der Vernetzung der extremen Rechten*, Münster, Anrast.

Oswalt, W. (1991), 'Definition des Begriffs Rechtsradikalismus/Rechtsextremismus', in M. Kirfel and W. Oswalt (eds), *Die Rückkehr der Führer. Modernisierter Rechtsradikalismus in Westeuropa*, Vienna, Europaverlag, 2nd edition, 28.

Payne, S. G. (1995), *A History of Fascism, 1914–1945*, Madison, University of Wisconsin Press.

Pennings, P. and K. Brants (eds) (1985), *Rechts-extreme jongeren. Theorie en praktijk van politiek gedrag*, Amsterdam, Vakgroep Collectief Politiek Gedrag.

Pfahl-Traughber, A. (1992), 'Der Extremismusbegriff in der politikwissenschaftlichen Diskussion – Definitionen, Kritik, Alternativen', in U. Backes and E. Jesse (eds), *Jahrbuch Extremismus und Demokratie*, Vol. IV, Bonn, Bouvier, 67–86.

Pfahl-Traughber, A. (1993), *Rechtsextremismus. Eine kritische Bestandsaufnahme nach der Wiedervereiningung*, Bonn, Bouvier.

Pfahl-Traughber, A. (1994), *Volkes Stimme? Rechtspopulismus in Europa*, Bonn, Dietz.

Pfahl-Traughber, A. (1999), 'Demokratiedefizit', *Blick nach Rechts*, 16:3, 4.

Piryns, P. (ed.) (1992), *Zwarte zondag. Beschouwingen over de democratie in België*, Antwerp, Dedalus.

Pridham, G. and P. Pridham (1979a), 'Transnational parties in the European Community I: the party groups in the European Parliament', in S. Henig (ed.), *Political Parties in the European Community*, London, George Allen & Unwin, 245–77.

Pridham, G. and P. Pridham (1979b), 'Transnational parties in the European Community II: the development of European party federations', in S. Henig (ed.), *Political Parties in the European Community*, London, George Allen & Unwin, 278–98.

Raschke, J. (1970), 'Parteien, Programme und Entideologisierung. Zur Analyse von Parteiprogrammen', *Aus Politik und Zeitgeschichte*, B-8, 3–23.

Rensen, P. (1994a), 'Een partij van fascisten, criminelen en tuig', *Nieuwe Revu* (2–9 February), 41–58.

Rensen, P. (1994b), *Dansen met de duivel. Undercover bij de Centrumdemocraten*, Amsterdam, L. J. Veen.

Roberts, G. K. (1994), 'Extremism in Germany: sparrows or avalanche?', *European Journal of Political Research*, 25:4, 461–82.

Rokkan, S. (1970), *Citizens, Elections, Parties: Approaches to the Comparative Study of Political Development*, Oslo, Universitetsforlaget.

Rose, R. (1991), 'Comparing forms of comparative analysis', *Political Studies*, 39:3, 446–62.

Roth, D. (1989), 'Sind die Republikaner die fünfte Partei? Sozial- und Meinungsstruktur der Wähler der Republikaner', *Aus Politik und Zeitgeschichte*, B 41–2, 10–20.

Roth, D. (1990), 'Die Republikaner. Schneller Aufstieg und tiefer Fall einer Protestpartei am rechten Rand', *Aus Politik und Zeitgeschichte*, B 37–8, 27–39.

Sainsbury, D. (1980), *Swedish Social Democratic Ideology and Electoral Politics 1944–1948. A Study of the Functions of Party Ideology*, Stockholm, Almqvist & Wicksell.

Sartori, G. (1970), 'Concept misformation in comparative politics', *American Political Science Review*, 64:4, 1033–53.

Sartori, G. (1976), *Parties and Party Systems*, Cambridge, Cambridge University Press.

Scheuch, E. K., and H. D. Klingemann (1976), 'Theorie des Rechtsradikalismus in westlichen Industriegesellschaften', *Hamburger Jahrbuch für Wirtschafts- und Gesellschaftspolitik*, 12, 11–29.

Schikhof, M. (1997), 'De centrumstroming in de tachtiger jaren: enige aanvullingen en correcties', paper presented at the Politicologenetmaal, Soesterberg, June.

Schikhof, M. (1998), 'Strategiën tegen extreem-rechts en hun gevolgen', in J. Van Holsteyn and C. Mudde (eds), *Extreem-rechts in Nederland*, The Hague, Sdu, 143–56.

Schmollinger, H. W. (1984), 'Die Nationaldemokratische Partei Deutschlands', in R. Stöss (ed.), *Parteien-Handbuch. Die Parteien der Bundesrepublik Deutschland, 1945–1980. Band II: FDP bis WAV*, Opladen, Westdeutscher, 1922–94.

Schuijt, G. A. I. and D. Voorhoof (eds) (1995), *Vrijheid van meningsuiting, racisme en revisionisme*, Ghent, Academia.

Schulz, H. J. (1990), 'Alter und neuer Faschismus', in H. J. Schulz (ed.), *Sie sind wieder da! Faschismus und Reaktion in Europa*, Frankfurt am Main, isp, 8–20.

Seberechts, F. (1992), 'Beeldvorming over collaboratie en repressie bij de naoorlogse Vlaams-nationalisten', in R. Van Doorslaer (ed.), *Herfsttij van de 20ste eeuw. Extreem-rechts in Vlaanderen 1920–1990*, Leuven, Kritak, 65–82.

Seiler, D. L. (1980), *Partis et Familles Politiques*, Paris, Presses Universitaires de France.

Seiler, D. L. (1985), 'De la classification des partis politiques', *Res Publica*, 27:1, 59–86.

Seliger, M. (1976), *Ideology and Politics*, London, George Allen & Unwin.

Sippel, H. (1989), 'NPD und DVU – Bilanz einer schwierigen Beziehung', in U. Backes and E. Jesse (eds), *Jahrbuch Extremismus und Demokratie*, Vol. I, Bonn, Bouvier, 174–84.

Sjöblom, G. (1968), *Party Strategies in a Multiparty System*, Lund, Studentlitteratur.

Sprinzak, E. (1991), *The Ascendance of Israel's Radical Right*, New York, Oxford University Press.

Spruyt, M. (1995), *Grove borstels. Stel dat het Vlaams Blok morgen zijn programma realiseert, hoe zou Vlaanderen er dan uitzien?*, Leuven, Van Halewyck.

Spruyt, M. (1996), 'Het Vlaams Blok is overal', in *Geen voorrang voor rechts*, Brussels, SF, 39–52.

Stahl, V. (1997), 'Noch einmal davon gekommen', *Blick nach Rechts*, 14:20, 2–3.

Stake, R.E. (1995), *The Art of Case Study Research*, Thousand Oaks, Sage.

Stöss, R. (ed.) (1983/84), *Parteien-Handbuch. Die Parteien der Bundesrepublik Deutschland, 1945–1980*, Opladen, Westdeutscher, 2 Volumes.

Stöss, R. (1988), 'The problem of right-wing extremism in West Germany', *West European Politics*, 11:2, 34–46.

Stöss, R. (1991), *Politics Against Democracy. Right-Wing Extremism in West Germany*, New York, Berg.

Stouthuysen, P. (1993), *Extreem-rechts in na-oorlogs Europa*, Brussels, VUB-Press.

Suleiman, E. (1995), 'Is democratic supranationalism a danger?', in C. A. Kupchan (ed.), *Nationalism and Nationalities in the New Europe*, Ithaca, Cornell University Press, 66–84.

Svåsand, L. (1998), 'Scandinavian right-wing radicalism', in H. G. Betz and S. Immerfall (eds), *The New Politics of the Right. Neo-Populist Parties and Movements in Established Democracies*, New York, St. Martin's, 77–93.

Swyngedouw, M. (1992), 'Het Vlaams Blok 1980–1991: opkomst, groei en doorbraak', in R. Van Doorslaer (ed.), *Herfsttij van de 20ste eeuw. Extreem-rechts in Vlaanderen 1920–1990*, Leuven, Kritak, 83–104.

Swyngedouw, M. (1998), 'The extreme right in Belgium: of a non-existent Front National and an omnipresent Vlaams Blok, in H. G. Betz and S. Immerfall (eds), *The New Politics of the Right. Neo-Populist Parties and Movements in Established Democracies*, New York, St. Martin's, 59–75.

Taggart, P. (1995), 'New populist parties in Western Europe', *West European Politics*, 18:1, 34–51.

Tamir, Y. (1993), *Liberal Nationalism*, Princeton, Princeton University Press.

Ten Haaf, K. (1992), *… en morgen de hele wereld?*, Amsterdam, FOK.

Thomas, J. C. (1980), 'Ideological trends in Western political parties', in P. H. Merkl (ed.), *Western European Party Systems*, New York, The Free Press, 348–66.

Thomas, S. (1994), 'Artifactual study in the analysis of culture: a defense of content analysis in a postmodern age', *Communication Research*, 21:6, 683–97.

Tränhardt, D. (1995), 'The political use of xenophobia in England, France and Germany', *Party Politics*, 1:3, 323–45.

Ueltzhöffer, J. (1991), 'Rechtsextreme Parteien', in D. Nohlen (ed.), *Wörterbuch Staat und Politik*, Bonn, Bundeszentrale für politische Bildung, 566–70.

Van den Brink, R. (1994), *De internationale van de haat. Extreem-rechts in West-Europa*, Amsterdam, SUA.

Van den Brink, R. (1995), 'De Moon-sekte als souffleur van Janmaat', *Vrij Nederland*, 18 February, 12.

Van den Brink, R. (1998), 'The Netherlands', in J. Y. Camus (ed.), *Extremism in Europe*, Paris, éditions de l'aube/CERA, 237–48.

Vander Velpen, J. (1989), 'De wortels van het Vlaams Blok. Dillen, de behoeder van het collaboratie-erfgoed', in H. Gijsels and J. Vander Velpen, *Het Vlaams Blok 1938–1988. Het verdriet van Vlaanderen*, Berchem, EPO, 9–77.

Vander Velpen, J. (1992), *Daar komen ze aangemarcheerd. Extreem-rechts in Europa*, Berchem, EPO.

Van Donselaar, J. (1982), 'Racistische partijen in drie Europese landen', in J. M. M. Van Amersfoort and H. B. Entzinger (eds), *Immigrant en samenleving*, Deventer, Van Loghum Slaterus, 123–42.

Van Donselaar, J. (1991), *Fout na de oorlog. Fascistische en racistische organisaties in Nederland 1950–1990*, Amsterdam, Bert Bakker.

Van Donselaar, J. (1993), 'Post-war fascism in the Netherlands', *Crime, Law and Social Change*, 19:1, 87–100.

Van Donselaar, J. (1995), *De staat paraat. De bestrijding van extreem-rechts in West-Europa*, Amsterdam, Babylon-De Geus.

Van Donselaar, J. (1997), *Monitor racisme en extreem rechts. Eerste rapportage*, Leiden, LISWO.

Van Donselaar, J., F. Claus and C. Nelissen (1998), *Monitor racisme en extreem rechts. Tweede rapportage. Media*, Leiden, LISWO.

Van Eycken, F. and S. Schoeters (1988), *Het Vlaams Blok marcheert*, Deurne, Imprint.

Van Ginneken, J. (1994), *Den Haag op de divan. Een psychologische analyse van onze politieke top*, Haarlem, Aramith.

Van Holsteyn, J. (1995), 'Groeistuipen of stuiptrekkingen. Extreem-rechts en de verkiezingen van 1994', *Socialisme & Democratie*, 52:2, 75–85.

Van Holsteyn, J. (1998), 'Hans Janmaat, kamerlid', in J. Van Holsteyn and C. Mudde (eds), *Extreem-rechts in Nederland*, The Hague, Sdu, 47–60.

Van Hout, B. (1994), 'De dodenlijst van de Centrum Democraten', *Panorama*, 17–24 March, 12–17.

Van Kersbergen, K. (1995), *Social Capitalism. A Study of Christian Democracy and the Welfare State*, London, Routledge.

Van Riel, C. and J. Van Holsteyn (1998), 'In de raad. Over het functioneren van gemeenteraadsleden van extreem-rechts', in J. Van Holsteyn and C. Mudde (eds), *Extreem-rechts in Nederland*, The Hague, Sdu, 61–74.

Veen, H. J. (1997), 'Rechtsextremistische und rechtspopulistische Parteien in Europa (EU) und im Europarlament', *Texte zur Inneren Sicherheit*, I, 63–79.

Veen, H. J., N. Lepszy, and P. Mnich (1993), *The Republikaner Party in Germany. Right-Wing Menace or Protest Catchall?*, Washington, CSIS.

Verbeeck, G. (1994), '"Schaduwen uit het verleden". Extremisme van rechts: definitie, ideologie en geschiedenis', *De Gids op Maatschappelijk Gebied*, 85:3, 217–42.

Verlinden, P. (1979), 'Morfologie van de Vlaams-nationale uiterst-rechtse groeperingen', M.A. thesis, Catholic University of Leuven.

Verlinden, P. (1981), 'Morfologie van de uiterst-rechtse groeperingen in België', *Res*

*Publica*, 23:2–3, 373–407.

Verstraete, P. J. (1992), *Karel Dillen: Portret van een rebel*, Bornem, Aksent.

Virechow, F. (1999), 'Struktur und Funktion der Frey-Presse', in J. Mecklenburg (ed.), *Braune Gefahr. DVU, NPD, REP Geschichte und Zukunft*, Berlin, Elefanten, 28–40.

Von Beyme, K. (1983), *The Political System of the Federal Republic of Germany*, New York, St. Martin's.

Von Beyme, K. (1984), *Politische Parteien in Westeuropa*, Munich, Piper.

Von Beyme, K. (1985), *Political Parties in Western Democracies*, Aldershot, Gower.

Von Beyme, K. (1988), 'Right-wing extremism in post-war Europe', *West European Politics*, 11:2, 1–18.

Vos, L. (1992), 'De politieke kleur van jongere generaties', in R. Van Doorslaer (ed.), *Herfsttij van de 20ste eeuw. Extreem-rechts in Vlaanderen 1920–1990*, Leuven, Kritak, 15–46.

VSB (19XX), *Verfassungsschutzbericht 19XX*, Bonn, Der Bundesminster des Innern.

Wagner, P. M. (1992), 'Die NPD nach der Spaltung', in U. Backes and E. Jesse (eds), *Jahrbuch Extremismus & Demokratie*, Vol. 4, Bonn, Bouvier, 157–67.

Weinberg, L. (1993), 'Introduction', in P. H. Merkl and L. Weinberg (eds), *Encounters with the Contemporary Radical Right*, Boulder, Westview, 1–15.

Wetzel, J. (1994), 'Der parteipolitische Rechte in der Bundesrepublik 1945 bis 1989', in W. Kowalsky and W. Schroeder (eds), *Rechtsextremismus. Einführung und Forschungsbilanz*, Opladen, Westdeutscher, 89–102.

Willemsen, A. W. (1969), *Het Vlaams-Nationalisme. De geschiedenis van de jaren 1914–1940*, Utrecht, Ambo.

Zimmermann, E. and T. Saalfeld (1993), 'The three waves of West German right-wing extremism', in P. H. Merkl and L. Weinberg (eds), *Encounters with the Contemporary Radical Right*, Boulder, Westview, 50–74.

# Index

References to footnotes contain the letter 'n' following the page number. Page references containing matters of particular significance are in **bold**.